WOMEN OF THE FOUR WINDS

Annie Smith Peck

Delia J. Akeley

Marguerite Harrison

Louise Arner Boyd

WOMEN OF THE FOUR WINDS

Elizabeth Fagg Olds

Houghton Mifflin Company

Boston   1985

Library of Congress Cataloging in Publication Data

Olds, Elizabeth Fagg.
  Women of the four winds.

  Bibliography: p.
  Includes index.
  Contents: Annie S. Peck—Delia J. Akeley—
Marguerite Harrison—[etc.]
    1. Explorers, Women—Biography. 2. Explorers—United
Biography. 2. Explorers—United
States—Biography. I. Title.
G225.O43 1985   910'.92'2 [B]   85–69
ISBN 0-395-36199-0
ISBN 0-395-39584-4 (pbk.)

Printed in the United States of America

V 10 9 8 7 6 5 4 3 2 1

Book design by Linda Manly Wade

Maps by George W. Ward

*This book is dedicated
to my husband and my daughter,
who shared my enthusiasm for it
in many helpful ways.*

CONTENTS

ACKNOWLEDGMENTS

THE INSPIRATION for this book came from the members, the archives, and the library of the Society of Woman Geographers — all starting points for my fascination with the subject of women travelers and explorers. The four women whose stories are related here were all early members of this society. I am particularly grateful for the spiritual legacy of the adventuresome females whom I have known personally, for they have shown that our horizons may expand as boundlessly as our imaginations.

My next debt lies with those surviving relatives and friends of my subjects whom I was able to contact after much detective work. They responded generously through correspondence or interviews on the telephone or in person, loaning the explorers' invaluable diaries, scrapbooks, letters, and other memorabilia, without which much personal recounting would have been impossible. Gracious assistance came from Delia Akeley Howe's relatives and friends: her stepson, Carleton Howe, and stepdaughter, Katherine Howe Malone; her step-granddaughter, Patricia Howe Page; a great-niece, Dorothy Denning Stancheski; and Ann C. Bliven, sister-in-law of the former Martha Miller Bliven, who was Carl Akeley's secretary and a friend of Delia's. Equally responsive were Marguerite Harrison's son, Thomas Bullitt Harrison, and his wife, Jeanne, whom I interviewed in their Baltimore home amid many of Marguerite's antiques and pieces of art. Louise Boyd left no near relative, but I am indebted to various close friends and former colleagues for information about her, as noted in the Sources section in the back of the book. For Annie Peck, earliest of the foursome, the trail was colder, but I am particularly grateful to Frank de la Vega of the American Alpine Club; Jeanne L. Richardson of

ix

the Rhode Island Collection, Providence Public Library; and Alison Wilson of the National Archives for research help, as well as to the embassy of Peru in Washington, D.C.

Indispensable in my pursuit of information have been various museums, libraries, and historical societies, which responded to a flood of inquiries. Months of research in the Library of Congress, often with the assistance of Sara Pritchard, head of women's studies, laid the historical basis. I drew heavily on the resources of the Martin Luther King Public Library, Washington, D.C.; the Lenox (Massachusetts) Library; the Chatham (New York) Public Library; the New York Public Library; and the National Archives. Useful letters, clippings, and photographs came from the Society of Woman Geographers' archives. The Chicago Field Museum of Natural History, the American Museum of Natural History, the Brooklyn Museum of Arts and Sciences, and the National Museum of African Art all contributed information about Delia Akeley. William M. Vanderbilt of the Marin County Historical Society, San Rafael, California, catalogued that society's archive of Boyd material for me and rendered other research assistance.

Helpful, among others, in locating and assembling illustrations — a project in itself — were Alison Wilson and Sharon Gibbs Thibodeau of the National Archives; Walter Weinstein of the National Bureau of Standards; Ellen Murphy, Photo Librarian, the American Geographical Society Collection of the University of Wisconsin-Milwaukee Library; Nina Cummings, Photography Department, Chicago Field Museum; *The National Geographic;* and the Rhode Island Historical Society. For painstaking photographic work in copying faded, frayed, and sometimes half-destroyed old pictures, I am indebted to Columbia Photo Labs, Washington, D.C.

Informal advice in planning the route maps of the expeditions came freely from cartographers Dorothy A. Nicholson, Evelyn Bird, Sandra Shaw, and William Hezlep, while Meredith F. Burrill and Betty Didcoct Burrill advised on place names. Others who contributed in one way or another were: Gertrude E. Dole, Reba Forbes Morse, Ruth Trimble Chapin, Lucille Quarry Mann, Alison Spence Brooks, Luree Miller, Arlene Blum, Chris Prouty Rosenfeld, Noona E. Cheatham, William T. Dutton, Lindsay

Cooper, Jocelyn Crane, Hal Demuth, Ellen Sparry Brush, Marjorie Fountain, Gordon Fountain, Elgin Groseclose, Coleen Stone, Linda Grant de Pauw, Lucy Post Frisbee, Patricia King (Director, Schlesinger Library), James Dogherty (Board of Editors, *Smithsonian Magazine*), Glen B. Rhu (formerly Director, Smithsonian Books), and John McPhee (*The New Yorker*).

My daughter, Cynthia Craig Olds, assisted me in research at the University of Pennsylvania Library and offered comments on the manuscript. My husband, Lawrence Bruce Olds, also provided help on the manuscript and produced the route maps for the expeditions of Peck, Akeley, and Harrison. Cecilia Blewer and Pennell Davis were patient typists.

Heartfelt thanks go to my editors at Houghton Mifflin, Frances Tenenbaum and Janet Silver, for their sensitive perceptions of my aims, as well as their enthusiasm, encouragement, and skillful guidance. Finally, I am eternally indebted to Dr. Wilton Dillon, Director of Seminars and Symposia at the Smithsonian Institution, whose friendship and faith were instrumental in bringing my project to the good offices of Houghton Mifflin Company.

WOMEN OF THE FOUR WINDS

INTRODUCTION

FROM THE DAYS of the mythical Argonauts until relatively recent times, the business of discovery and exploration, whether legendary or real, inevitably featured an all-male cast. Women stayed at home, awaiting the adventurers' return, presumably stitching away on some interminable tapestry, in the tradition of that stoic image of patient resignation, Penelope.

But in the eighteenth and nineteenth centuries the situation began to change. Encouraged by improving means of long-distance travel by rail and steamship, certain women in Western cultures threw aside their needlework, abandoned the symbolic "hearth," and went forth to see the world for themselves. These individuals were decided exceptions to the rule, of course, for they were usually equipped not only with financial resources and education but also with a fierce spirit of independence and above all an unquenchable curiosity.

They were numerous enough, nonetheless, to constitute a well-defined breed, and today they are identified in a growing body of literature as "traveling ladies." Mostly Europeans, they undertook journeys into remote, often dangerous hinterlands, enduring physical hardship and wretched travel conditions. Among the more celebrated of these early travelers are Alexine Tinné, the beautiful Dutch heiress who in the later decades of the nineteenth century took two expeditions up the Nile in search of the river's source, only to be murdered in the Sahara Desert; Kate Marsden, the Englishwoman who trekked across Siberia to study exiled lepers in the Yakutsk region; Lady Ann Blunt, Lord Byron's granddaughter, the first Western woman to visit the Nejd region of Saudi Arabia, where she faced spear-wielding natives; Ida Laura Pfeiffer, who twice circled the globe in the mid-nineteenth century, dying of a

1

fever on the island of Madagascar; Lady Hester Stanhope, niece of William Pitt, who settled among the Druses in a fortified convent in the Levant, adopted Eastern dress and religion, and became a prophetess; and that redoubtable British traveler Isabella Bird Bishop, who visited central Asia, the Orient, the Hawaiian Islands, and the American West, writing nine travel books and becoming the first woman elected to Great Britain's prestigious Royal Geographical Society.

These dauntlessly peripatetic figures of Victorian times, and of preceding decades, were followed at the turn of the century by a still more numerous band, who were to write a new chapter in the history of women travelers. It is this new era, covering the period from 1900 until around 1930, that is the focus here.

The new women travelers were largely American. And they were different from most of their predecessors, who had tended to be romantic dreamers, more intrigued by the exotic aspects of travel, the "spell of the East," for instance, and with the novelty of independence than driven toward defined goals. The new women explorers, by contrast, were highly goal oriented, single-minded, and stoutly dedicated to specific objectives. They freed themselves from their Victorian upbringing to organize and lead expeditions of their own, with institutional or other backing if possible, but in any case asserting themselves as serious explorers.

They are important as a transitional group in the evolving advances of women, for they were the direct forerunners of today's trained women scientists and field workers. Although themselves heirs and successors to their Victorian counterparts, they cast off, as soon as possible, the quaint and inhibiting sidesaddles, flowing skirts, long tresses, and veils of their sisters. But they were not yet modern, either. Having after all been born in the Victorian era, they donned their knickers with misgivings, rode astride but wore concealing robes or jackets, and bivouacked with their porters and bearers with uneasy apologies. But meanwhile they managed to explore some of the earth's most unlikely spots, encounter adventures as wildly improbable as their predecessors' and contribute much to our knowledge of people, customs, and geography.

The four women in this book, each a pioneer in her field, represent a number of like-minded, vigorously mobile females of this

period. Presented here are the stories of Annie Smith Peck (1850–1935), a mountain climber; Delia J. Akeley (1875–1970), an amateur anthropologist and ethologist; Marguerite Harrison (1879–1967), an early documentary filmmaker; and Louise Arner Boyd (1887–1972), who introduced women into the study of the Arctic.

While almost forgotten today, they were far from ignored in their time. They were, indeed, considered remarkably singular and their deeds were covered with respectful wonder by journalists astounded not only by their feats but also by the fact that these women explorers were not hard-bitten, leather-skinned, strong-jawed Amazons but were as conservatively feminine as their own mothers.

With the passage of time, however — as so often happens with women's careers — the names and contributions of these explorers tended to sink from sight, their achievements questioned or minimized. Marguerite Harrison, who organized the expedition that filmed the great documentary *Grass*, was later termed a "hanger-on" by a disgruntled male critic. After Peru had named the north peak of Mount Huascarán in her honor, Annie Peck's ascent of it decades earlier was disputed by a come-lately team of German men. In those days, divorce was in such disrepute that Delia Akeley forfeited much of the credit for her African work with Carl Akeley to his second wife. As a female expedition leader in the male-dominated circle of Arctic explorers, Louise Boyd was slighted even by men whose careers were furthered through her assistance.

Although these four, and many of the new tide of adventurers, lived to ripe old ages into mid-century or later, their careers had flourished in the earliest decades. They were on the move, in most cases, before the late 1920s, when good roads, automobiles, and commercial air transport began to revolutionize travel; or at least they traveled when such advancements were in their infancy. Their journeys therefore were not so very different from what they might have been a century earlier. They had to make lengthy steamship voyages to reach major ports, perhaps long rail journeys inland, then continue on by horse, camel, dugout, litter, or on foot. Like their earlier sisters, they confronted spears, bandits, ferocious beasts, crocodiles, plagues. Their encounters with formidable

3

mountains, barren deserts, or icebound seas were no less hair-raising.

The essence of this era found voice in 1925 in the creation of the international Society of Woman Geographers by many of these brilliant women whose careers were at a height at the time. They might well have been called a society of woman explorers, for while their geographic interests were as diverse as the individuals, they were in one way or another all engaged in exploration. They sought intellectual companionship in a period when their global assaults were still regarded as decided aberrations from the norm. Margaret Mead and Amelia Earhart were among the earliest members. But less famous women were undertaking equally daring expeditions, among them the four whose stories are related here.

Though not trained as scientists, these women reflect in their work the quickening advance of science and geography, and their self-reliance reflects the emancipating influence of the fight for suffrage and, when it came, of World War I. They were living proof that women could be as physically durable as men in exposed situations, and as ready to forgo comforts when necessary. And their prolific writings proved them to be reliable, sensitive, perceptive observers and reporters. These turn-of-the-century traveler-explorers paved the way for the researcher-explorers of later decades — trained specialists armed with good equipment and advanced degrees, whose work takes them nearly anywhere in the universe, from the bottom of the ocean to the stars. The trailblazing adventures of women like those portrayed here, in a still newly accessible world, will remain unique, and their contributions deserve reinstatement in the history of American explorers.

ANNIE SMITH PECK

1850–1935

AT A BONE-CHILLING early morning hour, on August 31, 1909, a small American woman halted at the glacier's icy brink and squinted skyward. Mount Huascarán's massive, snow-crowned heights towered thousands of feet above, a double-peaked Andean giant, the highest mountain in Peru.

But for all its power, the mountain did not intimidate Annie Smith Peck. After carefully reckoning the ascent ahead, she signaled an advance and strode upon the great snow field, followed by her two stocky Swiss guides. Her moment had come at last! Although she had tried and failed five times before to scale Mount Huascarán, Annie Peck, with her customary self-confidence, was certain that on this try she would vanquish her adversary, the mountain's north peak.

"*Pobre* Miss Peck! *Pobrecita!*" (Poor little thing!), the townspeople at the mountain's base had exclaimed when they saw her depart for yet another attempt. For four years the citizens of Yungay, Peru, had watched this strange American lady in her relentless attacks upon the implacable, unscaled mountain. Mountain climbing held little interest as a sport or challenge for the Peruvians themselves, who dwelt at lofty heights as a matter of necessity. But many in Yungay had helped Annie gather together the last-minute items necessary for her climbs: food, climbing irons, flannel shirts, flannel yard goods, woolen stockings, and equipment for her Indian porters. For this trip, she had cut and sewn from local fabric what she modestly termed "unmentionables" to provide her porters warm underclothing. And someone had found her a kerosene stove to replace the one lost on her last try.

To today's climber, Annie Peck's rig would have appeared

7

pathetic indeed, a far cry from modern equipment and streamlined outdoor garments designed for warmth without weight. And as she was, moreover, chronically short of funds, even the "best" of her day was often outside her means.

But this woman, now nearly sixty, with graying hair and steel-rimmed glasses, was a monster of persistence. She was determined to become the first known human to ascend the summit of the forbidding Huascarán, which she hoped would prove to be the highest in the Western Hemisphere, the "apex of America."

And so she went on to reach Huascarán's summit on her sixth onslaught. Her achievement was heralded by *Harper's Magazine* as "one of the most remarkable feats in the history of mountain-climbing." Upon her death at eighty-four, the *New York Times* called her the most famous of all women mountain climbers.

The story of Annie Peck's metamorphosis from lady professor, model to young women in private school, and scholar of classical studies, into heroic mountaineer — all after age forty-five — is a classic of mountain-climbing lore. With her first serious attack on a major peak, the Matterhorn, in 1895, she had joined the roster of great alpinists and gained overnight fame. She was one of only three women in the nineteenth century to reach the summit of that formidable peak.

Annie's flamboyant defiance of Victorian society's decree that women be firmly harnessed to domesticity was a triumph of libera-tion. She refused to be constrained and undertook adventures that would test the strongest male, and were quite beyond imagining for most women of her generation.

Born into a well-to-do family of cultured and distinguished an-cestry in Providence, Rhode Island, on October 19, 1850, Annie was the youngest of five children and only surviving daughter of George Bacheler and Ann Power Smith Peck. On her mother's side, she descended from that pioneer of religious liberty and founder of the State of Rhode Island, Roger Williams. Her father descended from Joseph Peck, who arrived rather grandly in this country in 1638 from England, with his wife, three sons, a daughter, and five servants, to settle in Hingham, Massachusetts.

Annie's father, a graduate of Brown University and a member of the Rhode Island bar, served on the Providence City Council and in the state legislature. He also ran a wood and coal yard, a circumstance that made Annie particularly alert to natural fuel resources in South American countries where she later traveled.

As the youngest child and the only girl, Annie was pitted against three brothers in games and sports — a united male front that may have provoked her militant feminism as an adult, when she actively espoused equal rights and privileges for women. (Named Annie Smith Peck for her mother, she rarely used the name Smith. But after she had achieved fame, she billed herself as "Miss Annie S. Peck" or "Miss Annie Peck," placing a feminist emphasis on her unmarried status.) Competition with her brothers may also have inspired her to excel in physical stamina and courage, perhaps even to confront the grueling challenge of mountaineering.

She was sent to Dr. Stockbridge's School for Young Ladies in Providence, then to Providence High School, and went on to Rhode Island State Normal for two years, graduating in 1872. She taught briefly in the Providence public schools, then moved to Saginaw, Michigan, to become preceptress of the high school there. But she longed to go to college as her brothers had and soon resigned her job to enter the University of Michigan, which, after two decades of bitter debate, had opened its doors to women students in 1870.

Her desire to enter college was dampened only by the realization that she would be twenty-seven when she gained her degree. But in her typical manner she told herself, "Well, I'll be twenty-seven anyway," and took the plunge. She prepared for the onslaught with seven months' study which covered the equivalent of two years' college work and allowed her to graduate in 1878, in less time than the full four-year term. Majoring in Greek, she distinguished herself in every subject she took, both scientific and literary. Again specializing in Greek, she earned her master's degree in 1881, meanwhile teaching mathematics for a short time at Bartholomew's School for Girls in Cincinnati, Ohio. She then became preceptress of a Montclair, New Jersey, high school. From 1881 until 1883 she taught Latin and elocution at Purdue University, making her one of the first American women to become a college professor.

By 1884, in the tradition of the nineteenth-century American intellectual, she was ready for a period of study and travel on the Continent. She studied music and German in Hanover for some months, toured Italy, concentrating on the "antiquities," and in 1885 was the first woman to be admitted to the American School of Classical Studies in Athens. With this new polish, she returned home in 1886 to teach Latin at Smith College and to deliver "parlor" lectures on Greek and Roman archaeology, using stereopticon slides made from her own photographs. With the income from her lectures, she could continue to travel part of the year; by 1892 she gave up teaching and supported herself entirely by lecturing.

In 1893 Annie Peck was included in *A Woman of the Century: Leading American Women in All Walks of Life,* a biographical encyclopedia. She appears as the epitome of the female Victorian scholar: the gentle profile in her photograph reveals a poetic, thoughtful face, her hair done in a high bun — the proper physiognomy for a lady described as an "educator, musician, profound classical scholar, and distinguished archaeologist." In neither portrait nor description is there a hint of the fearless mountaineer yet to emerge.

The account of the young Annie Peck in *A Woman of the Century,* written before her climbing career had begun, suggests that her staid, conventional New England Baptist family was not in sympathy with her academic pursuits, her independent European travel, her bold self-reliance, her whole emancipated life. "Her course has been strictly of her own determination," the biographical account remarks, "receiving but the negative approval of those from whom cordial sympathy might have been expected, except for the encouragement and assistance rendered by her oldest brother, Dr. George B. Peck, of Providence, R.I." This physician brother, who, like Annie, never married, encouraged her through various phases of her career. After her rise to celebrity, another brother, principal of Providence High School and a teacher of Greek, a slight man who shared the family home with Annie when she was in town, manifested his pride by regaling his students with tales of her latest deeds, punctuated with quotations from Homer. But it appears that Annie's exuberant independence did not elicit financial aid from a family that was hardly poor, for certainly she was always skimping and scrounging. Even as a professor she earned what she described as a "mere subsistence," and as a lecturer her income was intermittent. Learning early how to stretch a penny would prove valuable to her in the coming years when she began organizing the costly expeditions required for serious mountain climbing.

The mountains first captured her imagination on her initial visit to Switzerland in 1885. The radiant Alps had an almost revelatory impact on her. She knew immediately she was made for mountains, and they were made for her. "My allegiance previously given to the sea, was transferred for all time to the mountains, the Matterhorn securing the first place in my affections," she declared. "On beholding this majestic awe-inspiring peak, I felt that I should never be happy until I, too, should scale those frowning walls which have beckoned so many upwards, a few to their own destruction."

She began by climbing smaller mountains in Switzerland and Greece, and after her return home worked through a succession of progressively higher altitudes, striding up Mount Shasta in California's Sierra Nevada in 1888 — at 14,162 feet, her first significant height. Mountain ascents were effortless and exhilarating for her and she treated them almost as if they were afternoon strolls. "The exercise was delightful and invigorating," she remarked of Shasta.

Even the Matterhorn, at 14,690 feet, did not faze her. In 1895 she realized her aspiration to scale the "frowning walls" of its peak, "where death can strike suddenly and surely." Although set in the heart of the south-central European continent, on the Italian-Swiss border, where climbers had been "rambling" or "wandering" for centuries, the Matterhorn had not been scaled until 1865, and four of the party had lost their lives. The tragedy placed mountaineering on a public blacklist for a time, causing mountain climbers to be looked upon "with scarcely disguised contempt by the world of ordinary travelers."

But in 1871, only six years later, the Matterhorn was scaled by an Englishwoman, Lucy Walker, in the nineteenth ascent. A few weeks later, she was followed by Meta Claudia Brevoort, an American, the first woman to traverse the peak, ascending from Zermatt and descending to Breuil. Both were accomplished mountaineers. When Annie became the third woman in the nineteenth century to

11

scale the Matterhorn, the feat brought her instant fame. And her costume created almost as much of a sensation as the climb, for Annie wore pants.

The endeavors of women climbers in the Alps had always been a matter of extra courage. Not only were women breaching a male preserve, but they had unfailingly climbed in skirts. Henriette d'Angeville, a French countess, was one of the first, climbing to Mont Blanc's summit in 1838 wearing, according to a painting of the era, a long dress with petticoats. To climb the Matterhorn, Lucy Walker, daughter and sister of mountaineers, wore an old white print dress which became a celebrated garment after her success. At the turn of the century, a Mrs. Aubrey le Blonde was forced to make two ascents of the Zinal Rothorn one day because she'd left her detachable skirt on the summit and without it could not possibly return to any "reputable inn in the valley."

A far cry from a print dress, Annie's outfit consisted of a hip-length woolen tunic, knickerbockers, puttees, and a saucer-shaped felt hat tied on with a veil. A studio photograph shows her posed against a mountain backdrop with her climbing irons and rope, a striking figure at a time when ladies wore floor-length skirts for even the most energetic undertakings. The audacity of Annie's choice of costume can be judged by the fact that on the very day newspapers in this country carried her modest cable announcing her triumph, a woman was being prosecuted in Arkansas for appearing on the streets in bloomers.

Following Annie's triumph, the Singer Company began to give away with every sewing machine it sold a packet of these pictures of Annie in her climbing gear so that, as one writer commented, "Ladies pumping away at the treadle could sigh with admiration at one of their sex who had launched into the world's more daring occupation." Thereafter, her lecture placards proclaimed her "Queen of the Climbers."

Annie termed the clamor over her deed "unmerited notoriety" and treated the whole business as a mere romp, a spur to a truly significant climb. At age forty-five, seeking a challenge that "should render me worthy of the fame already acquired," she entered her definitive and unswerving career as a mountaineer.

"The most feasible next project seemed to be the ascent of

*Studio shot of Annie Peck wearing the
controversial costume in which she
climbed the Matterhorn in 1895*

Orizaba in Mexico, its summit the highest point which had yet
been reached in North America," she later wrote. Mount Orizaba,
the spectacular white-capped mountain rising from tropical forests
above Vera Cruz, was then thought to be a lesser peak than
Popocatépetl, one of the two volcanoes guarding the Valley of
Mexico and Mexico City. Today, with more accurate measurement, Orizaba is counted the third highest peak in North America,
at 18,700 feet, while Popocatépetl, at 17,887 feet, is the fifth highest.

Annie polished off both these mountains in 1897. Her ascent of
Orizaba brought her to the highest altitude in the world to be

*At the same time that it wanted a hair-raising
story, the* World *derided Annie's accomplishment with its comic, wholly imaginary
illustrations. In this drawing, the artist puts
her in hat, veil, and parasol.*

reached by a woman up to that time. It was also her first attempt to
make her expeditions scientifically useful. She took along a mercurial barometer to measure the mountain's altitude, and her results,
calculated by the U.S. Weather Bureau, indicated a height of
18,660 feet, remarkably close to current readings. Afterward, she
called Orizaba an "easy goal."

"El Popo," as the Mexicans call it, was the next challenge. It had
been ascended as early as 1519 by Diego de Ordás, a member of
the Cortés party, so it was by no means "unconquered." But so far
as was known, it had not been scaled by a woman. To obtain
financing for an expedition to the peak, Annie went to Arthur
Brisbane, august editor of the *New York Sunday World*. At that
time El Popo was still occasionally emitting clouds of smoke and
possibly spurts of lava. Annie proposed planting the banner of the
Sunday World on its peak, and her exciting sales talk quickly won
Brisbane's support. She left his office with a contract to write the

*Annie seems to have changed her hat in this
sketch, which is captioned, "Seated on a heavy mat,
sturdy Mexican mountaineers haul their passenger
over acclivities that no woman could
traverse unaided."*

story of her perilous ascent and with an advance to cover the
expense of outfitting and of a trip to Mexico.

The dangers of the death-defying ascent were played to the hilt in
ads in the newspaper announcing the forthcoming story, priming
readers for the exclusive account when it could be told. The night
Annie's report was expected to come in by cable, Elizabeth Jordan,
an assistant editor who had spent a good deal of time with Annie
before her departure, was on duty, prepared to remain at her desk
until dawn to edit the copy. A full page of the newspaper had been
left open for the "vivid recital of the appalling difficulties." Lay-
outs were also ready featuring El Popo legends and the history of
other famous climbs.

When the story began to arrive by cablegram, Jordan said, she
started to read them with shaking hands, fearing the worst. The
"worst," as it turned out, was the shocking simplicity of the account. Annie had reported her climb with scrupulous honesty. She

never imagined the *Sunday World* would be disappointed in anything less than a hair-raising yarn. "As it turned out, it wasn't a difficult climb at all."

She had started from the hotel at the volcano's foot at early dawn, flattered to find half a dozen hotel guests assembled to speed her on her way. When they set out with her up the mountain, Annie expected them to turn back at any moment. Instead, they kept right along at her heels. At noon, lunch baskets appeared and a gay picnic was enjoyed on the warm rocks. No lava marred the day. The party continued upward with festive enthusiasm. Approaching their goal by late afternoon, they glanced upward to the crater's edge to behold a surprising figure: a small boy whose mother had earlier sent him back to the hotel. Finding a shorter route, he had scooted up in advance of the climbers and now waved greetings to the latecomers.

Aghast at this devastatingly guileless tale, Jordan rushed to the editor who had penned copy for the announcements about the "unequalled triumph in mountain climbing" and watched his face as he read. When he could finally speak, Jordan recalled, he said in a "strangled voice, 'You're going to fix this thing, aren't you?' " And, of course, she did. She blue-penciled the picnic party, the lunch baskets, the happy stroll up the mountain. She even heartlessly expurgated the little boy.

Annie already was scanning the horizon for more ambitious ascents. She was eager to explore new terrain, rather than merely follow in male footsteps.

"My next thought was to do a little genuine exploration to conquer a virgin peak, to attain some height where no *man* had previously stood," she asserted. The question was where. Her eyes turned toward South America. By the end of the nineteenth century, few peaks in this immense continent had been viewed by scientists, much less ascended. Some were then wholly unknown to geographers and were nameless. Moreover, altitudes of known peaks were often still a matter of guesswork. Almost anywhere in the Andes, the explorer could find unfamiliar, if not actually untrodden, ground, peaks known only to the natives who dwelt in sight of them.

Bolivia's Mount Sorata, thirty miles above Lake Titicaca, was brought to Annie's attention. Its summit still unachieved, it was thought Sorata might be the highest mountain in the Western Hemisphere. The only potential known rival was Aconcagua in Argentina, scaled for the first time in 1898 by the E. A. Fitzgerald expedition. In 1899 when Annie determined to attack Sorata, she had every reason to believe it might outstrip Aconcagua. (Sorata is the name given by English-speaking geographers; in Bolivia the mountain is known as Illampu.)

Annie now launched an aggressive fund-raising program. "Newspapers and magazines refusing to be interested in the matter to the extent of the $5,000 I believed essential to the enterprise, I conceived the idea of raising money by subscriptions of $100 each," she later wrote. Although ingenious, her methods were sensationally unsuccessful. Only a few people responded. "Advertising men by the dozen including representatives of Sapolia and Castoria, food people, manufacturers of shoes and of chocolate, and wealthy private individuals in vain were invited to lend their names and resources to the expedition." To some her scheme seemed merely "foolish and unprofitable," while to others she appeared outright insane, she said.

For four years she struggled unsuccessfully to raise funds for a Sorata expedition, lecturing from coast to coast under professional management in order to maintain herself. A pleasant break came in 1900 when she traveled to Europe as the American delegate to the Congrès International de l'Alpinisme in Paris, with side trips to climb the Funffinger Spitze in the Austrian Tyrol, Monte Cristallo in the Dolomites, and the Jungfrau in Switzerland.

In May 1903 she found that with a spurt of help from friends her coffers were adequately filled for an expedition to Sorata. Since she'd lived in readiness for this moment, she instantly cabled two Swiss guides, already tentatively lined up, and also invited a professor of geology reputed to be an expert photographer with knowledge of botany and entomology. She'd actually conversed with the professor only about an hour, a scanty introduction that would prove most unfortunate.

Scarcely a month later, on June 16, 1903, "half dead with the fatigue of hasty preparations," Annie Peck boarded the *Segurança* at New York, joining the two Swiss guides, Lauber and Maquig-

Annie sets out for Bolivia from New York on the Segurança *on June 16, 1903, with the professor and two Swiss guides.*

naz, and the professor, as leader of her first major expedition. Maquignaz had accompanied Sir Martin Conway on an unsuccessful attempt on Sorata five years earlier.

Annie was overflowing with cheer and optimism. By her own account, she was always "favored of fortune." She was bound to succeed now as always. In addition to her usual quota of woolen garments for layering her body, she had with her Admiral Robert E. Peary's Eskimo suit brought from the Arctic, which the American Museum of Natural History had loaned her at his suggestion, a particularly valuable addition to her climbing wardrobe.

Another novelty was a Japanese stove for each pocket, small cloth-covered tin boxes heated by a roll of prepared fuel, good for a couple of hours when clasped by hands encased in warm mittens.

For nights, her sleeping bag consisted of two pairs of blankets inside a canvas cover. A Primus oil stove, pots, an aluminum lantern with candles, field glasses, compasses, rifle and revolvers, whistles "in case of separation," smoked glasses, and four cameras were further equipment. Easily prepared and digestible foods included rolls of *erbswurst* (a sort of German K ration), dry soups, tea, coffee, cocoa, brandy (for exhaustion), and the "absolutely essential" chocolate.

Annie proudly described the various tools of science assembled "for observations in geology, geography, and meteorology." Two mercurial barometers were brought for ascertaining the height of the mountain through comparison of atmospheric pressure at the base station and above. One was loaned by the U.S. Weather Bureau, the other made especially for Annie, "probably the only one in the country reading down to ten inches," useful only for such heights as the Himalayas or Andes. In case the awkward barometers were broken, there were two hypsometers to find the temperature of boiling water at various altitudes and thus determine height above sea level, and to further measure Sorata's height, a transit instrument that measured horizontal and vertical angles. Two aneroid barometers, smaller instruments used to measure atmospheric pressure, were also included for both weather forecasting and in determining elevation, and to measure the humidity of air, three psychrometers. In her "physico-medical" department were two clinical thermometers to take body temperatures, a sphygmograph to observe "the strength and character of the pulse," and a sphygmomanometer to ascertain blood pressure. For such a small party, the array of scientific objectives suggests that aims were a bit scattered and overambitious.

Annie was also prepared to "attempt the use of oxygen on the mountain," though she admitted this could be difficult. Her contrivance for this sounds comical today, but then her description is not as complete as one might wish. Knowing that cylinders of oxygen under pressure are heavy and inclined to burst at considerable elevations, she planned instead to "transport to our highest camp materials for its manufacture, with rubber bags to contain the gas." She does not say what materials for the manufacture of oxygen these might have been. But in any case, "the bags with a capacity of six or eight gallons were arranged to be carried on the back and were provided with tubing and mouthpiece," a self-service unit presumably designed so that the climber would inhale the oxygen from the bags by the mouthpiece. The bags may have been concocted by Annie herself, for she wrote that the Davidson Rubber Company of Charlestown, Massachusetts, "assisted in their design." Indeed, the entire oxygen scheme may have been her own notion. Unfortunately, it was to prove unfeasible, for "the idea was necessarily abandoned." Today oxygen is considered unnecessary except for the very highest altitudes.

The shipboard photograph of the expeditionary party, taken as it left New York, portrays a professionally armed and plucky-looking group, Annie holding one of the long mercurial barometers, with another strapped to her shoulder. She nevertheless looks very dainty in a long full skirt sweeping the deck, a high-neck blouse with leg-of-mutton sleeves, brooch at throat, and a flat, ribbon-trimmed straw sailor hat — a Gibson girl strangely loaded with ungirlish gear.

Annie's account of this first assault on the Andes, and of others that followed in her effort to conquer the highest peak in South America, is detailed in her book *Search for the Apex of America* and in various magazine articles. Her trials were marked by repeated betrayals by faithless guides and lazy porters.

At that time, for any explorer, the journey to the destination could prove as much of an adventure as the actual exploratory work itself, sometimes more. Annie's trip from New York to Mollendo, Peru, took just over four weeks: by steamer to Colón, Panama; by rail across yellow-fever-ravaged Panama, with glimpses of the "French canal" under construction; then aboard one of the irregular little West Coast steamers that made endless stops at small ports down the coast to load or unload freight, at any one of which they might be delayed by quarantine problems related to the prevailing bubonic plague.

They arrived at Mollendo, Peru's second busiest port, on July 18, to find "without doubt the very worst" debarkation of any port so far. Perched thirty feet above the rocky shore, Mollendo had no harbor. Passengers reached the town by means of barrels, which lifted them over seas "too turbulent even for an iron pier."

From Mollendo they took the Southern Railway of Peru to Puno on Lake Titicaca, the world's highest lake, lying on the boundary between Peru and Bolivia. The journey across Peru was nearly straight upward: by 4:30 the first afternoon, the train arrived at Arequipa, already 7500 feet above sea level. Annie wanted to pause a week here to acclimatize the party and, as a training exercise, to climb Arequipa's beautiful El Misti, 19,199 feet high. But the professor and the guides insisted on pressing on, so the next morning they continued the trip to Puno. Mounting ever higher up and over the western range of the Andes, Annie found "novelty, interest, at times grandeur" in the scene — Indian villages, droves of llamas, pasturing alpacas, occasional vicuñas, distant snow-covered massifs — but she confessed that "to pass within sixty hours, from the sea to an altitude of 14,600 feet [their highest point] is sufficient to disturb the interior economy of all save the soundest constitutions." Only the professor complained of a violent headache, however, giving Annie a sense of disquiet about his fitness to attempt high altitudes.

They first glimpsed "gigantic Sorata" the next day during the steamer voyage from Puno over "noble Lake Titicaca," as Annie called the great body of water, fourteen times the size of Lake Geneva. Sorata rose from a range of towering mountains to the east, the Cordillera Real, "where Mont Blanc would be lost among the foothills." Even to the guides Sorata "looked formidable and well worthy the preparations for its conquest," Annie noted, and she was pleased when Lauber remarked it was "worse than he expected."

They sailed all day on Titicaca, landing the following morning at the Bolivian port of Guaqui, at the south end of the lake. A train ride carried them across a vast brown plateau to the rail terminus, where they mounted an antiquated carriage that conveyed them to the singularly situated La Paz, the highest city on the globe at 12,500 feet, but located at the bottom of a canyon 1000 feet deep. At a distance from the Bolivian capital, "magnificently overtopping" the canyon's steep walls, was the "great and radiant snow-crowned" Illimani, by today's reckoning (21,201 feet) higher than Sorata (20,867 feet). The party had made excellent time, but Annie soon faced troubles with her companions.

Her mountaineering schedule naturally had to be attuned to the Bolivian calendar, essentially a two-season year, rainy and dry.

Although situated in tropical latitudes, a large portion of the country lies across the Andes, including the high, cold plateau between the eastern and western ranges to which Annie was bound. To benefit from the maximum period of dry weather before the November beginning of the rainy season, she should have left New York in May, but her financial problems prevented her from leaving until early June. Still, good traveling time brought her to Mollendo only a week behind her ideal arrival date of July 11.

Now in La Paz still in good time, she was jolted when scarcely a week later the professor announced he would have to leave for home on August 20. It was already July 31, they were still many miles from even the foot of Sorata, and he was allowing only twenty days for the ascent and no time at all for a second effort in case of bad weather or initial failure. Annie protested: he had come at her expense and was expected to remain until the mission was accomplished or abandoned. He offered to withdraw, returning home at his own expense; but if he stayed for the specified time, he declared, she must pay his way back. Annie so needed this man's photographic skills that, however reluctantly, she had to acquiesce, even though the "specified time" was likely to be insufficient. To have his help so briefly after "the expenditure of thousands of dollars and months of travel was a terrible and unexpected blow," she wrote, but with that ever-buoyant faith in her special luck, she told herself that perhaps she would be able to reach Sorata's summit within the brief time allotted.

Next, however, Maquignaz, who had been stoned by unfriendly Indians on his previous expedition to Sorata, demanded an escort of soldiers for the ascent. This nuisance of a request was settled by word from the authorities that soldiers were neither needed nor available.

As Annie plunged into last-minute preparations, the professor vanished on the final day on a personal excursion, leaving her to rush about La Paz, "to the great astonishment if not horror of the Bolivians, who never hurry," she wrote. She was not able to get to bed until 2:00 A.M. on the morning they were to start, "poor preparation for an arduous journey," she remarked sourly, since she had to arise at six.

An undeniably impressive cavalcade clattered out of the hotel

Annie with her two Swiss guides and the professor in La Paz

patio next morning, August 3, at 10:30 A.M. At the head, nobly mounted on horseback with a fine embroidered saddle, rode the muleteer, or *arriero*, hired at forty-five dollars a week for his services plus the use of his eight mules and one Indian. Also on horseback rode a lieutenant of the Bolivian army, resplendent in a white uniform, spurred, with saddlebags and sword, on loan from the Bolivian secretary of war. He was to take observations near Sorata's base, which would be measured against others taken at the summit. The Swiss guides, with rifles tied to saddles, revolvers in pocket, came next, each riding a mule, as was the professor, also armed. Next came Annie on muleback, garbed in knickerbockers and riding *astride*. She tried to soften the impact of such aberrant behavior by wearing a long ulster opening to the waist at back, giving the impression of a divided skirt, which "I trust prevented my shocking the sensibilities of anyone." Three mules heavily laden with baggage, the Indian on foot who would watch the mules, and the fourteen-year-old son of the muleteer brought up the rear.

They stopped for the night at a *tambo*, a sort of hostel. Annie took the adobe bench in the middle of the single room; the others scattered their bags around on the floor. No stranger to unconventional situations, she was quickly sound asleep.

New doubts about the professor's mountaineering qualifications arose next morning as they gazed at the tremendous snow fields looming above. "My, it looks cold up there," he remarked. Only a tenderfoot would make such a naive comment, Annie reflected with a deepening sense of foreboding.

Two more nights in *tambos* of varying cleanliness, and by the third day they were poised to ascend Sorata's north side, Annie's choice because this side had not been examined by other mountaineers. But now Maquignaz insisted that since he was familiar with the southwest side he could practically guarantee an easy climb to the summit by this attack. Reluctantly, Annie relinquished the north ascent. Eight additional Indians were hired to carry baggage up the lower cliffs from the point where mules would be dismissed. It was a Monday morning, a full week since they had said good-by to La Paz, when they finally left from their last shelter, the *finca,* or ranch, Umapusa. And then they were lacking the muleteer who had spent the weekend drinking and didn't show up in time to leave with them.

Their first camp was in a narrow valley hemmed by high walls. Aneroid barometer readings found them at 15,350 feet, higher, Annie quickly calculated, than any of the Alps except for Mont Blanc.

Up at six, chafing to begin the next five-thousand-foot climb, Annie discovered with alarm that the professor was still huddled in his sleeping bag. He complained of the cold and "indigestion." Annie cynically diagnosed *soroche,* the ubiquitous ailment of the Andes, although the professor disagreed. Even the ordinary rail traveler in the Andes can be stricken as trains climb to altitudes of ten thousand feet and over. Resembling seasickness, *soroche* may cause headaches, often nausea and vomiting, sometimes fever; in extreme cases, hemorrhage, apoplexy, or heart failure. But Annie didn't expect it to strike a presumably seasoned climber.

Then, as she and the guides began to rearrange mule packs for the porters to carry on their backs, the porters went on strike. They claimed the snow was deeper and half a mile lower down the slope than usual, an unexpected hazard since they were wearing only

24

sandals (not until later climbs did Annie begin to furnish footgear). Actually, they were demoralized by the professor's defection. Being a man he must be the one really in charge, they thought, the true boss; and he didn't want to continue, so why should they? Maquignaz began to insist again on soldiers.

At last, filled with "rage and mortification," Annie had to give up. "To manage three men seemed beyond my power," she later wrote. "Perhaps some of my more experienced married sisters would have done better." As they descended, the delinquent muleteer who might have helped translate her instruction to the Indians met them on his way up, too late to be of use.

Arriving in La Paz after dark — Annie was thankful her "ignominious defeat" could be suffered out of public view — they learned that bubonic plague had closed their exit port of Mollendo. This alarmed the Swiss guides, who feared they might be caught in Peru for months and decided they must join the professor in a quick departure from the still-open port of Antofagasta, Chile. After disagreeable arguments, including quarrels about pay for the porters, Annie paid them all off and saw them go on August 20, glad to be rid of them. Snowstorms now began sending avalanches down the mountain, signaling the end of climbing. The rainy season was closing in early after an unusually wet "dry" season. The best moment for climbing in this poor year was lost. Her team had denied her a success she always believed would have been easily attained. She withdrew with a vow to return another year.

Annie left La Paz hoping to find an alternative exit port by way of Arequipa, a route that allowed her to climb El Misti and descend into its crater, half a mile in diameter and eight hundred feet deep. The crater proved more exciting, in fact, than the ascent of the mountain itself since the summit could be reached comfortably by horse or mule, classifying it as a climb for amateurs. But from the summit she viewed glittering peaks in tempting array: Chachani, more a range than a peak, a bit higher than El Misti; Pichupichu, lower, tinged with reddish-yellow desert sands; and Ubinas, a distant volcano. Her reckoning of El Misti's elevation by her hypsometer was 19,200 feet; current readings cite 19,199. Returning from the summit, she descended to the Harvard University Observatory station, where she stayed as a guest, more fatigued

25

from riding downhill on muleback than from any climb on foot of as many hours.

Since Mollendo was closed, Annie decided to leave Peru for home by the port of Quilca. This entailed a horseback journey across the vast "Pampa of Islay," a desert trip that could present hazards of many kinds. A party of American men who had just arrived in Arequipa from Quilca warned her not to attempt anything so difficult. Annie recorded that their leader told her "they had ridden 102 miles across an absolute desert in the unprecedented time of twenty-six hours; that there was no place to pause en route, but they had slept, unsheltered, for a brief period; that there was danger of being lost on the trackless desert and of perishing from hunger and thirst, of being overwhelmed by sand storms, of freezing at night and roasting by day; in short, he would strongly advise me to reurn to La Paz, for the two days' stagecoach ride to Oruro, the three days by rail to Antofagasta, and the four days additional on the steamer, with all the extra time and expense involved, rather than attempt this terrible journey." The professor and guides had used the Oruro-Antofagasta route.

This tale of horror served only to whet Annie's appetite. She assured the gentleman "that if his feat were so extraordinary, there was the more reason for my duplicating it, since, not having climbed my mountain (Sorata), I was eager for adventures."

She was perfectly ready to go alone with only a muleteer and a mule to carry her trunk, when she heard of an American man also planning to go north by the next boat from Quilca. She got in touch with him and they arranged to travel together. Explaining her forwardness, she said, "In strange lands, far from home, where Americans are few, as in these regions in 1903, one is apt to feel that all men from the United States are brothers, more or less . . . Most men under such circumstances are disposed to be polite."

Having thus reassured herself on the safety and ethics of traveling with a male stranger on a nonexpeditionary jaunt, she prepared to strike out across the Pampa of Islay, an area of twenty-five-hundred square miles between the Tambo and the Vitor rivers, a segment of the great Peruvian desert, which itself stretches twelve hundred miles along the entire coast. Their *arriero* with animals was awaiting them at a designated train station in the desert, from which they set forth on very good horses, a welcome change from the mules of Bolivia. It turned out to be a thoroughly enjoyable trip. To Annie's delight the desert was "the genuine article," with dunes rising to fifteen or twenty feet and moving at the rate of about two inches a day as they were blown by the steady breeze. The muleteer did admit he was lost at one point, but with a distinct track leading westward, Annie felt no "forebodings of disaster" and they rode blithely along.

But at heart Annie's spirits were drooping. The nearer she got to New York on the trip home, the more dispirited she became. After such lengthy planning, elaborate preparations, expenditure of money, and after traveling ten thousand miles, not to have attained Sorata's summit was "mortifying" and the failure literally made her ill. She blamed an attack of shingles on the whole affair. However, it took only a few days' rest to put her back on her feet anxious to return for another battle with Sorata. "I *could* not leave it as it was, having merely confirmed in their opinion those persons who had previously regarded me as insane," she explained.

On June 21, 1904, only a few months after her return to New York, she sailed again for Peru. She had scraped up a paltry twelve hundred dollars by begging from old Providence friends and through article assignments for the *New York Times* and the *Boston Herald*. She relied on the hospitality of her previous hosts and her knowledge of the countries to see her through. If conditions permitted, she might even scale still another untrodden South American peak after conquering Sorata.

Sailing down the rugged Peruvian coast, she was permitted a seductive glimpse of Mount Huascarán. In the double spine that runs down the length of Peru, it was one of the chain of mountains in Peru's White Range (Cordillera Blanca). Lying between the White Range and the coast is the Black Range (Cordillera Negra), jagged and snowless. Annie estimated the height of the Black Range to be between fifteen and eighteen thousand feet, which meant that Huascarán, peeping from behind, must be gargantuan. Certainly this was a challenge to keep in mind.

In La Paz once more, after the usual delays owing to fumigation, uncertain steamer schedules, and problems of overland travel, she located a new assistant and companion, an Austrian who would replace the ill-starred professor. She felt the need to have a white male companion, as she was still unwilling to travel alone with the Indians. Stories of Indian cannibals, robbers on the *puna* (high plateau), and Indian unrest were frequent. This time, she equipped herself against troubles with mutinous porters. She added a wooden cross to her equipment, to be planted at the summit of Sorata to allay the Indians' superstitions against the ascent. Four quarts of alcohol, three for the porters, the other to light the kerosene stove, were also added. In deference to local custom, she also purchased a bag of coca leaves. Without coca, she had learned, the Indians would refuse to do arduous work. Writing about this years later, after encountering it on other South American climbs, she said: "Chewing coca leaves (from which cocaine, not cocoa, is derived), the Indians can defy hunger, thirst, sleep, and fatigue, travelling continuously for several days, if need be, with little food or drink. I have read that when provided with coca the Indians do not care to eat, but in my considerable experience with both Quichuas and Aymaras I found them always to have excellent appetites, however much coca they consumed. If *able* to go without eating they evidently did not wish to, eagerly devouring anything within reach." This last remark reflected cynical recollections of the copious provender she had supplied on various expeditions.

A decidedly less splendid cavalcade departed La Paz this time than in 1903: in addition to Annie, only the Austrian, a majordomo from a nearby *finca,* and several Indians. But by the first night of encampment, they were already far higher than at the same time the previous year, having taken a shorter route. Annie, who never bothered with physical training between climbs, at first felt the lack of recent exercise, but she nibbled chocolate and bread to keep her energy up. After some dispute, and to Annie's annoyance, they slept on a ledge too narrow to pitch the tent, and awakened to find themselves covered with six inches of snow.

Annie was dismayed when the Austrian, panicked by the snow, proposed that they turn back. She proposed that they wait a day for better weather. The Austrian agreed to this, but once under way on the following day, he insisted on pitching camp shortly after noon. Fretful about wasted time, Annie occupied herself taking altitude measurements; she judged this third camp to be at about

18,100 feet. After supper she took her usual pulse and temperature readings; her pulse had been rising, she found, from 60 on shipboard to 72 in Arequipa, 88 in La Paz, to 120 on the mountain. Her temperature was a degree above normal. She spent a restless night, with a twitch in her thigh, possibly a touch of *soroche*, she thought.

After their morning tea and soup, the party started out roped by an eighty-foot length, the Austrian in the lead, the major-domo next, Annie in the rear. The Austrian soon demonstrated his ineptitude once again. Swallowing a protest, Annie watched him take an ill-chosen course. Instead of going straight up a ridge, he cut to the right, making a traverse across a steep incline where soft snow in the midday heat could provoke an avalanche. Apprehensively she watched him flounder. Annie had already realized that this man "in common with many of his sex . . . does not take kindly to suggestions, and dearly loved his own way." Soon he had sunk to his waist in snow and announced he would climb no farther. It was too late in the day to reach the summit in time to get back to the tent before dark, he declared, and moreover "he did not propose to risk his life for any money!"

They were near the top of the ridge and only a few hundred feet from the summit. Even proceeding to the peak of the ridge would give them a view of what came next, Annie argued. Without waiting, she struck out for the crest of the ridge, expecting the two men to follow. She soon faced an incredibly steep slope of almost bare ice, where she could take only about three steps without pause. But, carefully planting her ice ax ahead, she pressed on. Suddenly her ax sank into a void, and looking down she gazed at a crack in the snow at her very toes. She was in line with a great crevasse but had counted on a snow bridge to hold solid. It had not. Turning to ask for help from behind, she beheld to her "horror and disgust" that her rope trailed idly in the snow. The two men had unhitched and stood where she had left them, watching her.

Annie was furious at this betrayal of climbing ethics. "On a steep and dangerous slope, on the very brink of a crevasse into which a careless step would have plunged me," she later wrote, her outrage unabated, "and no one on the rope! A little less caution and I should be in the bottom of that crevasse now." There was no question of going farther. Indignation surpassed other emotions,

29

she said. "Even a Swiss guide would not advance alone in such a place."

Particularly infuriating was the fact they were probably within two hours of the summit. She had been ready to continue for three more hours in any case, if necessary — at least, until five o'clock — and was quite prepared to descend by moonlight. Heroics were in order when one was so close to success, she declared. "If worse came to worst, compelled by exhaustion or bad weather, I believed we could make a cave in the snow, which might be warmer than the tent, and in this stay until morning. One must be prepared to take a little chance when undertaking the conquest of a great mountain." But she had no choice but to begin the steep, rocky descent, two nights and a forty-five-mile mule ride from La Paz. She had neglected to protect her face and was badly sunburned. She now wanted to get back to La Paz as fast as possible, and they pushed hard.

Years later she was still trying to fathom the mentality of the quitter. "That he had refused in the best of weather to go on when we were at the highest point, or to persist a day or two longer in the conquest of the mountain, when we were on the ground, has always seemed strange." The Austrian was not of the same stuff as Annie Peck, one may say for certain. But then, as Amelia Earhart would declare, "Miss Peck would make almost anyone appear soft."

Back in La Paz, Annie watched snowstorms sweep over the mountains, announcing the dry season's end. She now abandoned Sorata, not only for the time being but forever, for she now realized there were higher peaks in South America to scale. On her second trial on Sorata's slopes, she had attained a much greater height than in 1903 — 20,500 feet by her reckoning — and without skilled assistance. Sorata's height today is given as 20,867 feet, so if Annie's measurement of her altitude was correct she fell short of the summit by only 367 feet. A pity! "Oh, how I longed for a man with the pluck and determination to stand by me to the finish!" she lamented. Unfortunately, her wish was not to be fulfilled.

Though the season was late, she determined to take on another goliath before leaving South America. Her candidates were Bolivia's Sajama and Peru's Huascarán, both unscaled. Sajama was clearly the easier goal. It was the more accessible and had only moderate slopes. But Sajama stood in isolated and uninteresting country. The view from the summit could prove disappointing, "tame and unworthy of the toil required to reach the goal," she thought, although it was at a respectable height estimated between twenty-two thousand and twenty-three thousand feet.

The journey merely to reach Huascarán, on the other hand, would be formidable. Huascarán was also higher and more difficult to scale. But it lay in a region of scenic grandeur that, she had heard, rivaled any part of the Western Hemisphere. An ascent would attract wide attention to the area. While hoping that Huascarán would prove the highest peak in the hemisphere, she made her choice partly as a service to Peru and its tourist potential. "Although the probability of a successful ascent of Sajama was great, while that of Huascarán was doubtful or worse, I decided to undertake an expedition to the latter, as being in every way more valuable, except from the standpoint of personal success," she explained afterward.

Annie was still nursing cold sores and blisters on her face and recuperating from the exhausting descent down Sorata and the long mule ride back to La Paz. But she prepared to leave Bolivia for Lima, Peru, within a week, hoping to enlist a new escort and interpreter along the way. Since Huascarán lay in the northern Peruvian wilderness, many miles from the coast, she hoped to find her companion in time for him to accompany her across this region as well as on the climb itself. The entire trip entailed the long rail journey from La Paz to Mollendo on the coast, a boat trip up the coast to Callao, a stay in Lima, then a sail up the shore to Samanco, the port of entry for her trek to Huascarán, and an extensive overland trip to Yungay, the town nearest the foot of the mountain.

After repeated efforts to find a companion, Annie had reconciled herself to proceeding from Lima without one, when on the evening before the weekly steamer was to sail from Callao she spotted a prospect. He was a brawny-looking American, speaking fluent Spanish at the hotel desk, and she quickly sized him up as a good gamble. Annie approached him with an offer to pay for his companionship on her expedition, and she was relieved to find him willing. He was a soldier of fortune, of sorts, who had knocked

31

about South America as a miner, a seaman, and a worker at a variety of jobs, not educated but pleasant. He was named Peter. They sailed together the next day from Callao for Samanco. It was September 3, 1904.

Awaiting them in Samanco were saddle horses and baggage mules from the *hacienda* of San Jacinto, a sugar plantation owned by a British sugar company. Annie had enlisted the aid of the company agent in Lima, a Peruvian named Señor A. B. Leguia, later to become president of Peru, who had wired ahead for the animals to accommodate her. Otherwise she would have been stranded in the tiny port of Samanco for there was neither rail nor carriage road to Yungay.

Located in the deep, narrow Huaylas Valley, only one to four miles wide, lying between the Black and White ranges, Yungay was to remain crucial to Annie's fortunes for years to come. All of tiny Samanco assembled to gape at the mules being loaded and to watch the departure of the strangers on horseback, trailed by a great heavy wooden box on a cart. There was a cart road only as far as Moro, thirty miles inland, where baggage would be roped to burros.

The Huaylas Valley brought Annie far into the interior of Peru — five days by horseback to the first town, Cajabamba, with night stops first at the sugar plantation, then at a simple hotel in Moro, and thereafter in Caras in homes of English-speaking residents to whom Annie had letters of introduction. After crossing desert country, the party entered mountainous ridges. They made one thirty-five-mile uphill climb, but on entering the Huaylas Valley they were forced to pick their way down a path so precipitous they had to dismount when burro trains passed to avoid being hurled into the chasm below.

This country was far more interesting than the Bolivian desert, and as they entered the Huaylas Valley, through which winds the Santa River, the largest river in Peru that flows into the Pacific, Annie became rapturous over its beauty. The ride from Caras to Yungay, over a hard-surfaced road at last, sent her into transports, marveling at the equable climate at seven or eight thousand feet where tropical and subtropical fruit flourished. The scenery sur-passed Chamonix in Switzerland, and the mineral riches rivaled the

Annie's own shot of the twin-peaked Huascarán

Klondike, she declared. Introductions again settled her comfortably in a private home, that of the Vinatéa sisters, in Yungay.

Now for the first time Annie could appraise her adversary, Huascarán, at close range in all its dazzling splendor. She admitted that her heart sank in apprehension: "When I first saw from Yungay magnificent Huascarán towering far above the valley, I was filled with dismay at my own temerity in dreaming for a moment of its conquest. Many thousand feet rise the rocky slopes and the well-rounded earth covered buttresses, supporting the broad ice-clad sub-structure of the twin peaks, which at a startling angle pierce the blue sky above. The immense glacier below the peaks was so visibly and terribly cut by a multitude of crevasses that it seemed impossible for the most skillful, much less for men wholly inexperienced, to find their way through such a maze."

But she vigorously set about preparations, and by September 28, scarcely more than three weeks since departing from Lima, she was ready to set forth. If her caravan leaving La Paz for Sorata had created a hubbub, the imposing parade now departing the tiny town of Yungay for Annie's first attempt on Huascarán was a major sensation. Prominent local men mounted on horseback accompanied the party, led by the governor of the state of Ancash and including the local newspaper editor. The governor made sure the parade, numbering more than a dozen, circled all the main streets before reaching the outskirts, where he and the other figureheads dropped out.

All local pundits believed ascent of Huascarán was impossible, yet everyone had an opinion about which side was the better on which to make an effort. Annie chose the east side because getting there would take her through the "wonderful scenery" of the Llanganuco Gorge.

By the second night, when they pitched camp at fifteen thousand feet, they still had not reached the snow line. Annie, sharing her silk tent with the newspaper editor and another Yungay man who had hung on, got little rest. All the next day they toiled up the moraine of the huge glacier sweeping down Huascarán, seeing and hearing masses of snow thundering down to the left while the middle was impassable because of frightfully crevassed glaciers higher up. In her later accounts, with seemingly total recall, Annie described the step-by-step advance and the dangerous traverses, detailing the contour of every cliff and perpendicular wall, each immense snow cornice along the way, and recollecting the plan of attack.

Her ultimate goal was the north peak. "Apparently the most feasible route," she wrote of the spot above, "was to follow up the moraine and the rocks at the right until we were well towards the *col* or saddle. Then it would be necessary, for the avoidance of a great *berg-schrund* [a deep and often broad crevasse or series of such crevasses] in the centre, to cross the crevassed glacier 10,000 feet below the top of the *col* to its left hand corner, thence, after getting above the *berg-schrund,* to take a diagonal towards the top of the saddle. Camping here we should the next day attempt which ever peak from this point appeared the more practical."

That night, at seventeen thousand feet, Annie shared her tiny tent with four others and again got practically no sleep. The next day, the fourth day of climbing, they advanced another thousand feet to the east side of the north peak and hoped to proceed to the saddle on the fifth day. But immense avalanches were coursing down the mountain under and around the saddle, and so they were forced to give up the preferred route and consider climbing the dreadful rocks. Then heavy snow began to fall and raged on for several hours, covering the rocks and ending the climbing day, and also delaying their start the following morning.

The snow had melted in the sunshine the next morning and they were ready for the final effort, when Peter balked at carrying Annie's climbing irons and camera. "He refused to carry anything except himself," Annie reported. She told him that if he carried nothing he was "not of the slightest assistance" and that carrying her necessary equipment was one of his essential duties. Peter had already been obstreperous more than once, but this refusal was crucial. He was so hopelessly inexperienced with the rope that Annie had already decided to go without it rather than trust him. Now with neither rope nor climbing irons available, Annie was stymied. Further advance was out of the question. The newspaper editor had stuck with the party until this point but now found he dared go no farther. His presence was not necessary, but Peter's was, as Annie found carrying even the slightest weight burdensome. Once again she was confronted with the uncompromising reality of faint-hearted males.

Recalling the superstitious natives of Mount Sorata, she had had a new cross made in Yungay for this ascent, and now she proceeded carefully to the edge of the glacier to plant it in the ice. Then, with a sad heart, she gave the order to retreat.

The editor later wrote rhapsodically of the episode of the cross: "The courageous American woman, notwithstanding that below her feet was a precipice reaching down to the glacier, took the cross . . . and resolutely traversed this dangerous place where at every step she was liable to go down to certain death." Annie's response to this report was typically honest. "I remember nothing of any place that seemed especially dangerous . . . In one place, indeed, I passed along a very narrow ledge with a nice drop below, but the footholds were quite sufficient and with a steady head, without which I should hardly be climbing, there was not the slightest danger."

Annie savored the descent down the "wonderful mountain," occasionally stopping to enjoy the view on the east side. Already she knew she would not be coming this way again; the west side clearly afforded the better route for her next attempt. And she did not feel as mournful as before, for although not attaining any spectacular altitude, she had been rewarded by "beholding scenery more magnificent than any which had previously come within my vision either in Europe or America."

Peter was paid off as quickly as possible. He was equally happy to depart. He had proved of scant service. Scared out of his wits most of the time, he swore he would not take such a trip again for a million dollars.

Not so Annie. Only five days later, rested and fired with new determination, she was at it again. She now abandoned her notion that an American or European white male should be along as an escort. She would take her chances with the Indians. Yungay friends assured her the Indians were safe; she had no need even to carry her revolver. And so she started up the west approach with five Indians as her only companions and porters. Though inexperienced in mountain climbing, these five Indians turned out to be the most reliable men she had had as porters so far, and during the two nights they spent on the mountain, she shared her seven-by-nine-foot tent with them without a qualm.

The little party fought valiantly to reach the saddle by the west slope. But a treacherous labyrinth of crevasses on the enormous glacier slowed their progress. Snow squalls beset them all along and by four o'clock of the second afternoon a fierce snowstorm blew in and lasted hours.

During the bitter cold night, Annie lay awake pondering the situation. They were an entire day and two thousand feet below the top of the saddle. After that, still another day would be needed to make the summit. Two more nights on the ice would be unspeakably cruel for the thinly clad Indians. Annie came to her own harsh decision this time. There was no question: again she must turn back; the weather was against her.

They camped at 17,600 feet, according to her aneroid barometer, and the next day, to avoid crevasses, climbed to 18,000 feet, she reckoned. Thus she had stood "where no mortal before had stood" and reached an altitude "possibly higher than any man or woman now residing in the United States." She still thought Huascarán to be higher than Aconcagua, and thus the highest in the hemisphere. On the ninety-mile horseback trip back to the coast, she planned her next assault. With dependable Indians, free of

MISS ANNIE S. PECK, A.M.

THE WORLD-FAMOUS MOUNTAIN CLIMBER, LECTURER, AND WRITER, OFFICIAL DELEGATE OF THE UNITED STATES TO THE INTERNATIONAL CONGRESS OF ALPINISTS, 1900, PRESENTS THE FOLLOWING LECTURES

Each Illustrated by 100 or more Wonderful Views which cannot be Duplicated in this Country. The Lectures may also be given without Illustrations

Bolivia and Mt. Sorata	To the Summit of the Matterhorn
Peru and Mt. Huascaran	
See Harper's Dec. 1906	Afoot and Alone in Tyrol
Panama and the Canal	
	Switzerland, with Ascent of the Jungfrau
Mexico, with Ascents of Popocatepetl and Orizaba	
	Athens, The Acropolis, and Ten other Lectures on Greece
The Passion Plays of Europe	

Also Business Opportunities in South America and the Pan American Railway.

MISS PECK IN CLIMBING COSTUME

Holding a second degree from the University of Michigan, the first woman to study at the American School of Archæology in Athens, having occupied the Chair of Latin at Purdue University and Smith College, Miss Peck is called by competent judges one of the most scholarly and accomplished women in the United States. Practically single-handed and alone she has accomplished extraordinary tasks. She has ascended higher on this hemisphere than any other American man or woman— to a height of approximately 20,500 feet on Mt. Sorata, in Bolivia—while in Peru she has made one first ascent and explored a section of country practically unknown here.

Miss Peck may be addressed at Hotel Albert, New York

superstitions about mountain summits, properly clothed and equipped (which her porters had never been), she was sure she could make it to the top. With sufficient food, gear, and ice axes, she believed, these natives could be so efficient that she could again dispense with Swiss guides (which she still considered desirable if funds were available). She would return early in the dry season, May or June, with the sun far to the north, the heat of midday not so fierce, the crevasses fewer, and the glaciers better covered with

37

snow. In these conditions, she figured, she should make a comparatively easy ascent to the saddle, and from there, with care, to the summit. Optimistic as always, she returned to Manhattan.

But here she confronted the same struggle for funds all over again. Despite her best efforts, she received no support, and 1905 passed without success. She was well into 1906 when *Harper's Magazine* offered her seven hundred dollars, not enough for Swiss guides — or for very much else, for that matter — but sufficient to send her forth on the instant. She called on *Harper's* on a Monday, signed a contract on Tuesday, and sailed on Thursday, May 25, 1906. Her capital was half that of the previous trip, but there was always Peruvian hospitality to see her through.

She entered Peru this time by the small port of Chimbote. Its lovely harbor simply implored development, she decided, and she foresaw a bonanza for any capitalist who had the courage to move in. "Were I a young man with $1,000 to start, I can conceive of no more favorable place to go and make my fortune than Chimbote," she wrote prophetically. Chimbote today is one of the half-dozen largest cities of Peru, having far outgrown Callao, the earlier port of favor.

Horses from the San Jacinto sugar plantation, again summoned by telegram from her former friendly hosts, were awaiting at Chimbote, and with them were mules and two men from the plantation. The first day's ride to the plantation was thirty miles, her first long horseback ride in the year-and-a-half interval since the last lengthy ride from Yungay to the coast. She arrived hardly able to stand from stiffness and exhaustion. But she continued the next day on the ninety-mile ride to Yungay. In Yungay her old friends the Vinatéas welcomed her warmly, and she began preparing for her third attempt, the second on the west side.

While preparing this trip, Annie learned that a man from a nearby town had telegraphed his wish to join her on her ascent, but she was urgently advised against accepting his company. He had once been "violently insane" and was still considered *loco*. Annie was charmed and decided, after all, she could still use an English-speaking companion. Always the optimist and no judge of character, she promptly got in touch with the man and invited him to come along.

With a new cross, five new Indian porters (her former men had, unfortunately, dispersed to other towns), and the so-called *loco,* she got under way at last, although two weeks later than she'd hoped. The start for the mountain from the Matarao mine, her former jumping-off point, was made on July 20. This time her Indians were well clothed. She had brought five pairs of heavy shoes from New York and had fashioned leggings of dynamite cloth cut into strips. Alpenstocks, ice axes, and climbing irons were provided, with strips of rawhide substituted for straps to fasten the climbing irons. Two pounds of coca leaves were among the provisions for her companions as well as for herself; she'd found the coca to be an "invaluable stimulant at great altitudes" and in her pragmatic way chewed it herself when needed. Pease meal, toasted maize, tea, sugar, Grape-Nuts, and cocoa were also included. The *loco* seemed intelligent and eager.

But the Indians were not to be compared with the stalwarts who had preceded them. They would do nothing unless told, and when one worked the others looked on. She had to dispatch one for water, another for firewood, assist them in pitching the tents, even show them how to place the iron stakes. In her new single-person tent, she was very cold the first night and had no sleep. Next morning the *loco* somehow managed to slide fifteen or twenty feet down a bare rock before they even got to the ice. Soon after their lunch of canned beef, parched maize, and chocolate, the Indians rebelled and wanted to halt for the night. The *loco* gave them a rousing lecture in Quichua, their native language, and they continued. But after Annie herself went into a dramatic slide, halted by the rope, but alarming to the Indians, they again began to protest and insisted on an early halt for the night, claiming fatigue.

Since it was still early after the tents were pitched, Annie added rice to the soup, but the water (snow) refused to boil and after two hours the rice was still raw. She sipped a couple of spoonfuls and retired to her tent, placed near the larger one occupied by the men. Now on the glacier rather than the edge of the ice as on the previous night, she felt a buffeting wind that was much colder. She wrote feelingly of the miseries of retiring on a glacier in a tiny tent: "To sit in cramped quarters with bundles and bags by my side, take off high laced boots, change stockings, get into Eskimo trousers,

39

pull out and make use of my toilet articles, cold cream, Pond's extract, Japanese stoves, comb and braid my hair, when half dead with fatigue and stiff with cold, — well, it was the hardest kind of labour. Every few minutes I was obliged to rest from exhaustion. Inside my bag I was still cold, especially my nose. A vicuña fur glove at length served as protection. I had additional clothing, but to get out of my sleeping bag and put it on was too great a task." (Being a proper Victorian lady, needless to say, she does not reveal how she took care of her functions of elimination.) Dressing in the morning meant getting out of her sleeping bag, combing her hair, putting on her boots. With nothing but snow available, she skipped any washing up.

When she blew her rising whistle at dawn, there was no response. Nor to her shouts. Peering into the Indians' tent, she discovered they had gone on strike. They would not stir, would not stay another night on the ice. Annie was outraged. These men had better clothing and equipment than any she had ever hired, and yet none had complained as loudly as these. She berated them vociferously in Spanish. She offered to pay them double, then triple the amount agreed upon. But they were adamant. The *loco* drew her aside and disclosed he had overheard their discussions in Quichua in the night. Not cold but fear gripped them, he said. They believed they would change to stone if they went higher. The *loco* himself complained of colic from eating the half-cooked rice.

Annie now desperately bargained with the head Indian, who had seemed a superior sort, and finally convinced him to carry her camera. He also consented to be tied with the rope despite his fear of being dragged to his death by another's fall. Leaving the other porters in the camp, Annie, the *loco,* and the head Indian started forward, the two men halfheartedly. Presently the *loco* went into an unnerving slide halted only because Annie stood firmly at her end of the rope. The episode did nothing to lift spirits, and the Indian had to be coaxed to remain on the rope and to carry the camera; he consented only after the promise of extra payment. Crevasses and detours delayed them so that by 1:30 they were still an hour or longer from the big rock at the foot of the north peak Annie initially had hoped to reach that day. They must get back to camp by three, otherwise the porters might well desert, abandoning the tents and gear on the glacier.

Disconsolately, Annie boiled snow to determine the elevation with her hypsometer, took some photographs, ate a hasty lunch, and began the descent. Reaching camp, she gave the order to retreat. The malcontents broke all records for packing, but even so the *loco,* claiming illness, and the head Indian, with some other excuse, started headlong down the mountain. It was left to Annie to rope herself and the four Indian porters and to lead them down. They spent the night on the edge of the snow and arrived at the mine the next morning. Her two supposed escorts had arrived the night before and headed onward. The fiasco ended with a loud quarrel with the porters about final pay, and Annie once more must have been wringing her hands at this new betrayal by undependable males.

Thus buffeted, but ever resilient, she was within a very few days ready for another attempt. And, still more surprising, prepared to accept as a companion — of all people — the *loco.*

The suggestion was his. Shortly after her return to Yungay, a letter from him arrived from his home in Carhuas enthusiastically proposing another expedition. Two days later he appeared in Yungay accompanied by a mine superintendent who also wanted to go along. Annie was cool at first. A new effort that might add only an additional thousand feet up the mountain was not worth the hard work. After the sleepless nights, exhausting days, and new facial burns and blisters, not to mention wasted funds, she would settle for nothing less than the summit.

But here was another chance. She soon succumbed. The *loco* hadn't been impossible, after all. Instead of Indian porters, they would use *cholos* this time, half-breeds with equal strength, greater courage, and no superstitions, she was told. These porters, unlike the others, would be required to sign a contract agreeing to pay a fine of twenty *soles* if they did not accompany Annie to the highest point of the saddle between the two peaks. Once at the saddle, they would bargain further for the summit, she thought. Annie was in transports once more at the prospect of a fourth attempt on Huascarán.

Forebodings of disaster began even before they got under way from the Matarao mine. The *cholos,* fearful of travel after dark, arrived a day late. Once started, before they reached the snow line, the *loco* vanished for hours, the mine super got colic from drink-

41

ing cold water, and Annie again encountered stubborn resistance in getting the porters to obey. The second day the mine superintendent dropped out entirely, leaving with Annie's climbing irons. Snow fell; the men refused to proceed because the tent had become wet and heavy. They called an early halt.

On the third day, the *loco* began giving real trouble. In the lead, he disputed Annie's choice of routes, untied the rope, and left the party. The *cholos* rebelled, demanding higher pay or they would drop half the equipment on the glacier. After bitter argument, Annie had to yield. Presently the *loco* was heard furiously shouting and whistling. His voice, it was discovered, was coming from the depths of a fifty-foot snow wall where he was cutting steps downward. He urged the others to follow this unreasonable course, but everyone, including Annie, retreated in terror. The man seemed to have gone mad.

The porters, now thoroughly demoralized, pitched the tents before Annie could stop them. As they settled into camp, their wandering companion's voice could be heard calling from time to time from a great distance and from across areas broken by impassable hollows. Later the voice drew nearer. Darkness fell, and as Annie could not get the men to take her lantern and candles to go search for him, she hung the lantern on an ice ax and anxiously stood waiting, wondering if her climb was to end in tragedy. The man's behavior was clearly that of a person bereft of reason. About nine o'clock they heard his cry on the next ridge, and he was brought safely to the tent. Annie now searched for a small bottle of whisky she carried for emergencies, but in vain; the *cholos* had stolen it. The *loco*, moreover, had lost her precious barometer.

Annie saw the situation as hopeless. There was no knowing what her unbalanced companion might do next. The *cholos* were anything but dependable. They had drunk up almost all the fuel alcohol essential for the next four days, the time still needed to reach the summit at their present rate of progress. Her hypsometer indicated they had attained an altitude of only around 17,500, a poor record for the two days.

And the calamity-beset expedition had not seen the last of disasters. One of the *cholos* dropped his pack into a deep crevasse, losing among other valuables the field glasses borrowed for the

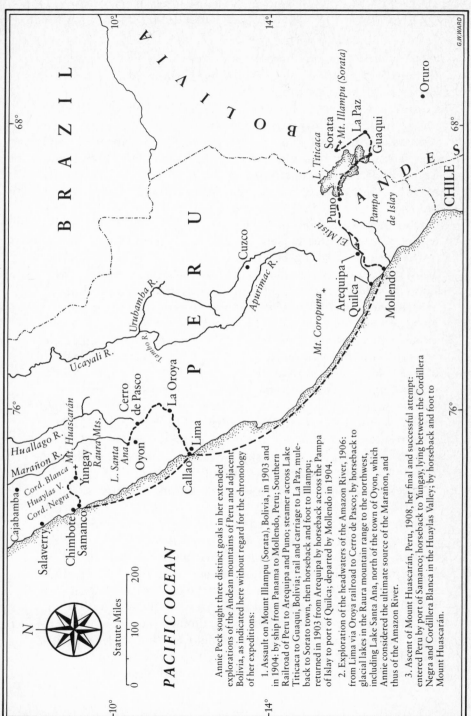

Annie Peck sought three distinct goals in her extended explorations of the Andean mountains of Peru and adjacent Bolivia, as indicated here without regard for the chronology of her expeditions:

1. Assault on Mount Illampu (Sorata), Bolivia, in 1903 and in 1904: by ship from Panama to Mollendo, Peru; Southern Railroad of Peru to Arequipa and Puno; steamer across Lake Titicaca to Guaqui, Bolivia; rail and carriage to La Paz, muleback to Sorato town, then horseback and foot to Illampu; returned in 1903 from Arequipa by horseback across the Pampa of Islay to port of Quilca; departed by Mollendo in 1904.

2. Exploration of the headwaters of the Amazon River, 1906: from Lima via Oroya railroad to Cerro de Pasco; by horseback to glacial lakes in the Raura mountain range to the northwest, including Lake Santa Ana, north of the town of Oyon, which Annie considered the ultimate source of the Marañon, and thus of the Amazon River.

3. Ascent of Mount Huascarán, Peru, 1908, her final and successful attempt; entered Peru by port of Samanco; horseback to Yungay, lying between the Cordillera Negra and Cordillera Blanca in the Huaylas Valley; by horseback and foot to Mount Huascarán.

Annie S. Peck Route Map

trip. Once more Annie had to lead the men down the mountain without help from the *loco*, who rushed downward on the excuse he needed to wire his wife.

In Yungay Annie now learned it was the *loco* himself who had set the *cholos* to demanding higher wages, for he was extracting a commission. He also claimed to know where the barometer had been left, and that he could rescue it for payment. Finally she heard he had declared he would like to kill her. He was sent by his family to some "baths" to calm his excited condition, and when Annie returned to Yungay in 1908 she heard he had become completely deranged, possibly from the strain of the expedition. With such an escort, Annie counted herself lucky to have returned alive.

The idea of climbing Huascarán with the help of local talent alone now had to be abandoned. Annie would return another year, but with other assistants, preferably Swiss guides. She had finally learned her lesson. Meanwhile, before leaving Peru, she intended to visit the famed copper mining center, the Cerro de Pasco Mining Company, at 14,500 feet the world's highest mining camp. No animals could be hired for the great distance of the direct ride from Yungay, so she had to return to Lima. She lingered in Lima for the visit of United States secretary of state Elihu Root, enjoying the social whirl of the capital, then took a train to the beautiful Rimac Valley, site of the Cerro de Pasco town of fifteen thousand. Here at an altitude impossible for many to endure, "on a cold bleak plateau with its grey leaden sky," had been created a settlement wholly drawn by the mineral riches of the region.

Eagerly investigating the town and mining operations, Annie was riding muleback one day when her saddlebags slipped off. Remounting after she'd secured the bags, she was suddenly thrown and dragged when the mule bolted. She rode back to Cerro in the bottom of a native cart, having suffered fractured ribs, bruises on her left arm, and deep gashes on her forehead and right hand.

But eighteen days after the accident she undertook an excursion to the Raura Range northwest of Cerro de Pasco with two young American men from the smelter who, though "destitute of experience," thought a mountain climb would be "fun." Her still-sore ribs did not deter her from a horseback trip that would be ninety to one hundred miles each way, and into rugged, little-known country. In this outpost region of "numberless and nameless peaks" she would find one to scale, she felt sure — although not one of Cerro's fifteen thousand inhabitants could help her with definite information. Of more importance, the expedition would take her into the possible headwaters of the Amazon River system, formed by the union of the Marañón and Ucayali rivers. At this period, little scientific work had been done to determine the source of the Amazon, one of the world's most extensive and complex river systems. Annie may well have been the first American woman to venture so deeply into this glacial lake region, then incompletely identified on maps, and her shrewd chapter on the journey forms a useful footnote to the long quest for the river's course. Even so, after Huascarán and Sorata, this was a gleeful twelve-day picnic.

She chose for her destination what she came to regard as the Amazon's initial source, a glacier on the second highest mountain of the Raura Range above Lake Santa Ana, whose water fed the Marañón. The Marañón River appeared to her to be the primary tributary because it extended the farthest west from the mouth and carried a greater volume of water than the Ucayali — though how she determined the latter point she does not say. The lake lies only about one hundred miles from the Pacific Ocean and a "short distance north" of the town of Oyon, she said, and she located it on her own map. Although the glacier was largely hollow and very dangerous, the climbing party attained a probable altitude of eighteen thousand feet. Annie then went on alone to the summit of a rock mountain of sixteen thousand feet, an ascent she made easily. It was her first summit in South America, the first time in all these climbs she had reached a mountaintop; though no mammoth among the Andes, it was higher than Mont Blanc.

Lake Santa Ana and the Raura Range are not listed in contemporary atlases. But support for Annie's assumptions came after World War II from an English writer-explorer, John Brown, who studied the Raura glacial lake region, including Lake Santa Ana, describing it in his book *Two Against the Amazon* (published in 1952), and including schematic sketches of the topography, although he regarded Lake Ninococha, lying just beyond Santa Ana and closer to the glacier, as the initial source. Today, the still-disputed question of the Amazon's true source counts strong supporters for the Ucayali-Apurímac tributary on grounds that it is the longest tributary, and they name Mount Huagra, some 130 miles south of Cuzco, as the origin of the Apurímac.

The two young American men in Annie's party found that the climb was not the fun time they had anticipated. They slid and shrieked and cursed all the way up the glacier, and they were left behind for the rock climb. Later they said they were astounded "that a woman could have such courage combined with such discretion and prudence." Annie did not agree "that those qualities are so rare among my sex." The guide remarked: "The Señorita is neither a man nor a woman; she is a cat." Annie had once been flattered by a guide in the Adirondacks who claimed, "She went where a chipmunk couldn't go!" Such comments confirmed Annie's conviction that mountain climbers are born, not made.

After four failures, Annie was still obsessed with the dream of mastering Huascarán. Returning to New York in December 1906, she feared that no one would take an interest in further efforts. Then to her joy, she learned that *Harper's* had published her article about her aborted attempt on Huascarán. Still more wonderful, they were ready to help on a new effort, although with less than the three thousand dollars she thought necessary to hire Swiss guides. But with their prestigious backing she felt optimistic about raising other funds. She was determined not to return without guides.

However, as always, the flow of money into her pockets was slow, and the months dragged by. She was well into the spring of 1908, with the last possible departure date to catch the dry season approaching, when a special delivery letter arrived, announcing new funds. The benefactor was a wealthy New York woman, Mrs. Anne Woerishoffer. Annie dedicated her *Search for the Apex of America* to her.

With funds now secured, Annie immediately cabled for Swiss guides, again by prearrangement, then dashed to Washington to seek the benediction of President Theodore Roosevelt, an honorary member of the recently formed American Alpine Club, of which Annie was one of the founding members. Why Annie needed his encouragement, or exactly how it assisted, is not clear from her somewhat enigmatic comments. Although the great sportsman was "not quite committed to Woman Suffrage," she wrote, "he was not the sort to decry women's ability, or when it had been proved, to throw stumbling blocks in her way." At any rate, he received her, for whatever it was worth.

So short was the time and so vast the preparations for this attempt, that even by noon of the day of sailing, June 27, 1908, Annie could not imagine how she would make the ship on time. She later complained that shipboard photographs published in newspapers made her "look about a hundred years old," since she was "a perfect wreck after months of labor and worry, several weeks of rush, and not a wink of sleep the night before." (She was actually fifty-eight.)

Since she started each of her climbing efforts in such a state of exhaustion, one wonders that she never trained between climbs or worked at keeping fit. "I have been asked about training for my mountain climbs," she said. "I heartily recommend such a course, but for myself, except when I climbed the Matterhorn, have had no opportunity. On my four trips to South America, I have gone on board ship at New York a perfect wreck; each time save in 1906, a little worse than before, having practically no exercise between voyages. But trifles like that and some that are worse must be endured with equanimity."

Favored with the "usual fair weather" (she imagined herself perpetually endowed with good weather), she was buoyantly confident of success on this voyage back to Peru.

In Yungay, at the home of her old friends the Vinatéas, she hastily acquired some pink cotton flannel to complete the outfits she'd assembled in New York for her porters. Cutting and sewing them herself, she made the "unmentionables" she'd failed to bring and could not buy in Yungay, where heavy woolen undergarments were not to be found. The climbing party moved on to the Matarao mine on August 6 and early the next morning started the ascent to the snow line, beginning her fifth attack on Huascarán.

In short order, the familiar male arrogance manifested itself. The Swiss guides rejected Annie's suggested line of ascent and pointed out a better way. As a result, they camped at a higher point than was desirable and had to make an unnecessary traverse the next day. Like her previous assistants, the Swiss dismissed her three

47

*The single-tent encampment at the edge of the glacier, on Annie's
fifth attempt to climb Huascarán in 1908*

abortive efforts on this, the west, side of the mountain (her first
attempt had been on the east side) as if they counted for nothing.
"One of the chief difficulties in a woman's undertaking an expedition of this nature is that every man believes he knows better what
should be done than she," Annie complained in exasperation.

Trying to cut back on expenses, Annie hired only two porters
this time, Domingo and Anacreo, planning to have the Swiss help
carry equipment. This meant doubling back on the track to bring
baggage forward to each new stop. One of the guides, Rudolf, lost
no time in objecting. He was not a porter, he declared, nor would
he double his route. On the heels of this dispute on their first day
on the mountain, Annie discovered she'd brought the wrong film.
Without photographs she could not document the view at the top.
She offered Domingo extra pay to return for the correct film and he
left immediately. In his absence, however, they would have only
one porter.

Annie hated having to take charge of the stove whenever the task
fell to her, but the shortage of porters forced her to do so through-

out this ascent. It had always meant that at night when others had retired, or early in the morning before they arose, she was nursing snow into a boil. And now for some reason the tedious melting of snow took three hours rather than the usual two of previous climbs.

> Imagine me then, early and late, sitting in or on my sleeping bag, coaxing the stove to melt snow for soup and tea! While the others were resting or were bringing the second installment of baggage, I sat by the hour, cramped and motionless, save for pumping a little pressure to the gas or adding chunks of snow to the kettle. How that stove would smoke, blackening the kettle and everything around; how we waited hour by hour for our soup at night, and after the others had gone to sleep, how I still sat melting snow for the water bottle next day! My work, though less arduous than the men's, continuing through a greater number of hours, was a severe tax upon my strength, obviously much less than theirs to begin with.

The old cry: Woman's work. Always over the stove!

But worse surprises awaited her. Next morning, their third day on the mountain, Rudolf announced he was too ill to continue. To Annie's astonishment, he departed forthwith. A Swiss guide suffering *soroche,* the mountain illness? A man who had lived his whole life in the mountains! While she was absorbing this shock, Domingo returned with the wrong film, despite explicit written instructions.

Disgusted, Annie opted to go on anyway, with one guide and no film. She, the other guide, Gabriel, and the two porters pressed on roped together into an area of terrible ice walls, chasms, and crevasses until they faced a wall nearly perpendicular in slope. Gabriel cut steps into the ice, but these were so steep Annie could hardly get one foot above the other. Gabriel, doing double duty in Rudolf's absence, appeared exhausted as the day wore on, and even remarked at one point that he was "about finished." He doggedly refused to chew coca leaves, as Annie and the porters were doing. After enormous exertions, they reached the top of the saddle at one o'clock Friday. As everyone was exhausted, they decided to start for the summit of the north peak on the following day.

At 6:15 in the early morning cold, they began the final ascent, roped, with Gabriel in the lead cutting steps in the ice. "Appalling" slopes confronted them, many surmounted by even more fearful jutting precipices. At noon, perched in midair, they ate lightly without much appetite, although they'd been on scanty rations for some time.

With each passing hour, Annie grew more concerned about Gabriel's weariness. It was still two hours to the summit, and, if they continued upward at this hour, the descent — the worst in her experience, as they were at a greater height — would have to be made after dark. Annie concluded she must give the order to retreat; the hazards of further progress were too great. They reached the tent exhausted, suffering acutely from the arduous downward trip.

Despite the advantageous altitude of this camp, Gabriel was too prostrate for another try for the peak next day. Too few porters made Rudolf's absence devastating, and their food was nearly gone. After nine nights, Annie saw that they had to give up. Bad luck continued on the descent: two sacks slipped into crevasses, one containing, among other articles, Admiral Peary's Eskimo suit and, even worse, the stove. Without a stove they could do no more climbing, and there were none in Yungay that burned kerosene or alcohol. Passing one campsite after another and recovering articles left at each, they at last reached Yungay, to the relief of those awaiting them.

Yungay had been in a state of alarm at their protracted absence. In going over the saddle, the party had vanished from the telescopic view of observers three days before and nothing had been seen of them since. Certain of disaster, the town had telegraphed to Lima, and the message had then been cabled to the United States, that Annie Peck and guides were last seen at an altitude of twenty-five thousand feet on a mountain said to be twenty-six thousand feet in height. Even Annie, who held great expectation for Huascarán's superior height, had never supposed that such an altitude was likely. The error would create no end of trouble for her, giving rise to accusations that she had exaggerated claims about Huascarán's elevation. Her own maximum estimates — later proved wrong — were of between twenty-three and twenty-four thousand feet. (Current citations give 22,205 feet.)

Her annoyance at the mistake was much mellowed by her appreciation of the genuine concern of her Yungay friends. A wanderer with little left of home or roots, she reflected rather sadly, "My peaceful death in my native city or elsewhere would occasion far less excitement than my brief disappearance aroused among those friendly folk." Once on one of her return voyages from South America, Annie had been asked by a fellow passenger, "Where is your home?" and she'd answered, "Where my trunk is." The gentleman had insisted: "But where is your real home?" She had reiterated, "Where my trunk is." Later, she realized she'd come to think of Yungay as her home.

Although by now fully accustomed to Annie's repeated assaults on their mountain, the people of Yungay were astonished to learn that, after a single day's rest, she had started preparations for her sixth attack. This time she would take four porters instead of two.

"Probrecita!" they exclaimed, the good citizens who had watched her battle over the years. The inexpensive Peruvian telegraph system, which compensated for lack of roads, bristled with the search for another stove, and soon a Norwegian model that burned kerosene with a gas flame was found in a nearby town — possibly the only one in the entire Huaylas Valley. Annie rapidly created two additional "unmentionables," and after ten days' organizing was ready to go, with Rudolf, now recovered, prepared to participate.

Annie was particularly optimistic now because in many ways she considered her party better equipped than ever before. But her own clothing, if not the party's entire gear, would have shocked even an amateur hiking group today. She wore, one might say, every warm garment she could find in her closet: "three suits of lightweight woolen underwear, two pairs of tights, canvas knickerbockers, two flannel waists, a little cardigan jacket, two sweaters, and four pairs of woolen stockings," none water or wind resistant. She would miss the Eskimo suit, as it had been her only real protection against wind and water. Her face and head covering was the most improbable of all: a knitted woolen ski mask purchased in La Paz, with

*On her final, successful ascent, Annie's
costume included a woolen face mask with
"a rather superfluous painted moustache."*

useful eye holes, mouth slit, and nose flap, but decorated with, as
she herself admitted, "a rather superfluous painted moustache."

They set out for the Matarao mine on Friday, August 28, Annie
more confident than ever, although she was running only a month
earlier than her 1904 failure and was long past her ideal climbing
month of June. But the mountain appeared better covered with
snow than before and in the best shape for scaling she had seen it.
At the last minute, a friend loaned her a heavy poncho, a most
unlikely garment for a professional climber. But later the poncho
would help save her life.

On Saturday Annie decided she was feeling a "bit faint," so postponed departure from the mine until the next day, a decision encouraged by dark clouds hanging ominously over the mountains. At eight the next morning, they set forth for the snow line. They made such excellent time that they arrived at their old first campsite at the early hour of two in the afternoon, had their soup and tea before dark, and turned in early.

By 7:15 the next morning, Monday, August 31, they were advancing upon the glacier. The Indians all wore climbing irons she had made for them, but Annie herself did not: the strap was too tight for her foot, which had come perilously near frostbite on the previous ascent. By four o'clock they were approaching their fourth camp, still ahead of their previous time. Despite high winds, their second night was not too uncomfortable.

All was still going well the next day when Lucas, one of the Indians, started across a doubtful ice bridge with his heavy pack. He was on the rope with Rudolf and Annie, when he suddenly disappeared into the crevasse below. Rudolf and Annie held firmly to the rope which was attached to Rudolf's ice ax. Gabriel quickly signaled for the men on the second rope to untie. This rope was dropped to Lucas who, though hanging head down, coolly tied it to his own rope, and then righted himself so he could be pulled out. But he had lost his pack — which contained the new stove.

Gabriel, who would time and again prove the hero of this ascent, daringly descended some thirty feet into the chasm. He could not bear to lose their stove. After a fearful interval, he came back up with the pack, out of breath from the tremendous effort at this altitude, but saving the expedition. By nightfall they had camped at the top of the saddle. In only two days from the snow line, they had arrived at the point Annie previously had failed time and again to reach.

The next day, Rudolf once more jeopardized the trip. As they pushed forward, Annie wished to change into the vicuña mittens specially made for her in La Paz, which Rudolf was carrying in his rucksack. In an incredible fumble, Rudolf dropped one of these vital articles and in an instant it was whipped from sight by the gale wind. Annie was too angry to speak; but she would wait until they got down to unload her fury.

Then about two in the afternoon, with the summit quite near, Rudolf proposed stopping, for no apparent reason. Gabriel had to urge him on. As they approached the peak, Gabriel suggested it would be wise to take observations before ascending into the full blast of the wind on top, and Annie agreed. Rudolf then untied the rope and disappeared, while Annie and Gabriel struggled to light the candle for the hypsometer, a chore Rudolf could have helped facilitate by holding the poncho against the wind. But the wind was so high and time so short they finally had to give up. It was already three o'clock and Annie, thinking of the dreaded descent, decided to forgo taking the altitude rather than risk further delay. They quickly packed the hypsometer and prepared to make their triumphant emergence on Huascarán's peak.

At this moment Rudolf appeared and announced he had gone on to the summit alone.

Annie's outrage knew no bounds. She was flabbergasted. Such a violation of ethics! By all the laws of courtesy, as well as by her own explicit instructions, she should be the first to step upon the peak. Instead, this cowardly man who had defected at sixteen thousand feet on the previous ascent, necessitating a second climb, and who had almost slumped out today, then by his absence had prevented the crucial altitude observations, not to mention his carelessly losing Annie's mitten — now he had stolen the honor of first to the top.

It was a mere token, of course, for only a short distance lay between Annie and the summit, but the action was nonetheless base and inexcusable. Annie postponed her remonstrance in view of the freezing cold and howling wind. But by the time they reached the bottom, Rudolf was beset by such serious problems of his own she never had the heart to speak her mind.

As Annie stepped upon the broad ridge, possibly forty feet wide, that constituted the summit, she had only one thought: "Shall we ever get down?" Her sense of accomplishment was overcome by fear of the descent that awaited them. The last stretch to the summit had been so dangerous and difficult she wondered how they could possibly negotiate it downhill after dark. She was so absorbed in this thought, she even forgot to have Gabriel take a photo of her at the peak. She did snap pictures of views from the four quadrants, then without a moment's rest began the downward journey. It was already 3:30. They had spent seven hours scaling the peak and would certainly be overtaken by darkness on the way down.

She later recalled that nothing she had imagined was as terrible as the actual experience. The retreat down the icy slopes along the small hacked-out steps, down the steep rocks, across hollow ice — the whole descent was a torture she would never forget. For quite a while she had realized her left hand had lost all feeling in the absence of the vicuña mitten. At last thoroughly frightened, she donned the poncho, an Indian-style blanket with a slit in the center for her head, under which she could protect her hand. Later she was certain the poncho saved not only her hand but her life, providing much-needed warmth as the bitter night came on. But it also constituted a peril, its folds causing her to fumble and slide.

"My recollection of the descent is as of a horrible nightmare," she wrote afterward.

The little moon seemed always at my back, casting a shadow over the place where I must step. The poncho would sway in the wind, and, with my motion as I was in the act of stepping, would sometimes conceal the spot where my foot should be placed. Although my eye for distance is good, my foot once missed the step. Slipping then on the smooth slope so that I fell, as usual in the sitting posture, crying out at the same time to warn the guides, I expected nothing serious, but to my horror, I did not remain where I was. Still sitting I began to slide down that glassy, ghastly incline. As we were all nearly in the same line, I slid at least fifteen feet before coming to a halt, when checked by the rope. Now to get back! The guides called me to get up, but being all in a heap with the rope tight around my waist, I was unable to move. The guides therefore came together just above and hauled me up the slope. Thankful again to be in the line of the steps, though more alarmed than ever, I went onward, resolved to be more careful. But again I slipped, and again slid far below. While from the beginning of the descent, I had greatly feared the outcome, after these slips my terror increased. Several times I declared that we should never get down alive.

Five or six times more she slipped, always with staunch Gabriel holding the rope and saving her. At one point Rudolf sped past in a great slide but Gabriel held both Annie and Rudolf secure, or the three would have dropped thousands of feet.

It was 10:30 at night when they gained the saddle and the tent, too tired to eat or, at first, to sleep. Seven hours, many in the dark, they had spent picking their precarious way down the ice! Rudolf's hands were badly frozen, the left the worse, his fingers black. He had laid down one of his mittens on the slope to fasten his shoe, and lost it to the wind. Annie had witnessed this stupidity, but after dark a second mitten had blown away, and he had said nothing about the loss.

Annie, the two guides, and four Indians huddled in the tent all night, battered by a howling wind and too spent to rub Rudolf's hands to help stimulate circulation. All the following day and night they remained prostrate in the tent; the alcohol had mysteriously disappeared so they were without fire, and therefore without water, soup, or tea.

By the next day, Friday, they bestirred themselves to continue downward. The three-hundred-foot perpendicular wall now had to be descended. Their three ropes tied together reached 180 feet to an intermediate ledge, and one by one Gabriel and Lucas lowered each person over the edge, Annie going last. Halfway down, Annie found the rope going dangerously slack and untied it as a signal to pull it more taut, while she perched in a precarious niche in the wall to wait. But the two men above could not see her and did not hear her shouts, so drew the rope up, thinking she was safely ensconced with the others. At last Gabriel realized the situation and lowered himself to the rescue. It was their last heart-stopping episode. They reached their first campsite safely, having gone forty-eight hours without fire and water.

In Yungay by the next day, they rushed Rudolf to a doctor. His foot had also frozen. Annie, aghast at the tragedy which took the bloom off her triumph, was also annoyed. "Incredible and inexcusable" were her words for such carelessness by a professional guide. In one way or another, Rudolf could have cost all of them their lives. He had refused to wear extra socks, despite Annie's admonitions, and had left an extra flannel shirt in the tent, as well as four pairs of extra mittens. Annie had warned him at every turn and so was partly consoled that "it was his own fault, and not a necessary consequence of the climb." Charitably, she pondered if the altitude had "rendered him stupid, as at lower levels he had seemed as thoughtful and as careful as Gabriel." In the end, despite treatment, amputation was necessary for the left hand, a finger of the right, and half of one foot. Annie left Yungay after making arrangements for his care and Gabriel remained to help get him home. He was not able to leave until December.

In her farewell to the mighty Huascarán, her tormentor for nearly a decade — "that magnificent mountain, conquered at last, after so many years of struggle, days and weeks of hardship and now at such cost" — Annie said she felt like shaking her fist at it and saying, "I have beaten you at last and I shall never have to go up there again."

Harper's Magazine of January 1909 carried Annie's article "The First Ascent of Mount Huascarán," with the adulatory editorial comment: "The conquest of Mount Huascarán will stand as one of the most remarkable feats in the history of mountain-climbing. That this first ascent has been accomplished by a woman renders it still more wonderful. Undaunted by her failure to reach the summit of Huascarán in the summer of 1906, Miss Peck started out some months ago in the interests of *Harper's Magazine* to try again. The news of her success has already been cabled around the world, but this is Miss Peck's first account of her daring achievement."

An exact and vivid reporter, Annie opened by describing the problem she faced.

The conquest of a mountain like Huascarán is truly a gigantic task. Although more favorably situated than many others in that it rises directly above a city of considerable size (Yungay), the fact that 9,000 feet of snow must be surmounted, of which the lower edge is higher than the loftiest elevation in the United States proper, and that the real climb begins only when one has surpassed the summit of Mont Blanc, renders the undertaking one of extraordinary hardship and difficulty. Not all mountains of approximately the same height present similar conditions. It is an astonishing circumstance that Mount Aconcagua, though much farther from the equator and with the reputation of a greater altitude, possesses no such vast extent of snow-field and glacier, so that anyone who is able to endure the rarity of the air may walk without danger over ashes, rocks and streaks of snow quite to the topmost ridge. Far otherwise is it with Huascarán.

As for the height of the mountain, she said that since she had been denied the chance to take observations of altitude at the summit, her estimates had to be postulated on observations taken at the saddle, at which point she judged the elevation to be approximately twenty thousand feet. The distance from the saddle to the peak, according to guesses by the two Swiss guides and from her own surmise, appeared to be about four thousand feet. Thus she speculatively and conservatively set the probable height of Huascarán as above twenty-three thousand feet, "higher than Aconcagua (22,800), and the loftiest mountain known on this hemisphere." Still on a speculative note, she commented: "If, as seems probable, the height is 24,000 feet, I have the honor of breaking the world's record for men as well as for women."

Annie published a similar article in the June 1909 *Bulletin* of the American Geographic Society. She might have known, had she been more sophisticated, that any claim to a world's record, however tentative, is a red flag to the competitive spirits of the globe. Annie was now up against a greater foe than Huascarán itself. In the jealous, suspicious world of exploration, little is left uncontested. Annie, a woman, was an immediate target. Yet her most belligerent antagonist was another woman, Fanny Bullock Workman. While Annie was building a reputation in the Western Hemisphere and the Alps, Fannie Bullock Workman and her husband, Dr. Hunter Workman, were capturing mountaintops in the Himalayas, having already long before "done" the Alps and other European peaks.

Annie's claim of having reached a record altitude aroused the redoubtable and disputatious Mrs. Workman to a towering rage. She moved like an avalanche to crush the idea that any woman held title to an ascent higher than her own. Money being no object for the wealthy Workmans, she solicited help from the head of the

Société Générale d'Études et de Travaux Topographiques of Paris, M. Henri Vallot, to check out Huascarán's pedigree. At her expense, an expedition was dispatched to Peru in July 1909 to triangulate the disputed rampart. Results were published in an expensive tome.

The pages of *Scientific American* now became the arena for one of the memorable conflicts in mountaineering annals. In her hammer-fisted style, Mrs. Workman issued the first challenge. Her team, she reported, had determined the height of the north peak climbed by Miss Peck to be 21,812 feet; of the south peak, still unscaled, 22,187. "Miss Peck's highest ascent to date therefore stands, north peak Huascarán 21,812 instead of 24,000 feet, as she estimated it; she has not the 'honor of breaking the world's record,' either for men or women, for my two highest ascents of respectively 22,568 and 23,300 feet debar her from that honor in the case of women, while a number of men have made ascents exceeding her highest," she declared.

Annie blasted back. Since high winds had prevented the taking of hypsometric observations on the summit, she certainly had not expected the scientific world to regard her estimate as an exact measurement. "If anyone did so, I cannot be responsible," she wrote. As for Mrs. Workman's checkup on Huascarán, she was scornful: "It was, of course, quite within the province of anyone to take so great an interest in the matter as to spend some thousands of dollars in sending engineers to Peru to make a triangulation of the mountain, and to publish this as the absolute height of Huascarán," she said. Indeed, she questioned the accuracy of *any* triangulation, quoting a Mr. A. L. Mumm of the English Alpine Club:

"The results of triangulations do not always agree, and even when they practically coincide, they cannot be accepted as absolutely unimpeachable. There is good reason to suppose that the effect of refraction is not yet sufficiently understood for allowances made for it to be perfectly accurate; the higher and more remote the summit, the larger is the possibility of error. Bearing these facts in mind, it will be apparent that anyone who starts to form a decided opinion as to what persons are entitled to the honor of having reached the highest elevations has a very pretty tangle to unravel."

Annie finished her remarks by observing that her request that Mrs. Workman supply supporting figures of her own unpublished observations of her Himalayan ascents had not been answered. This was an allusion, undoubtedly, to contentions and debates that had surrounded certain of the Workmans' so-called new discoveries as well as some of their altitude claims.

Dr. Workman himself pitched in at this point with a lengthy letter to *Scientific American* refuting Mumm's view about the error potential in triangulation and further attempting to discredit Annie. All this was disquieting to her, but she did not outwardly show that it had done much to dampen her sense of victory.

Annie was mournful over the money spent, however. The $13,000 the Workmans had sunk on reassessing Huascarán's height was a fortune she could have stretched endlessly. It was such "a large sum to spend for triangulation of a single mountain in which it cost but $3,000 to climb. With $1,000 more for my expedition, I should have been able with an assistant to triangulate the peak myself. With $12,000 additional I could have triangulated and climbed many mountains and accomplished other valuable explorations."

But she accepted the Workmans' figures. "It would thus appear that Huascarán is not so lofty as I had hoped," she conceded. However, she maintained that her years of effort had conquered a mountain at least fifteen hundred feet higher than Mount McKinley, and twenty-five hundred feet higher than had been climbed by any man residing in the United States. And no one could take from her the fact that it was the first ascent ever made of the mighty Huascarán, the highest peak in Peru.

This last victory was all that mattered to the government of Peru. In the excitement that followed her achievement, which had focused the eyes of the world on Peru, and before she had departed the country, she was received by the president, her former friend, Leguia, the British sugar company agent in Lima who had often helped with horses. He presented her with a gold medal, twenty-two carats fine, bearing the words: *"El Gobierno del Peru à Annie*

*Annie poses prior to a lecture, holding the
silver stirrup presented by the Lima
Geographical Society.*

S. Peck — *Nadie llegó antes que ella à la cumbre del Huascarán, 2
Stbre, 1908"* ("No one arrived before her at the summit of Huascarán," was Annie's translation). The accompanying presidential decree praised the North American's stimulation of exploration in "the lofty summits of Peruvian Andes, especially . . . the Nevado Huascarán."

Annie became the first woman to address in Spanish the Lima Geographical Society, illustrating her lecture about Huascarán with stereopticon views. Interest was so great that more people were turned from the door than were allowed to enter, and a hundred or more remained standing outside. The following day, the society presented her with a solid silver stirrup in the form of a slipper, a traditional design from the Spanish colonial era. (In 1928, twenty years after her triumph, the society named Huascarán's north peak in her honor, *Cumbre Ana Peck,* using her first name lest there be any mistake that a man had accomplished the feat. Reporting this, the *Washington Post* noted that the "Ana" was inserted because "the committee was unanimously desirous of leaving on record the fact that this magnificent effort was made by a woman.")

Nearly sixty years old when she finally surmounted Huascarán, Annie was not about to accept some mythical age line when she could take things easier. She began to recount her trip immediately on her return and after finishing various articles on Huascarán wrote her engrossing account of adventures in South American mountaineering, published in 1911, *Search for the Apex of America: High Mountain Climbing in Peru and Bolivia, Including the Conquest of Huascarán, With Some Observations on the Country and People Below."* She wrote with a fresh eye, in sharp and exciting detail, giving glimpses of Bolivian and Peruvian life in the first decade of this century, and of the primitive travel conditions, as well as stirring accounts of her various climbs. It is a book of particular interest to anyone curious about early mountaineering in the Southern Hemisphere.

But it was not an easy moment in her life. She did not immediately find a publisher, an embarrassment in itself, and meanwhile she was struggling to meet her weekly room rent of seven dollars until she could get an advance on acceptance. Also despite her outward stance of victory regarding her Huascarán accomplishment, she was in fact deeply pained by the challenges to her integrity. During 1909 and 1910 she poured out her anguish in long letters to Commander Robert E. Peary (later Admiral) whose challenged claim of reaching the North Pole in 1909 after many attempts Annie compared to her own debated climb of Huascarán. "I thought when I had climbed my mountain my troubles would be over, as doubtless you did when you got to the Pole, never dreaming that fate could pay you so shabby a trick," she wrote Peary on July 14, 1910. In another letter she reported, "Mrs. Workman has continued to be rather hateful about my mountain climbing. Of course she had a right to have it [Huascarán] measured if she wanted to but if you have a chance to speak a good word for me anywhere in Europe, I trust that you will do so, especially to refute any notion that I am less scientific than she. I have a far better education and I rather think as much brains, but unfortunately no money to take along topographers." She concludes with a touching appeal for a loan of two hundred dollars to tide her over until the book has been accepted.

Peary evidently responded to this request, for another letter to him voices warm thanks. But her hero declined her request that he write an introduction to her book, on the grounds that he did not "feel sufficiently posted in regard to mountaineering to write appropriately on the subject." This disappointment did not deter her from publishing a long, blistering article in the *Brooklyn Eagle* refuting the claims of Dr. Frederic Cook, who she said was "not to be trusted" in either his assertion that he had climbed Mt. McKinley or reached the North Pole. In the Peary-Cook dispute that still surfaces today, Annie's loyalty to Peary was unflagging.

After Huascarán, Annie returned to South America periodically to lecture and do research for her books. In 1911 she planted a pennant proclaiming "Votes for Women" on Peru's second highest peak, Nevado Coropuna (21,079 feet). In 1912 and again in 1916 she delivered three lectures in Spanish to the Library of the National Council of Women in Buenos Aires, and addressed a thousand businessmen on the leading U.S. industries. Another South American swing in 1922–1924 again promoted mutual knowledge between the hemispheres. Her authority was enhanced by the publication in 1913 of her excellent guidebook *The South American Tour,* illustrated with her own photographs taken from Panama to Tierra del Fuego, and in 1922 by her useful economic survey, *Industrial and Commercial South America* — both heading the Pan-American Union's recommended reading list. Her books and steady schedule of lectures made her one of the foremost interpreters of Latin American life.

As Annie was now approaching eighty, one might have expected her activities to subside a bit. Instead, she embarked on one of the great adventures of her life. From the earliest flutter of an airplane wing, she had followed developments in aviation with fascination.

63

Perhaps it was the similarity of attempts to elevate the human body that intrigued her. A few weeks after she first sailed for South America in 1903, she noted with interest that the Wright brothers had tested their first plane on Kitty Hawk Hill, North Carolina, attaining a free flight of fifty-nine minutes. Five years later in 1908, about the time she was climbing Huascarán's north peak, the Wrights, now in France, attained flights of up to seventy-seven miles' duration, with later flights in Italy, Spain, and England. They returned to the United States covered with honors, and in 1909 were preparing to stage a spectacular flight over the Hudson River in connection with the Hudson-Fulton Celebration, commemorating Henry Hudson, who first explored the Hudson River in 1609, and Robert Fulton, who launched the *Clermont,* the first steam-driven ship, on the Hudson in 1807.

Annie, now back in New York, fresh from her Huascarán triumph — "then being in the height of my glory," she said — called on Wilbur Wright at the Hotel Vanderbilt a day or two before the Hudson River flight was to take place. Annie aspired to be the first woman in America, possibly the world, to fly as a passenger, and she proposed that she accompany Wilbur Wright across the Hudson. She seemed to have been unaware that a Mrs. Hart O. Berg had already captured the "first in the world honor" by flying with Wilbur Wright in Aubours, France, on October 7, 1908, for two minutes, three seconds. Tying her full skirt around her legs against the wind that thrashed the passenger seat, Mrs. Berg had inspired a Parisian dressmaker present at the flight to design the idiotic "hobble skirt," which would enjoy only brief popularity. Annie had probably not even heard of Mrs. Berg since Wright took up many passengers while in France, and Berg's record would have been made while Annie was deep in the mountains of Peru.

In any case, Annie laid her petition before Wright, no doubt in her most winning manner. But she was nonetheless disappointed. "Mr. Wright received me with much courtesy," she later reported, "but to my inquiry if I could go with him he responded that he would take me if anyone; but he would make the flight alone."

If she couldn't be the first, "why be the thousandth?" she felt, spurning mere "joy rides" as air travel became less novel. She did nothing more about flying, continuing to make her South American trips by rail and ship. An invitation from Colonel Charles A. Lindbergh would have been promptly accepted, for even an hour's flight, she admitted later. "Had he been aware that I had climbed higher on my two feet than he in his airplane, perhaps he would have asked me," she once remarked half in jest.

In February 1929 came the announcement that air service from Panama south would soon be inaugurated. Local air service had been developing within and between the South American countries, but soon long-distance flight that would obviate slow sea trips was to be available.

This new chapter in aviation inspired Annie to fly at last. She decided to make her tenth visit to South America a tour by air, not merely flying around the edge of the continent, as a few men had done, but using the local services within each country, reporting on individual interior connections and on the interesting aspects of each leg of the trip. It was a herculean undertaking, particularly since Annie, dedicated to thorough research, was determined not to miss a single airline engaged in regular service in a single South American or Caribbean country. (She actually skipped Venezuela, for some reason.) She would even include points far from the usual tourist spots as well as the large cities and ordinary meccas. She would also take the train to include some important site not attainable by air but a reasonable side trip for the visitor.

The whole amazing experience she afterward described in her *Flying over South America: Twenty Thousand Miles by Air,* published in 1932. The account, written immediately after she returned from a trip that would have frazzled most others, is a lively story of seven months' travel, from November 1929 to June 1930, over twenty thousand miles in a dozen varieties of airplanes. It was the longest journey by air yet credited to any traveler from the north, but none of it, even the spectacular crossing of the eighteen-thousand-foot Andes, carried her as high as she'd reached by foot on Huascarán or Nevado Coropuna.

She returned an aviation enthusiast, stating emphatically that age had nothing to do with adjustment to or enjoyment of air travel. Her picture in the *New York Sun* showed a delicate-looking old lady with white hair in a neat bun atop her head,

Annie at age eighty, on her return from a twenty-thousand-mile flight over South America

wearing rimless spectacles, choker beads, and her treasured Peruvian gold medal pinned proudly on her lace yoke. She was eighty when she finished this great flight. All over South America she had made news, greeted by officials as "amiga del America del Sur," and the "heroine of Huascarán." The airlines must have loved this elderly voice proclaiming the ease and comfort of air travel.

The fact was, however, that Annie had had to rise before dawn for nearly every leg of the journey to arrive for flights that always started with first light in order to make the most of daylight in the absence of landing lights. Planes were mostly small, frequently sea planes, and sometimes she was the only passenger. She spent nights in every kind of hotel. Flying schedules were informal, easily post-poned in the face of thunder or lightning, or a pilot might turn back if ominous clouds were ahead. (All navigation was by ground contact.) One pilot turned back because he had failed to deliver a package. There were two forced landings, neither seeming to bother Annie a bit, although one was in an empty field, the other in a river. She always sat as far back as possible on the left side, so that whether going down the west coast or back up the east she caught the important shot with her camera. Her photographs taken through the plane window, along with others collected along the way, illustrate her book.

The trip had been tiring, however, so much so she nearly missed a dinner arranged by her friends to celebrate her eightieth birthday at the Hotel Commodore in New York, on November 24. She wrote her thanks for a congratulatory telegram sent by the Society of Woman Geographers (to which she had been elected in 1925): "Unfortunately I collapsed November 12 from ten years' over-work, spent five unhappy days in a hospital, and practically got out of bed to go to the dinner. A hair dresser came and the maid of a friend, who helped me dress. My friend called to take me to the dinner of which I dared eat only a mouthful or two and brought me back. I was good for nothing until February."

Annie was at last beginning to wind down. She climbed only smaller mountains after this trip. Her last was Mount Madison (5,362 feet) in New Hampshire, in the Presidential Range of New England's White Mountains. She quit climbing only when her phy-sician warned that altitude might affect her heart and lived quietly in a Manhattan hotel, occasionally sending letters to newspapers. A German climbing party's claim of a first ascent on Huascarán in 1932 triggered a new dispute over Annie's own claims. But the American Alpine Club, among other authorities, had supported Annie's report and, as the *Standard Encyclopedia of the World's Mountains* declares, "history has been inclined to give Miss Peck the benefit of the doubt."

Sedentary life palling, by March 1934 she was off on a cruise alone to the islands of the West Indies and Trinidad, and a few months later, in September, went with a companion to Newfound-land. Her eighty-fourth birthday, in October 1934, was celebrated by her fellow members of the New York group of the Society of Woman Geographers at a reception in a member's studio. Newspaper pictures imparted a happy impression of Annie smiling, hair smartly finger waved, an enormous orchid at her shoulder, her face lighted by eighty-four glowing candles on a huge birthday cake.

In January 1935, three months later, she started a seventy-five-day world tour. But after climbing the steep road to the Acropolis in Athens, which she had visited years before, she turned back. Her health had been failing. On July 18, 1935, she died in her apartment at the Hotel Monterey in Manhattan after a short illness. She was cremated and her ashes were buried in Providence. Her brother, William Thane Peck, was her nearest surviving relative.

Her will left "minor sums" to two nieces and the residue of her estate valued at $38,245 to the Massachusetts Hospital for Women in Roxbury, Massachusetts, a sum that, though modest, was surprising for someone who had earlier begged for loans to pay her rent.

Annie Peck has been judged from highly disparate points of view, as a doughty heroine or an implacably driven tyrant. About the diversity of her natural talents there is no disagreement. In the words of Mary Edith Butler's open-letter tribute shortly before Annie died, "She is a versatile woman, scholar, writer, lecturer, mountain climber, swimmer, oarswoman, horsewoman, splendid conversationalist, at home in the drawing room, the ballroom, at the bridge table; adaptable to a tent on an ice field or to a long journey on the back of a burro under the blistering sun that South Americans know best."

Argument exists on the subject of her ambition to tread the untrodden. Was she a dreamer who dared, who had to test herself, to climb "because it was there"? Or was she a crassly ambitious person ready to sacrifice others for her goals? After her scaling of Mount Huascarán was hailed by the world as a major feat, the *Athenaeum*, a leading magazine of the day, commented: "She has done all that a man could, if not more. She had sagacity, and with it, 'nerve' and 'grit.' "

At the opposite extreme is the harsh judgment in the Radcliffe *Notable American Women* biographical dictionary:

Miss Peck's success as a mountain climber was achieved in the face of inadequate financing, too little equipment, and inexperienced assistants and porters. Her book *A Search for the Apex of South America* (1911) is a chronicle of near disasters. She exposed herself and others to needless danger and suffering by making do with what she could afford: her financing came from the contributions of friends and from magazines such as *Harper's* which paid in advance for her articles, and was often less than her minimum projected expenses. Lacking accurate information on the terrain, oxygen for high altitudes, and, often, adequate clothing for her native porters, she drove her men relentlessly, impatient with their inexperience and unwillingness to follow her judgment in all matters. The less than full acceptance of her leadership she attributed to resentment against her as a woman. For her desire to succeed overcame concern for personal danger, lost packs, altitude sickness and other hazards of mountain climbing, and she had little sympathy for those who did not share her ambition. Certainly there was a steely element in her nature that inspired grudging admiration rather than affection.

In answer to this, one might say that comparable indictments — in part or totally — might be made against many male explorers. Most of them drove their assistants. All were consumed with a lust for success or they would not have embarked on journeys that were bound to involve danger and suffering. Byrd, Peary, Pizarro, Cortés, Columbus, Marco Polo — any explorer with serious ambitions, dead set on winning his goal, has been by nature singleminded and egomaniacal. Considering the hazards and frustrations of the trade, there is no reason to suppose the same ruthlessness would not be essential for a female explorer — perhaps more necessary because she is a woman. One can accept that the character of an explorer by definition requires a steely edge that might not be lovable.

Whatever her flaws, Annie Peck's legacy is an image of intrepidity and daring. Her example was a powerful encouragement to women in this country to enter outdoor activities, particularly mountaineering.

One can be glad that Annie was spared the sight of the destruction of her beloved Yungay, the hospitable town at the foot of Huascarán. On May 31, 1970, a catastrophic earthquake smashed its way ashore from the Pacific seabed, destroying a six-hundred-mile stretch along the Peruvian coast. The intense movement started a landslide on Huascarán that buried Yungay and part of a nearby town under a sea of mud, snow, and rocks. Of the several thousand inhabitants, only a few hundred survived, and where Yungay once stood only four palm trees remained.

DELIA J. AKELEY

1875–1970

November 21, 1924 — After a restless night with porters running after women in the village, then handclapping and singing, I felt a wreck when Ali came to my tent and called "Memsahib, time to start." The rascal got us up at 3:30 and we were in the canoes by 4:15. But never have I been so thrilled by a water journey. Everything looked weird and mysterious. The cries of the birds and monkeys were strange. Before daylight an old hippo bellowed and came with a rush, and the men nearly upset the canoe driving it against the bank, ready to jump. The river had risen during the night and was running a good ten or fifteen miles an hour; current pretty stiff for those who managed the dugout. In half fading moonlight we passed the most beautiful river scenery imaginable; trees one hundred and fifty feet high with cables of vines and creepers hanging from the great limbs and streaming out on the water like a huge curtain that almost shut out the light. Sometimes the boys would strike this mass of green with the punting poles. Huge lizards and often snakes would drop into the water, or a troop of monkeys or sleeping birds would go chattering and screeching away. Ants, some with a wicked pair of nippers, and worms, flies, spiders and other insects would drop upon us. Startled fish would jump out of the water, sometimes into the boat. We finally saw an open spot on the Somaliland side and made camp, with my tent under the thorn trees and almost at the very edge of the river bank. It takes hours to look after the wounds on my feet. My big toe is really worrying me greatly and I am afraid of real trouble. Insects are the curse of this country and the feet of the natives and also of my men are repulsive with wounds and sores. My porters clean their clothes of lice by putting them in the sun and putting dirt all over them. They wash their bodies but not their filthy clothes. Consequently, they have cooties, fleas, and other parasites and it takes half a day to keep myself free from them for the men of necessity are handling my things. Kerosene, iodine, peroxide, permanganate, and cigarette ashes are used freely and still they get the best of me. Even as I write this, the lantern's light attracts things which would both sting and bite. Today I fought a tetse [sic] fly all the way upstream. I turned up my collar and rolled down my sleeves and then kept a bush of leaves waving wildly all the time, and still he was so persistent that he lit on my thin silk shirt sleeve twice and he had a nice feast on the boy in the bow of the canoe.

The year was 1924 and Delia Akeley was near the beginning of her journey across Africa. Her journal, scrawled in faint pencil, often by lantern light in tents and rest houses, was laboriously written while she traveled — at this stage by dugout up the crocodile-infested Tana River through eastern Kenya, where she camped at night on the riverbanks with her black porters, her only companions.

A slender but sturdy American woman five feet five inches tall, with pale, delicate skin and sapphire blue eyes, Delia Akeley was doggedly pushing her way across the immense continent without benefit of safari agents, white hunters, or trained guides. A newspaper photograph published before she left the States showed her to be a middle-aged matron, elegantly dressed, her white hair piled beneath a stylish hat, a pince-nez on her nose.

Delia journeyed in classic caravan style, her porters bearing her tents, cooking gear, luggage, rubber bathtub, photographic equipment, and silver dining service on their backs. Over land, she resorted to donkeys, camels, *tepoi* (litter), and foot. When she emerged from the stupendous wilderness of the Belgian Congo (modern Zaire), at the town of Boma at the Congo River's mouth, nearly a year later, she became the first Western woman — possibly the first woman — to have traversed the African continent alone from the Indian Ocean to the Atlantic.

Delia chose her route from Lamu on Kenya's coast in order to explore primitive areas still little penetrated by outsiders — in some cases where local peoples had rarely or never seen a white female, certainly not one traveling on her own. She sought out hidden Pygmy tribes in the fierce Ituri Forest in the isolated northeastern Belgian Congo and lived among them for months, sharing their daily chores, hunting with them, playing with them, and fending off their efforts to discover if the rest of her body was white like her hands and face.

Delia's announcement in Manhattan that she would be setting forth alone to cross the landmass of Africa by foot safari had provoked snickers of disbelief among African explorers. In the mid-1920s, much of Africa remained almost primeval, a mysterious land of wild beasts, wild terrain, and wild people. Few men, and certainly no woman in her right mind, would essay such a journey alone. But when the Brooklyn Museum of Arts and Sciences announced it was sponsoring her expedition, Delia Akeley had to be taken seriously. This would be the first museum-sponsored collecting expedition ever to be led by a woman, an extraordinary break with past practice. Delia would shoot, preserve, and ship back to Brooklyn specimens of mammals, as well as of native crafts, while photographing and studying tribal Africa.

In fact, Delia was no newcomer to African exploration, no novice at stalking and preserving trophies, even the largest of African beasts. Her mammoth bull elephant, taken on Mount Kenya, a record shot at the time, was then and still is on display in Chicago's Field Museum of Natural History. So was a towering bull cape buffalo she shot on the Tana River, an animal considered by some African hunters to be even more dangerous than the African bush elephant. Great tusks from another elephant attributed to her gun stood in the American Museum of Natural History, New York. Numerous bird and small mammal specimens she had collected in Africa were also in these museums.

Delia had gained her hunting experience during two earlier expeditions to East and Central Africa, first in 1905–1906 and again in 1909–1911, led by her famed husband, the taxidermist, hunter, and sculptor Carl E. Akeley. As a young woman, Delia had roamed the veldts and jungles with her husband on his museum-sponsored safaris in decades when Africa was even less "opened up" than in the mid-1920s. With no previous experience of guns, she quickly became a crack markswoman. Her unflinching presence at her husband's side was an invaluable asset in his strenuous hunt for prime museum specimens.

Now, more than two decades later, a divorce from Akeley behind her, she was returning on a trip that might well come to be counted a small epic in the annals of African travel. No understanding of her flowering into independence is possible without knowledge of her early years with Akeley. Without the experience she gained with him on safari in Africa she would never have acquired the skills that enabled her successfully to attack the African continent alone. Moreover, her marriage introduced her to polite and international society, to scientific and museum circles, tutored her in the organization and management of expeditions, and established her initial ties to Akeley's beloved "Brightest Africa." She was hardly a "born explorer" — that epithet so many male explorers were pleased to claim for themselves — but she easily adapted to the demands of her chosen profession and went on to make a name for herself after her divorce.

The bold independence and self-direction Delia displayed as an adult can only be glimpsed in what we know of her childhood, since she was deliberately silent about her past. Unlike other American female explorers, who came from upper-middle-class backgrounds, Delia could claim no heritage among the gentry, a fact she was always at pains to conceal.

Only once did she breach her habitual taciturnity in print. In a 1932 publisher's newsletter, she revealed she had been born on a farm near "a small midwestern town in Wisconsin as the youngest of nine children." She omitted the name of the town, but asserted that "washing dishes and making beds for a family that did not hesitate to criticize my efforts was to my mind a waste of precious time." This unusually candid statement, so filled with hostility, sheds a light on her early and permanent rift with her family.

We know she was born on a farm near Beaver Dam in southern Wisconsin and named Delia Julia Denning. (She never used her full middle name, only the initial.) Her birth date is not certain, but relatives think it was December 5, 1875. Her parents, Patrick Denning, a farmer, and Margaret Hanbury Denning, had migrated from Ireland, probably in the late 1840s or 1850s. They worked their way westward to the settlement of Beaver Dam, then a mere hamlet, and took up a stake nearby, a fine stretch of acres facing the Beaver Dam Lake. Devoutly Catholic, they had found a community of Irish, Polish, German, and Greek settlers where the Catholic church was entrenched.

This was the landscape of Delia's childhood, high, flat prairie lands where scattered unpainted farmhouses were insulated from biting winter winds by leaves or straw piled against their foundations. Groves of oak and evergreens in the yard protected the houses from the summer sun. The Denning house still stands, a simple wooden structure of modest size, today well kept and in use, with barn-red aluminum siding and white aluminum awnings.

Possibly Delia's arrival, a ninth child and a girl, might not have been wholly welcome. If gravestones in Beaver Dam's cemetery are accurate, Patrick Denning was sixty-one when Delia was born and his wife over forty. Another mouth to feed in a family whose fortunes may already have been strained could have seemed less than a blessing.

A scrappy, tomboyish child, Delia was dubbed "Micky" or "Mickie" (even she used both spellings), a nickname doubtless inspired by her combative, headstrong Irishness. "A little devil," one living relative described her. Her ready temper and implacable need to have the last word were all well known in Beaver Dam, according to tales told in the village.

The way she settled scores with the village boys who teased her is a good example of her feistiness. The boys were sent daily to the community well for water. Returning with brimming buckets slung from yokes across their shoulders, they encountered Delia, who rushed from hiding to pitch dirt or trash into the heavy pails, ruining the water and sending the boys back to the well, while Delia raced off in triumph.

When she was in her nineties, she described — with the gleefulness of a child — how she got even with brickyard workers who taunted her near her father's farm. One night she stole her father's shoes and carefully stepped on every single brick made that day, leaving an ugly footprint in the hand-molded damp clay, ruining the entire day's production.

A day of reckoning came when she failed to bring water to the farm hands as her father had asked her to do. There was a scene, and in a raging tantrum Delia, aged thirteen, ran away from the family farm, from dish washing, bed making, and scolding. In 1888, the probable year of her flight, such rebelliousness in a young girl would have been rare.

And she remained away for the rest of her life, never seeing her parents again. Her mother died in 1895, only a few years after her daughter's departure. Delia was in Africa when her father died in 1909. She had lost a brother, who committed suicide, a year earlier. (However, suicide was so unthinkable in the Catholic community that she may not have learned of it until years later.) In her mid-fifties, a woman of the world and a successful author, Delia dedicated her second book, *Jungle Portraits,* to her mother. The cryptic dedication to a mother she had not seen in more than forty years is the only sentimental bow she accorded her family in all those decades.

The angry young runaway of thirteen managed to reach Milwaukee, fifty-five miles away, not an impossible distance to walk, or to hitch a ride on some passing farm wagon or mule train. Here she was discovered by a barber, Arthur J. Reiss.

Reiss took her under his wing, found her a job washing dishes, and a few months later married her. The date was October 17, 1889, and Delia was probably fourteen.

Except that Arthur Reiss was considerably older than his child-wife, almost nothing is known of him or about her life with him, not even the duration of their union. Delia never alluded to this marriage during her years of fame. She simply began her life story with her marriage to her second husband, Carl Ethan Akeley.

How this uneducated farm girl and barber's wife met Akeley, then a serious, hard-working taxidermist and sculptor at the Milwaukee Public Museum, is unclear. The most dependable story is that during the 1880s she went with her husband on hunting trips to northern Wisconsin, on which Akeley accompanied them from time to time. Comradeship of hunting and love of the out-of-doors may have brought the men together; perhaps Reiss was Akeley's barber.

At some point came a divorce, and on December 23, 1902, Delia and Akeley were married. He was thirty-eight, she twenty-seven. Photographs of Delia show a pretty young woman with a gentle,

Delia Akeley at twenty-seven in 1902, when she
married Carl Akeley. He carried this picture
in his pocket watch until his death.

feminine countenance, lovely soft eyes, a slightly upturned nose, and a mass of light-brown hair done high above a level brow. A determined set of the mouth, perhaps, and a sturdy aura of health suggest a mental outlook and physical capacity to cope with the demanding, if exciting, role her life with "Ake" would require.

Like Delia, Akeley was born on a farm, near Clarendon, New York, and as a boy he had hunted and loved nature. Delia's earthiness and her rural upbringing may have attracted him. She quickly recognized his talents, submerged herself in his career, and catered to his needs, interests, and dreams.

Long before they were married, she was aiding Akeley with his private projects in taxidermy to develop his theories for mounting animal specimens for museum exhibition. Akeley had left his family farm at nineteen to learn taxidermy and had worked in the prestigious Ward's Natural Science Establishment in Rochester, New York, which then supplied the best American museums with nearly all their mounted specimens and natural history collections.

Akeley quickly saw a way to improve the crude taxidermy then practiced. He left Ward's after several years, partly because he was not allowed to experiment with his own techniques. He moved to Milwaukee and got a job in the Milwaukee Public Museum, where he began developing his system to replace the "old straw-and-rag-and-bone" method, which he likened to an upholsterer stuffing a sofa. In this old system, dried skins were simply stuffed with soft material until they roughly approximated the shape of the live animal. No attempt was made to give the impression of the true skeletal underpinnings or musculature of the original. The figure was then plunked down in the museum without any effort to impart an authentic or lifelike pose or to relate the animal to its natural habitat.

In his own little shop after museum hours, with Delia's help and encouragement, Akeley developed his more refined technique. First he reproduced the subject in clay. From this he built a manikin of muslin, glue, and papier-mâché, molding to follow the exact anatomy. Carefully treated skins were then stretched over this shape, producing a figure indefinitely durable and with a deceptive likeness to the live animal. Gradually perfecting this artistically honest technique, Akeley would ultimately revolutionize taxidermy.

By the time Akeley was offered a taxidermist's post at the Chicago Field Museum of Natural History, Delia had become a built-in resource, and sometime after his move to Chicago in 1895 she followed. Here she continued to immerse herself in his personal project, although she was eager for him to go to Paris and study sculpture. She even urged him to resign his $2,000-a-year job, but "Mr. Akeley," as she always referred to him in her writing, felt they had no money for such an indulgence.

Describing Akeley's new conception, and her own contribution, Delia later wrote,

> For some time Mr. Akeley had been developing plans for a series of habitat animal groups which he believed would revolution-

ize such work in museums. Taking the deer for his subject, he planned four groups which would show a family of deer just as they look in the forest in summer, spring, autumn, and winter.

The work was experimental and he could not afford to hire anyone to help him. But with my help he felt sure that he could not only make a tremendous contribution to the advancement of museums, but that together we could earn enough money to pay our expenses while he was studying in Paris.

His faith in the results of my cooperation was so convincing and inspiring that I agreed to forget Paris for the time being and go to work. We rented a wing of the large carpenter shop for a studio, and while he was busy at the museum I went to the northern woods of Michigan to collect accessories.

I made photographs of the forest, made plaster casts of leaves, flowers, and grasses. I garnered samples of bushes and plants and quantities of moss and lichens, and then packing them carefully carried them on my back to the railway station, where I shipped them to Chicago.

Mr. Akeley invented the process for reproducing them in wax, and I spent four years doing the manual labor. Each group is an exact reproduction of what I found in a given spot. There is variety in each leaf. No detail, no matter how minute, was omitted. Even the tiny bud which can be found at the base of the stem on each leaf is there.

While I was doing this work it was necessary to work in a room where the temperature was hot enough to keep wax soft and pliable. Before I could mount the leaves on the branches I sprayed each one with color from an air brush to give them variety.

Melted, tinted beeswax was poured over cotton batting compressed in metal dies to make each replica. This laborious method produced remarkable artificial foliage, scientifically accurate and very durable, and so realistic that even colleagues were sometimes fooled. Such exactitude brought an exciting new look to museum displays.

Before this, museum foliage had been procured from the millinery trade. These stiff flowers, leaves, and stems could pass muster for ladies' hats but were quite unconvincing as a slice of nature.

Adding insult to expediency, they were stuck about the animal cursorily, without thought to a naturalistic approximation of the real environment. Delia reckoned that more than seventeen thousand leaves were made by the wax technique for the deer habitat groups, of which she alone must have manufactured the bulk, although toward the end of the project Akeley had to hire extra workers paid by the hour.

While slaving away at this ambitious piece, Delia was as yet not married to Akeley. But the sale in 1902 of "The Four Seasons," as the exhibit was entitled, to the Chicago Field Museum opened the way for their marriage in December of the same year. Since the purchase price was too meager to cover either Akeley's or Delia's time, the only real profit was in the prominence it brought Akeley. The artistry and authenticity of the display, so striking a departure from the unlifelike mountings of the past, marked the real beginning of Akeley's fame as a sculptor and taxidermist. The achievement could never have been realized without Delia's help.

But Akeley now knew that he must collect his own specimens in order to project the animal as realistically as possible. He must travel to the native habitat, make his own kill, work in the field where he could study the animal in its natural environment. He had to measure and record skeletal data on the site of the kill, know how to remove skins, preserve them, and convey them back intact to the museum.

The Akeleys soon were offered just such an opportunity when they were commissioned by the Field Museum to go to East Africa and assemble an exhibit of African elephants. Delia, in her capacity of valuable assistant as well as wife, would accompany her husband to collect birds, butterflies, and "curios."

Akeley had already journeyed once to Africa. Soon after arriving at the Field Museum, he had been invited on a collecting expedition to British Somaliland in East Africa. As a member of a large, old-style safari expedition, with porters, native guides, gunbearers, and scientists, he hunted for five months in 1896, returning enamored with an Africa still almost virginal, a wilderness thrilling to any naturalist.

He was especially intrigued by the African pachyderm. He longed to study this monolith in its jungle home and bring it to the

Delia in Kenya on her first African expedition

attention of the American public. One of the least studied of the African beasts, it was vastly different from the smaller, docile, easily trained Indian elephant of zoo and circus. The African elephant, with its quick intelligence, would inspire Akeley with more respect, admiration, and fear than any other animal — fear that was well founded, for an African elephant would very nearly cause his death. And only Delia's courageous rescue would save his life.

The Akeleys left Chicago for London on August 13, 1905, to outfit themselves. They had little information about what awaited them in Africa, and what kind of reception to expect. Still under British protection, tribal peoples lived undisturbed in Kenya colony and Uganda, where the Akeleys were headed. Arab power associated with the ivory trade and its notoriously cruel practices had been broken by 1893 through the incursion of the Belgians, Germans, and British into Africa. The Kenya-Uganda Railway had been finished in 1901 only after lions had devoured no less than twenty-eight Indian coolies and scores of native workmen. White settlers had arrived in Kenya by 1903. By 1905, when the Akeleys arrived, primitive Africa still lay a few steps away from the rail tracks, the wholesale destruction of its lavish wildlife only just begun.

By October 18, the Akeleys were camping on the Athi plains, twenty-five miles from Nairobi. They had taken the Kenya-Uganda train from the port of Mombasa to Nairobi, hired porters there, and set up camp near the Athi River, the only water to be found in the vast grassy area during the dry season.

Delia had outfitted herself with a sophisticated wardrobe of safari togs: tailored jackets, long skirts, boots, pongee shirts, knickers, puttees, pith helmet — and dainty undergarments. "I always wore silk underwear in the jungle," she later declared. Clearly, the little farm girl had acquired a sense of style and fastidious taste. Photographs of her taken at the time reveal a good-looking, sporty thirty-year-old, her tomboyish silhouette softened by the pile of long hair atop her head.

So in disrepute is big-game hunting today that it is with a certain queasiness that one hails a woman as an uncommonly fine hunter. The pitifully depleted native animal populations of Africa and the specter of threatened species are testament to the mindless extermination that has taken place in this century. But the greedy and careless were bitterly condemned by the sober hunter even in Delia's day.

Delia herself never shot for the sake of slaughter, but for food, self-defense when necessary, and most usually for museum collections. Collecting, the Akeleys thought, would provide posterity with an idea of the Africa that was even then rapidly disappearing. Delia frequently declared that she detested killing and denounced "the guns of the mighty Nimrods who kill for the sheer joy of killing."

The urgent necessity of learning to handle a gun became evident to Delia while the Akeleys were camping on the Athi plains. She had set out one day from camp with a black guide, the essential companion assigned to protect her from predators' attacks, when an alarming sound arose from the bushes. "We were going quietly along the bush-covered banks of a stream looking for birds, [when] a lion growled at us, and I became petrified with fright," she recalled.

Familiar with lions, my gunbearer caught my arm and we backed away. It was then I decided to use my rifle. So the next day I went

*In Kenya, riding astride but in a modest divided skirt, Delia rests
with her gun boy and her guide under a giant baobab tree.*

*The Akeleys' safari on the move. Foot porters carry
all the equipment on their heads.*

out, first asking Mr. Akeley what animals I might shoot. Highly
amused, he assured me that I might shoot anything but an ostrich.
An hour later, I came across an eland and brought it down with
my first shot. When Mr. Akeley saw it he grinned rather wryly
and said I would have to pay a fine of $25.00, for elands were
protected by the government.

From then on I hunted animals and learned how to preserve
their skins. I learned from my gunbearer the names of the different species, how to stalk and trace them on the veldt and in the
forest.

Soon, instead of being left in camp or on her own to pursue
butterflies and birds, Delia was included as an invaluable adjunct
to her husband's elephant hunts. She backed up his big elephant
guns with her smaller .256 Mannlicher Schoenauer rifle. When
occasion called for her to take the initiative, she performed like a
seasoned hunter.

This new active role delighted her. "From the first I realized I
was not on a joy ride," she said. "I realized that a woman who
could not take care of herself could be a handicap. Each member of
the expedition was doing his utmost to make for success and I must

*The Akeleys' encampment forms a tent city on the
rolling Kenya plains.*

do mine. I knew that the success of the expedition meant my husband's success."

For nearly a year and a half, during 1905–1906, the Akeleys roamed over the great game fields and through the jungles of southern Kenya colony. They moved their large safari from encampment to encampment like a small army, a porter-borne field outfit that included gun boys, tent boys, watchmen, porters, and others needed for the complex of duties to support the enormous excursion. The indispensable "boys" took the place of horses, mules, or donkeys because the tsetse fly made use of beasts of burden impossible.

The Akeleys used the railway where they could. For instance, after two and a half months on the Athi plains, they moved by rail to Kajabi, forty-five miles inland, then a month later to Lake Elementeita, fifty miles northwest of Kajabi. They continued on at intervals by rail, setting up new encampments along the line, or going by foot to the next site as terrain and hunting dictated. By August 14 they had arrived at Fort Hall, a week's march from Mount Kenya.

The abundance of elephant life was overwhelming in the towering forests on the slopes of the eighteen-thousand-foot Mount

Kenya. Carl Akeley was so enthralled by the herds of these majestic monsters in this dreamlike landscape that he later resigned his Field Museum job to devote himself fully to collecting elephant specimens.

In her first week in these "most glorious forests in all Africa," Delia brought down the two magnificent elephants that were among the finest specimens captured on the expedition — a spectacular achievement for a beginner, or for any hunter, for that matter. But more than mere "love of adventure" was required to stalk elephants, Delia later wrote. Helping her husband study herds for desirable specimens could be exhausting and dangerous. On poor ground an elephant can outrun a superior horse. Over any terrain it can cover fifty miles in a day. A trail could lead across swamps reeking of rotting vegetation, where trackers could sink up to their necks in the deep holes left in the mud by the elephant's giant legs. To keep up with the swift beasts, Delia walked all day in dripping clothing, clawing her way up steep, slippery ridges, slithering over muddy paths, tobogganing down slick or rocky inclines, or plunging into icy mountain streams.

"The odds are all in favor of the elephant," she said. Man is out of his element in the "gloom-filled wilderness of vegetation, where the very silence and sentinel presence of the vine-draped trees" can intimidate. The elephant, on the other hand, is at home, its great strength and huge bulk allowing it to plow its way through the tangled overgrowth with ease. The hunter can only follow on the elephant's rough trail. In this crisscross maze, one can unwittingly stumble upon a whole herd without warning, since their round, treelike legs and wrinkled gray hide provide excellent camouflage. Before the hunter can flee, an elephant can charge with such swiftness it can stamp the victim to death, or pick him up in its trunk and pound his body to shreds on the tip of its tusk.

A serious stalk could become a dawn-to-dark endurance test, Delia found, particularly rough on the white hunters whose restrictive clothing made them clumsy. (The naked natives slipped fearlessly and silently through the jungle, protected, they believed, by their all-powerful fetishes.) A chase could last so late the hunters had to bivouac in the open beside the trail. "When our followers were too tired to clear a place in the bush for our tents, we slept, as they did, on the hard ground beside the blazing camp fire."

Delia with her first elephant taken on Mount Kenya in 1906

*Delia is anointed with the pulp from the tusk of her first Mount
Kenya elephant, in a ceremony presided over by the intrepid
Scottish hunter Richard John Cuninghame, who was a member
of the expedition.*

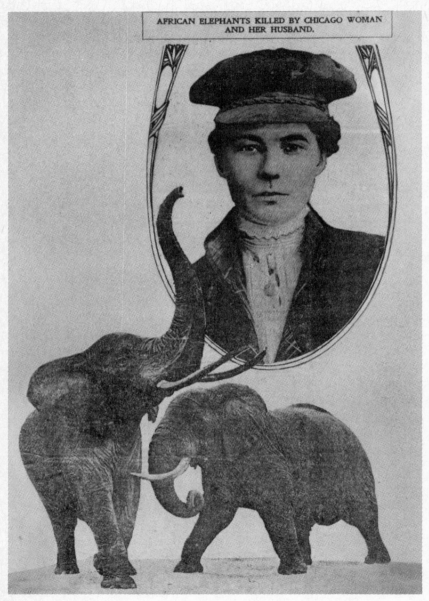

AFRICAN ELEPHANTS KILLED BY CHICAGO WOMAN
AND HER HUSBAND.

*Delia's bull elephant, mounted with trunk raised, as exhibited at
the Field Museum in Chicago*

Worse even than stalking and killing a monster that might be nearly twelve feet tall and weigh several tons was saving its skin. Once an animal was slain, the entire camp was galvanized into a frenzied race against deterioration. The animal had to be skinned where it lay no matter how perilous the site, or the hot sun would cause swift decay. Even while work was in progress, the underside could begin to decay. And a carcass left unguarded for the briefest time was certain to be ravaged by predators. Speed was essential.

Quantities of salt were needed to preserve the skin, as well as knives to remove the fat, lighten the skins, and hasten drying. After an important kill, Akeley and the entire caravan worked through the night. After the skin had been cured, it was rolled and sewn in canvas, the skeletal measurements taken, and the skull and principal bones packed into bundles and mounted on poles for porters to carry.

After five weeks on Mount Kenya, the Akeleys worked their way to the Tana River, and then proceeded downriver in search of buffalo, taking six weeks to obtain the six specimens desired. Back at Fort Hall by November 22, they proceeded with 175 porters to Nairobi with the collections. In Nairobi the treasures were packed for shipment by rail to Mombasa, a specialized task in view of their perishability. The first consignment left on the S.S. *Admira* on December 21, to be transferred at Naples. It arrived in New York January 28, 1907, a consignment of eighty-four packages weighing upward of seventeen tons. According to Akeley's log, this large shipment reached the Field Museum "in perfect condition."

Preceded by their superb collection of skins and specimens, the Akeleys were welcomed back in Chicago in February 1907. Delia's contributions won permanent listing among the Field Museum exhibitions. Not only is her Mount Kenya elephant (genus *Loxodonta*), taken August 31, 1906, still catalogued (#41411) and on exhibition, but nineteen other of her mammal specimens are also still catalogued as well, including hyrax, grysbok, eland, hartebeest, impala, gazelle, and porcupine. Her large, interesting bird collection was studied and reported on in the Field Museum of Natural History Ornithological Series in 1909.

The Akeleys returned home profoundly convinced of the ultimate doom of the wild game of Africa and certain that most people of the earth would view these diminishing species only through museum preservation. They therefore leaped at the chance two years later to return to Africa to collect a family elephant group for New York's American Museum of Natural History. Akeley resigned his Field Museum job, Delia packed their belongings, and they moved to Manhattan. The expedition got under way the same year, 1909. Theodore Roosevelt, who had been captivated, at a White House dinner, by Akeley's stories of African hunting, would rendezvous with them, with his son Kermit, and shoot at least one elephant for the family group.

The Akeleys set out optimistically filled with anticipation. But the happy course of the earlier expedition was not to be repeated. This trip would grow into a series of nightmares, testing their every fiber of fortitude.

"We sailed on our dangerous mission early in August, little dreaming that the penalty for trying to unravel some of the mystery which surrounds the giants of the animal kingdom would be so severe," Delia afterward wrote. Their two-years' effort to secure the family group thrust them into "the most strenuous and dangerous kind of hunting," trying "to learn something of their life in the forests, and prepare their colossal hides for safe transportation out of the forests, over mountains, plains, and sea back to America.

"That we finally completed our task and made it possible for the American Museum to have the distinction of being the only institution in the world to possess a family group of African elephants was entirely due to Mr. Akeley's indomitable perseverance and pluck," she declared, not mentioning that her own bravery and stamina pulled them through crisis upon crisis.

"Visitors . . . who look upon these superbly mounted specimen can have no conception of the dangers and hardships we underwent to place them there, or the disappointment and heartache we endured during the two years we searched for them."

Akeley wanted four perfect specimens, a calf, a cow, and two bulls. The party met up with the Roosevelt Smithsonian Expedition on the Uasin Gishu plateau, 250 miles west of Nairobi, after Colonel Roosevelt had been five months in Africa collecting materials, many of which are still on view today at the Smithsonian Institution's National Museum of Natural History, in Washington, D.C.

On the second day, the colonel and his son brought down four elephants. Since the green skin of an adult elephant weighs a ton and a quarter, and can take twelve hours to remove, Akeley and his men performed a herculean task in saving two larger cows and a calf. Later, dried, rolled, and sewn into canvas, the skins and the heavy skulls, tusks, and bones were portaged out to a wagon track and loaded into a trekking wagon. A span of sixteen oxen hauled the load to Londiani for rail shipment to Nairobi. Akeley later mounted one of the cows for the family group.

The two safaris parted, pursuing their separate goals. Akeley now faced his big challenge: to find the giant bull needed as the dominant figure in the family group, an old tusker that at full growth might carry ivory weighing two hundred pounds, a goliath typical of the great bulls once found in every herd. But week after week passed without success. Elephants of enormous size had become the prize of the ivory hunters; only smaller specimens remained. The caravan trekked to the slopes of Mount Elgon, rising 14,178 feet on the Kenya-Uganda border, where herds formerly roamed. No luck. They returned to the Uasin Gishu plateau and proceeded into Uganda, where they hired porters at Entebbe. They marched along the Hoima Road to the Kafu River, down the Kafu, to where the old Masindi-Kampala Road crosses it, proceeding then to Masindi, a two weeks' journey without sighting elephants. They next spent a month hunting in the region of the Victoria Nile, between Masindi and Foweira, formerly a great region for big tuskers.

The hard, tense months began to take a severe toll on Akeley's strength and spirit. He fell ill with a succession of ailments — meningitis, spirillum fever, black-water fever — which converted Delia into a lonely, frightened nurse. Now without white companionship after the Roosevelt meeting, she passed days and nights scarcely closing her eyes as she sat beside the cot of her feverish patient.

Moreover, the search for the great bull elephant had become an almost maniacal obsession for Akeley. Delia began to wish she herself could bring down the mammoth and end the quest so the sick man could be saved. "Many occasions [when] . . . elephants were reported in the vicinity of our camp . . . I went out with the native guides to inspect them, always hoping I might be able to secure the desired specimen so Mr. Akeley could leave the country before it claimed him for its own," she said.

At times he would rise from his cot and rush off alone. This effort would bring on a relapse and he would have to be brought back to camp in a hammock and Delia "would begin the stubborn fight for his life all over again."

New problems soon arose. With Akeley ill, his task unfinished, they ran out of funds. The American Museum cabled that no new funds were available. Stranded in the heart of Africa, they decided to sell Akeley's small family farm in western New York to cover their debts. Their Nairobi outfitters agreed to subsidize them until they could return home and pay off.

Heading for the more healthful temperatures of the Uasin Gishu plateau, they unexpectedly ran into one of the most terrifying encounters of their elephant-hunting careers: an elephant that refused to be downed despite heavy gunfire. They were still in the region of Masindi where the elephants had a "bad reputation for charging on sight or scent." Akeley described the unusual episode frequently in later lectures as well as in his journal:

I had thought best to hunt alone in the beginning but after four or five weeks of rather intimate association with hundreds of elephants I became less respectful and just at the last I consented to take M. [Mickey] out. It was the morning of the third day out that we came into the spoor of a herd of seven or eight bulls and were following hard for perhaps two hours when the first alarm came. One of the boys heard them across the little valley into which we were descending. Porters and all unnecessary followers were "deposited" with instructions to remain quiet till sent for and we began the stalk. But it was not until an hour later that our tracker pointed out patches of elephant skin visible through the trees 100 yards ahead of us. It was high bush and grass country — good cover — conditions reasonably favorable. We made a stalk to within thirty yards of where they stood beneath a big tree milling about somewhat uneasy, fanning themselves with their great ears. The wind was uncertain so we did not delay longer than necessary in choosing an intended victim, an enormous fellow with very wide-spread tusks. He stood at the moment quarterface to us and I told M. to shoot two inches below the eye, which she did to within one-fourth inch. I followed with a shot in the neck as he fell. There was a crash and roar as the rest of the herd stampeded. According to all rules and regulations, the proper thing at this time would have been to rush in and finish our beast off before he should have time to recover from a possible nerve shock. But when one is accompanied by his wife in such a situation he may be forgiven for ignoring "rules." At any rate we did not rush in promptly.

I waited a bit to make certain that the coast was clear or rather that there was no foxy old tusker quietly awaiting our appearance as sometimes happens. It was not more than a minute but it was too long, for the old fellow suddenly got onto his feet and got away in spite of six shots rained into his shoulders and neck as he went. We took up the spoor and followed cautiously . . .

Ten minutes later we had him in view again and as we swung to the left in order to get the wind right for a close stalk — at the time it was blowing from us to him — we saw him head around facing us. He had winded us and in an instant he started, ears spreading and closing, trunk thrashing the bush right and left, screaming with rage.

Twenty yards away I fired a .475 and he stopped, then I threw more of the same as quickly and carefully as possible at the vulnerable spot which I should know so well and all the time M. sending in those little swift ones of hers as fast as she could work her gun and the result! He took them as a sand bank might — just a little spurt of dust when they struck him and that was all . . .

It was not more than a minute when he made a third charge. As he came out from behind a clump of trees swinging aloft in his trunk an enormous branch which he had torn off in passing, I fired midway between eye and ear, just above the zygomatic arch and pierced his brain. I was never so thankful to see an animal go down . . . As I stood by the carcass I felt very small indeed. Mrs. Akeley sat down and drew a long breath before she spoke.

"I want to go home," she said at last, "and keep house for the rest of my life!"

A yet more terrifying ordeal awaited them on the slopes of Mount Kenya, to which they returned after a month on the Uasin

*Preparing a shipment of specimens on the 1909–1911 African
expedition for the American Museum of Natural History
in New York*

Gishu plateau had improved Akeley's health. They had cut their
way to the ice fields near the summit, where they found elephant
tracks above the timberline and even in the sphagnum marshes at
14,500 feet and more. Akeley believed that the elephant's adapt-
ability to a greater variety of conditions than any other animal in
Africa accounted for its survival through the ages.

Descending through giant tree ferns along old elephant trails, the
Akeleys decided to make camp at six thousand feet and to order
the base camp, which had been left behind, brought up to this spot.
Meanwhile, Akeley returned to the upper bamboo levels to get
better photographs than he'd been able to take before.

Delia remained in the camp to manage the safari, which would
number over seventy black porters after the base camp was mus-
tered. She would be kept quite busy with this responsibility. Also,
native drums having announced far and wide that a white woman
was on the mountainside, the lame and sick flocked daily to the
camp to get medical help, as was the custom when a Western

woman appeared. She possessed little knowledge or medical supplies with which to comfort them, but administered what aid she
could, including some simple medicine which, she marvelled, the
people seemed to adore despite the potion's vile taste.

Working in her tent on her shell collection on the third afternoon, she noted that two of the several porters who'd accompanied
Akeley had arrived in camp. In a leisurely way they chatted with
the cook at the kitchen tent, then at length proceeded to Delia's
tent, the entire camp population at their heels.

"'*Tembo piga bawna,*'" Bill, her tent boy, announced "as calmly
as if he were telling me that the men had brought in some new
species of bird," she recalled. "'Elephant has ketch master'" was
the only information she could glean, except that the guides had
run away. Instantly she perceived the seriousness of the news and
rallied swiftly. Not a moment could be lost. Perhaps Akeley was
still alive. Perhaps she could reach him in time to save him. She
wrote for a doctor to be sent immediately, offering a large reward
to the runners if they delivered the letter to the nearest white
official before daybreak — a slim hope, in view of the natives' fear
of the dark.

Lining up the porters, she selected twenty of the strongest to
accompany her into the forest. "I did not ask if they would go. I
calmly chose those who were to go," she wrote.

Collecting food, medicine, bandages, clothing, tents, and other
equipment, she had the porters pack them into light loads which
were stacked in her tent. Then she sent the porters to bed. Her last
chore was to construct a stretcher of cotton sheeting; an abundance was always carried for trade goods. "While I knelt in the
bitter cold on the floor of my tent and worked by the feeble light of
a smoky lantern, the tall camp guard stood at the entrance shivering . . . The icy wind that blew off the glaciers carried a biting force
across the camping ground and against my tent. When the prowl-
ing hyenas came too close he would go out to the camp fire and try
to coax the wet wood into a blaze."

Near midnight she sent the guard to summon the porters. It took
a second call to bring them stumbling to the fire, shivering and
sullen. They were coastal men who felt the cold acutely and sometimes collapsed with chills. The mood was mutinous. When she

entered her tent to fetch her gun, Bill whispered that they planned to kill her if forced into the forest in the dark. They feared the cold, the wild beasts, and above all the blackness of the jungle night. They knew hyenas would consume her body, erasing any criminal evidence. Already the two guides who had brought news of Akeley had run away in fear, Bill said.

Delia recalled being swept by panic. Without the guides, there was absolutely no way to find her husband in the jungle. She must rally the other men, too, or she would not have sufficient numbers to bring back the wounded man, since every step of the way had to be hacked through the forests.

With a bravado she did not feel, she declared to Bill that she would go from hut to hut searching out the guides. Bill responded loyally that he would accompany her. Heart pounding, Delia strode out to face the rebellious group huddled around the camp-fire. "Fear gripped at my throat," she later recalled of this crucial moment, "but the thought of being too late spurred me on. Steadying my voice, and putting as much authority as possible into it, I announced that everything was ready and it was time to be off. Not one of the men moved or spoke! But I read my answer in their . . . scowling looks. Twenty primitive, superstitious men with murder in their hearts and the cold, black night against me. The seconds I waited seemed hours, and the tightening in my throat nearly strangled me."

Desperate to break the impasse, she resorted to ridicule. They were children, cry babies, she mocked. Capering about and crying like a child, sucking her thumb and pantomiming a complaining baby, she made fun of their cowardice, shamed them for not being men. It was an audacious strategy.

But at last one of the men laughed. Then several grinned. Delia seized the instant.

"*Tayari*" ("Ready"), she shouted. "Putting my hand on the shoulder of the big Swahili who I thought was the leader, I pushed him gently ahead of me toward the loads," and to her relief all the men followed.

With Bill carrying the lantern and in the lead, Delia brought up the rear to watch for deserters. They threaded along a tiny path in single file to the beehive-shaped thatched huts of the village. A heavy downpour had started and drowned sounds of their approach, making it the more hazardous to rouse sleeping inhabitants in the darkness. The villagers thought they were being raided when the throng burst into view. But Bill's speaking their language, Kikuyu, facilitated their inspection of the huts.

Finally, they found the wife of one of the runaway guides. Delia had to threaten to take the woman with her before the wife revealed a tunnel in a thicket behind the isolated hut, the hiding place of the guides. On hands and knees by lantern light, Delia, Bill, and one of the porters crawled through the passage to the end where the two guides were asleep. Delia had them tied together with a rope and dragged out into the night.

Now a new crisis arose. Counting noses among the huddled porters, Delia discovered some missing. When she sent for them, they refused to come. There was nothing to do but to go back for them herself, slipping away in the darkness and returning before the complaining men had missed her. Between their heavy loads and the cold, they were all ready to defect.

> Each moment we delayed in the bitter cold rain increased their anger and my danger, so without telling the men of my decision I found the back trail and ran as fast as I could on the muddy path toward the men, whose voices I could hear.
>
> About halfway, a hand suddenly grabbed my coat. Panic stricken, I struggled frantically, exerting every nerve and muscle to free myself from this new danger which threatened me. Suddenly under the strain on the old worn buttonholes, my coat opened and caused us both to lose our balance, but his hold on my rain soaked garment did not relax.
>
> In that awful moment, which I realized meant life or death not only to me but perhaps to Mr. Akeley, I was the first to regain my equilibrium. With a strength born of my fear, I struck out wildly with the stock end of my gun. As he released me and fell, I ran back to the waiting men.

Had it been one of her own porters or an enraged villager? Would there be another attack? She had to move forward without knowing. Shouting threats that disobedient porters would be punished by officials for desertion, she drew the laggards into a line. At around two o'clock in the morning, the rescue party at last got started in earnest, pelted by rain and hail and lighted only by the smoky lantern.

Once on the trail, the men now held steady. Despite all the dangers and miseries, hour after hour they struggled over muddy ridges, fought lianas — thorny creepers that tore flesh and clothing — scaled steep, boulder-strewn inclines, crossed canyons, and fell into elephant holes. Delia slid time after time to the bottom of such pits, mud and water to her waist, all the while "with rain falling like shot on the leaves, and the strange animal sounds coming from all directions."

Meeting animals on the trail, narrow and walled by dense growth, was a continuous threat. Or they could fall into a pit dug by hunters to trap animals. Or they might release one of the poisoned spears hung from trees to kill game.

When a large beast bolted from the trail and plunged into the jungle, the whole party went to pieces in terror. But the shock drew them together in a common emotion, and Delia began to lose her fear of the men. With daylight came new hope, and they paused for Delia to administer first aid to cuts and bruises.

But now the guides confessed they had no idea where they were and wouldn't budge another foot. They were resting in a trampled elephant clearing.

"Almost frantic, I got down on my hands and knees and circled the clearing," she recounted, "spreading the vines apart and inspecting every inch of ground in the hope of finding the imprint of a hobnailed boot on the soft earth, but the rain would have washed away any trace. Beaten and almost exhausted after our terrible, nerve-racking night, I sat on the ground and the tears I had been fighting so long blinded my eyes and the bitterness of failure entered my heart."

Just then she thought to signal with her gun and fired three shots rapidly. An answering shot echoed, and at intervals was repeated. Akeley was near! In about half an hour she stumbled into Akeley's bivouac, a scene of disaster.

She later described what she found to Roy Chapman Andrews, director of the American Museum of Natural History, and he

100

recounted the tale in his book *Beyond Adventure:* "Mickey told me that Carl was a dreadful sight. The elephant's trunk had scalped his forehead, closed one eye, smashed his nose and torn open one cheek so that it hung down and exposed the teeth in a horrible grin. Many of his ribs were broken. Several had punctured his lung and blood was running out of the corners of his mouth. She knew what that meant and it scared her worst of all."

As Delia cleansed and dressed her husband's wounds, she learned from the porters what had happened. Akeley had abandoned his picture taking to stalk a herd of enormous bull elephants. He was inspecting his guns when without the slightest warning an elephant was towering over him. When he tried to shoot, his safety catch froze.

As the elephant closed in, he grabbed the two tusks in both hands and swung between them as he went to the ground on his back. The mountainous mass bore down upon him, but the tusks struck some obstacle — a stone, roots, something hard — that stopped them. "I should have been crushed as thin as a wafer if his tusks hadn't met that resistance," Akeley said afterward.

Usually a charging elephant would gore or trample the victim or hurl him around in its trunk. Akeley knew an instance when an elephant threw its victim down, walked on him, and then squatted, rubbing back and forth until it had rubbed the body into the ground. But Akeley was fortunate. This one charged off after the porters, who had scattered.

The porters and gun boys ultimately returned and made camp around their crushed and torn master, but they left him lying unconscious for four or five hours in the cold mountain rain. They would keep guard over his body until Mrs. Akeley, whom they had summoned, would arrive, but, explained Akeley, "they did not, however, touch me for they believed that I was dead, and neither the Swahili Mohammedans nor the Kikuyus will touch a dead man." He lay bleeding and freezing while they warmed themselves at a fire.

Fleeting consciousness at last indicated to them that Akeley was not a corpse, and he was moved into one of the porter's tents, where he drank an entire bottle of alcohol, took hot broth and quinine, then sank into unconsciousness again. In a lucid moment the next morning, he ordered a gun fired at intervals, then sank into a comatose state. He finally awoke to find Delia sitting beside him.

The Scottish medical missionary arrived the following day, only forty-eight hours after the accident, thanks to Delia's quick message. The downward journey with the helpless patient on the crude litter was a three-day ordeal of cutting a path through the forest, often with the invalid in peril of rolling over a steep incline.

After her patient was comfortably settled in his tent, Delia took a bath and put on dry clothing for the first time in a week. Then she broke down and wept. "When the terrible strain on nerves and body was over and I knew that Mr. Akeley would live, I will acknowledge frankly I indulged in the luxury of a real cry. But the horror and suffering endured that awful night have never left me," she wrote years later.

Delia became nurse, safari manager, and provider of food during the three months Akeley spent convalescing on his cot in the mountain camp. Several times a week she had to go out and hunt for birds, antelope, and other game to provide a change of diet from the native sheep.

Akeley's life had been saved; but another life would be lost — not to an elephant but to the feared and hated crocodile. Fording crocodile-infested rivers was a game of Russian roulette. Scent of freshly killed meat provisions, or of specimens carried by the porters, drew the vicious creatures in droves. They were always ready to attack anything that stepped into the water. Humans, animals — anything would be dragged beneath the surface for their feast. Lounging submerged, they betrayed their watchful presence by the eye knob rising above the water. Before a crossing was attempted, Delia and her husband tried to clear a path by firing volley after volley into the water and raking the shoreline with bullets, hoping to drive the creatures from the caves under the banks where they hid. After this aggressive onslaught, the advance guard would enter the water brandishing sticks and yelling at the top of their lungs to ward off any loiterers. "Forming a double line they would beat the water and shout while the burden bearers, singing lustily, passed safely between them." The Akeleys would come last.

"The terror of some of these crossings still lives in my memory,"

Delia recounted later. Once, in haste to reach the other side, she slipped on a rock in midstream and was knocked off her feet by the strong current. "Had it not been for the presence of mind and agility of my gun bearer, who leaped forward and grabbed my clothing, I would have been swept away, perhaps to the very death which I so greatly feared."

Delia had shot her first crocodile on the previous expedition. Measuring over twelve feet, it seemed a giant. But later she killed a colossus over sixteen feet long, the largest the party would capture. On this second expedition, while camping on the upper Tana River, she witnessed the horror of a crocodile's attack on a human.

The episode started when Akeley shot a crocodile basking on the opposite shore. Two young porters, thinking to please their master, dashed into the river in a mad effort to retrieve the body. The other porters were already making wagers on the race before the Akeleys realized what was going on. Appalled that two of their men were in a river swarming with crocodiles, they immediately began to fire into the water.

The stronger swimmer reached the far shore and leaped triumphantly astride the dead crocodile's back. But the second, less proficient, was having to fight the swift, deep current to make headway.

Suddenly the Akeleys saw him "throw up his hands, clutch wildly at the air, and with a haunting, blood-curdling shriek that ended in a gurgle, disappear beneath the water." Not a ripple was left, although the shriek was still "echoing weirdly on the air."

The Akeleys were now faced with bringing the other swimmer back across the river before darkness made him prey to lions and leopards. Delia suggested sending to camp for her canvas bathtub to be used as a boat. But even before porters could be dispatched, the young man on the opposite bank stood up, flung the dead crocodile into the water and dived in after it. Catching the floating carcass, he guided it to the spot of the tragedy, then indifferently swam leisurely to the near bank, reaching the shore safely. But not safe from Akeley's fury. Outraged at this exhibition of recklessness, Akeley yanked the boy from the water, shaking him violently and reproving him for his foolhardiness. The boy merely grinned and pointed to the fetishes strung around his waist, complacent in his utter faith in his witch doctor's charms. Delia found herself frequently bemused, speculating about the power of this faith. This same youth later swam many times unharmed in the Tana River where crocodiles were swarming.

The differing ways in which Africans and Westerners perceived life and death was brought home to Delia that same night. Probably provoked by the day's shock, Akeley was seized by an attack of malaria. Maintaining her vigil outside his tent, Delia could hear the porters around their fires at their evening meal (their single daily meal) hilariously conjecturing which portion of their late comrade's anatomy the crocodile had chosen to eat first.

One porter (there was inevitably a comedian in every safari) reenacted the river scene, playing all the roles in turn. First he took the part of the two swimmers, then the betting onlookers, and then Akeley delivering a furious tongue-lashing to the foolish boy; next he became the victim, the shrieking prey being dragged beneath the water; and as a climax the camp entertainer turned into the voracious crocodile tearing his prey to bits. Delia could hear the audience roaring with delight.

At last, she could endure the brutal comedy no longer. "Some of the men lay back on the ground and laughed and pounded the earth with their heels, until in sheer desperation I shouted '*Basi kelele*' (cease making noise). Then still laughing they covered their heads with their blankets and went to sleep on the sun-baked earth beside their fires as if nothing had happened, while I entered the tent and, sitting beside Mr. Akeley's cot, listened throughout the night to the mutterings of his fever-tortured brain."

For her, the tense vigil beside the sick man contrasted with the Africans' fatalistic acceptance of death, accenting the differing values placed on human life.

It was during these two early expeditions with her husband that Delia was drawn into study of African animal life. Later she wrote vividly about elephants, crocodiles, the lesser monkeys, baboons, and other African animals she had studied closely. The primates interested her most enduringly and one little monkey in particular would actually alter her life.

Throngs of many monkey species lived along the Tana banks, in the forests overlooking the Great Rift Valley, that vast declivity cutting through Central Africa, and on the slopes of Mount Kenya. When free of duties, Delia would take a guide and gun bearer into the forest in the early morning to the feeding grounds where monkeys could be watched to best advantage. Stationing her companions to guard against stealthy attacks by leopard or hyena, she lay on her back for long hours watching silently. Although the forest floor was alive with "all sorts of crawly things whose bites and stings felt like red-hot needles piercing the flesh," the monkeys foraging noisily in treetops soaring perhaps two hundred feet held her enthralled.

Her observations on monkey behavior reflect the creative insights of an astute reporter and many of her conclusions have been corroborated in studies by today's scientifically trained ethologists. Like any nonscientific person confronted for the first time with the anthropoids, Delia tended to invest them with human qualities. There is today a school of animal psychologists who use human comparisons to explain animal behavior. Supporters of the behaviorist school, on the other hand, hotly protest any anthropomorphizing in interpreting animal intelligence and behavior and would not regard kindly Delia's point of view.

The more she watched the activities of the monkeys, the more she wondered at the resemblance of primate family life to relationships and roles in the human family. No matter what the monkey species, there seemed always to be a "male" role and a "female" role. The male was arrogant, bullying of the females, and domineered over his harem and offspring. An ill-tempered old male might chase away an offending female at the very moment she was diligently grooming him. Woebegone, the outcast would sit apart and wail "like a chastized wife." Despite this patriarchal image, Delia never saw a wild monkey be unkind to a baby or to a female with a baby in her arms (or, for that matter, a native parent ill-treat a child).

Baboons seemed to her particularly family oriented and amusingly human, especially in their preparations for the night. She sat up four nights in succession studying a baboon family that slept in a tree near her tent. They soon grew accustomed to her presence and ignored her light.

First came the mother, scolding and readying the little ones for "bed," the old males meanwhile making a careful inspection of the tree for snakes or other enemies. Then the females with babies and the younger animals climbed to the higher, safer branches. The older animals settled in the lower. A sentry sat closest to the ground, commanding a full view of the surrounding area, guarding against the possible leopard that could creep silently up the tree. At exactly the same hour each night, the sentry changed and a new guard took over.

Delia was convinced that the primates have a "language" and "converse" with one another. "One has only to watch the functioning of their social organization to arrive at the conclusion that the primates communicate with one another by sound," she said. She thought moreover that communication between humans and primates could be established, a theory under considerable experimentation today.

Her most successful approaches were with the baboons. Her method was very similar to that now used by primatologists, which is based on imitating the animal's own behavior. She tried "talking" with the sentry on duty in her neighboring tree when all was quiet and he seemed lonely. She grunted and copied other sounds the baboons had used with one another. To her delight, the sentry responded. She extended her efforts to interact by imitating movements and actions as well as sounds. She scratched under her arms, groomed herself, moved her head from side to side, and "yawned" loudly, mimicking the typical hoots, grunts, and belches at the same time, all with pleasing response. She was certain she had truly established some kind of rapport.

One day, in "conversing" with the old male leader of a troop of silver-gray baboons elsewhere, the old fellow became so beguiled he abruptly leaped forward to within ten feet of where she stood. She drew back in alarm. His manner changed instantly. Sensing her fear, he became hostile and might have attacked if one of her men had not run forward and frightened away the whole troop. In a genuinely scientific spirit, she exulted in this episode as a successful encounter in animal-human communication rather than as a lucky escape from injury or death.

Delia's study of the African primates in their native habitats in the early years of this century, as far as it extended, was a pioneering effort, particularly for a woman. She was years ahead of such leading contemporary women primatologists now working in the field as Jane Goodall (studying chimpanzees at the Gombe Stream Reserve on Lake Tanganyika's shores since 1960); Dian Fossey (student of mountain gorillas of the Virunga Mountains of Rwanda in East Africa, since 1968); and Biruté Galdikas, who has spent a decade working with the orangutan in Indonesian Borneo.

When Delia began her studies, a developed science of animal behavior (ethology) did not exist. And even in the 1920s, when she started writing about her observations, primate study was still rudimentary, only beginning to be shaped into the more structured, systematic discipline it has become. Equipped with today's scientific techniques and training, Delia Akeley, as a careful, persevering, and perceptive observer, might well have made an outstanding primatologist. As it was, she wrote engrossingly for a lay audience and from firsthand experience. Though limited to two books and a few articles in popular magazines, her writing blended zoology with a highly personal sympathy. She used a naturalistic approach rather than a laboratory or statistical critique, which gained her a wide popular audience.

A beautiful little vervet, captured along the Tana banks during the early days of the second Akeley expedition, stole Delia's heart and prolonged her study of primates for many years, ultimately in disturbing ways. This experience, which she finally related in her first book years after it had occurred, forms a strange and sorrowful chapter in Delia's life. Published in 1929, the book was called *J.T., Jr.: The Biography of an African Monkey.*

The little monkey had been taken by safari porters to help Delia prove her argument that the wild monkey is naturally more cleanly than the captive. Delia intended to release the animal immediately, but the exquisite baby vervet was so engaging she decided to keep it, and named it "J.T." for John T. McCutcheon, a well-known American cartoonist who was a member of the expedition at the time. J.T. at once became a camp personality, a charming little tyrant for whom Delia hired a nine-year-old Swahili boy named Ali to act as "companion and valet." Delia garbed the child for his official function by replacing his single garment, a string of beads, with a little khaki suit and a bright red fez with a tassel, and further

The pet vervet monkey that became the subject of Delia Akeley's book, J.T., Jr.: The Biography of an African Monkey

dazzled him with the stipend of a dollar a month. For these rewards, Ali endured all kinds of abuse from the pet, which rode in his woolly hair, tail dangling across his face. On the trail Ali raised an umbrella to protect her ladyship (J.T. was female despite the name) from the tropic sun.

Foolishly, no doubt, J.T.'s mistress vowed she would not punish the animal, no matter what the transgression, a resolve kept during the nine years J.T. remained with her. She would study the monkey's reaction to living with humans, not attempting to train it in human ways, she said. But gradually J.T. began eating breakfast at the table with the Akeleys and even sharing Delia's cot at night. With the passage of time, the monkey became ever more aggressive and spoiled, nipping any convenient wrist or ankle when provoked. These nips were not so serious as long as she was a tiny creature, but her bites became more vicious as she matured.

J.T. came home to Manhattan with Delia and was soon installed in a room of her own in the Akeley's ample top-floor apartment on

Central Park West. She not only had her own chair and spoon for breakfast but "helped" Akeley shave in the morning. Indeed, she took the place of a young child in the family.

J.T. grew increasingly destructive and increasingly possessive of Delia. At least, Delia thought jealousy explained why the monkey would tear up her best dresses. Her closet had to be kept locked, and the key hidden. Indeed, everything in the apartment that could be picked up by the monkey had to be kept under lock and key. The dexterous animal in her insatiable curiosity would even dismount complicated instruments. If a tempting object was left unguarded by mistake, the consequences could be catastrophic. An expensive new hat, delivered in Delia's absence and placed within J.T.'s reach, was found stripped of its floral and feather ornamentation when the mistress returned. An elegant new beaded gown likewise was completely denuded of all beads.

More and more a prisoner of the little autocrat, Delia at one point would not leave the apartment for three weeks while J.T. "grieved" for a deceased monkey playmate she'd given the animal. Ever wilder, J.T. pulled tablecloths with dishes from the dining table, robbed drawers, ripped curtains, flooded the bathroom, disemboweled goosedown pillows, emptied purses of guests. And bit any convenient heel if in a bad mood.

At length the animal bit Delia severely on the ankle. Delia stoically waited three days before calling a doctor. The leg was then so swollen and badly infected that surgery was required to save the limb. But Delia refused to leave J.T. to go to the hospital; the operation had to be performed in the apartment. Three months in bed and three more on a cane were the price of this episode. Only after another extremely dangerous bite on the wrist, which came near to severing a large vein, did Delia bow to the certitudes. Akeley arranged for the monkey to be sent to the zoo in Washington, D.C., and shipped the animal before Delia could change her mind.

When writing her book about all this, Delia was aware of the obsessive extremes of her infatuation with the pet. "I had given up practically all my social life and many of my friends to devote myself to the care and study of this interesting little creature," she wrote. But she didn't mention that she'd given up her husband as well, at least indirectly, because of the monkey. Its presence in the household had caused a disastrous deterioration of their relations.

Even while they were still on the expedition, her preoccupation with the monkey had disturbed Akeley. In his personal journal, in a section entitled "Jungle Letters" (a title he intended for a book), he wrote to "my own Mickie" at periods when they were separated during the safari. In one letter, particularly revealing of his love, he wrote: "Dear Mickie: I love you xxxx [kisses], I want you with me darling. So much separation is hell for me. I'm jealous of your thoughts. Yes, I'm even jealous of the monkey. Oh Mickie, can't you tell how much I worship you? Your letters are full of everything but yourself. I must know about you."

In the years following the expedition, friends watched in dismay the erosion of a formerly devoted union. Here was Akeley in the midst of a burgeoning career, with a wife who couldn't accompany him to social functions because she must remain at home with a monkey. Here was Delia the huntress, a public figure herself, mysteriously distracted by a pet. The strain could hardly have come at a more inauspicious point in their professional careers. They had returned from the 1910–1911 American Museum expedition exuding glamour as the intrepid husband-wife explorer-hunter team. Ake and Mickie, as they were called, had led two thrilling African expeditions together, hunted with Theodore Roosevelt and his son, brought down goliaths of the African jungle (Akeley got his bull elephant at last), dodged death in countless frays, including the drama of the elephant mauling — heroic adventures, all recounted by the press. It was neither of the two alone who was honored by the welcome-home banquet at the Blackstone Hotel in Manhattan on November 27, 1911, but "The Akeleys," an authentic hero and heroine, linked in fame as a couple.

In their years together, working day and night, Akeley had completed fifteen large African mammal groups for the Chicago Field Museum's Akeley Memorial African Hall (as it came to be named); led two expeditions to East Africa, one for the Field Museum, the other for the American Museum; made collecting trips in the United States for material for North American mammal exhibits, and, of course, completed the "Four Seasons." Two of his inventions were in commercial production, the Akeley Cement

*The Akeleys with friends in New York in 1911, after returning
from the American Museum African expedition
(Delia left, Carl seated)*

Gun and the Akeley Camera, both still in use today. And now he
was immersed in his greatest project, a monumental African hall
for the American Museum of Natural History which would preserve for posterity the wildlife of Africa in a wide habitat range of
groupings, authentic to the last twig. The central exhibit would be
the African elephant family unit, dominating the hall. This dream
had taken shape during his convalescence after the mauling. (And
although years passed before its completion, the Akeley African
Hall stands today much as he conceived it.) Through all the career-

111

*Delia Akeley in the years between 1911 and
1918, when she and Carl Akeley lived on
West Eighty-ninth Street in Manhattan*

building years of money shortages, drudgery, sacrifices, and strug-
gles, Delia had encouraged and shared, been the loyal, loving
companion, the invaluable colleague. Many of Akeley's friends
thought he would never have succeeded without her.

But now in Manhattan in her seclusion and absorption with J.T.,
Delia grew suspicious of her husband and at last focused upon a
certain female as the probable "other woman." As with most
marital disruptions, outside conjecture was divided on the issue.
Some thought her jealousy was self-inflicted; Akeley was not "that
kind of man." Others questioned whether her devotion to the monkey was a substitute for something missing in her marriage. No
ordinary man, Akeley was possibly no ordinary husband. He lived

submerged in his own private world of work, though described as "always kind and considerate" and with a "gentleness that made people love him." His biographer, Roy Chapman Andrews, described a solitary, single-minded, driving personality, a man who "did not lead a balanced existence" — the classic profile of a genius.

Whatever their differences may have been, Delia left in 1918 to do canteen work with the American Expeditionary Forces in Nancy, France, in the midst of World War I, enduring nightly raids by German fliers. After the Armistice she lectured on big-game hunting to the Army of Occupation, returning to the States in 1919. Now nearly forty-five, she was still youthful and handsome looking, although her long hair was now white.

Akeley, who had been drawn into war work, had shared quarters near the American Museum with the Arctic explorer Vilhjalmur Stefansson, then later moved into the Explorers Club. In early 1923 he filed a divorce suit against Delia, charging her with deserting him in July 1918, the year she left for France.

Delia promptly filed a suit in opposition, also charging desertion. She was granted a divorce on March 22, 1923, on an amended claim in which she charged cruelty as well. Friends dismissed her charge of cruelty as nonsense, the concoction of a spirited woman who felt wronged.

Whatever Delia's share of responsibility for the breakup, Akeley had another woman friend by 1921, Mary Lee Jobe, whom he married on October 18, 1924. He died on November 17, 1926, only two years later on the slopes of Mount Mikeno in the Belgian Congo — probably of exhaustion — while leading an expedition to collect mountain gorillas for the American Museum. His new wife, on her first visit to Africa, supervised his burial on Mikeno and helped wind up the expedition's work. When Akeley's will was filed for probate, it turned out he had written it in August 1921, before his divorce from Delia. In it he left his estate to Mary Jobe.

Six weeks after the divorce, Dr. George P. Englehardt, far-sighted curator of natural sciences of the Brooklyn Museum of Arts and Sciences, announced that the museum's expedition to East and Central Africa would be led by Delia J. Akeley, who would collect artifacts and certain big-game mammal specimens, and continue her studies of primitive negro races. In describing the expedition Englehardt said:

> While Mrs. Akeley's equipment includes the usual outfit of big-game hunters in the way of supplies, weapons, and cameras for still and motion pictures, her expedition differs essentially from others in that it is a "one-woman" expedition and her sole companions on trips into the interior will be natives selected and trained by her. Mrs. Akeley's inducement for a step so unusual is based on her past experiences that the natives, when treated with tact and kindness, will respond readily by being loyal and dependable and that it is much easier for a woman to gain their confidence and admittance into the inner circles of their homes than it is for a man. She is confident of securing much information concerning customs and habits of negro races, hitherto shrouded in mystery.

In contrast to this quietly matter-of-fact report, the press babbled that this veritable "goddess of the hunt," this modern Diana, was being dispatched to the jungles of East Africa. "With her silver hair modishly waved, her delicate rosy complexion, her soft voice, and quietly fashionable dark dress, she appeared anything but the common or motion picture conception of a lady lion-killer," the *Brooklyn Times* interviewer wrote. "A pair of *pince-nez* on her finely molded nose added rather the impression of the gracious private-school mistress. Only the direct glance of her blue eyes and the queer bracelet of yellowed ivory tusk gave any key to the exploring spirit that is sending her out once again into the deep heart of Africa, at a time of life when most women are ready to retreat to the side-lines."

The spectacle of a white-haired lady trotting off to a lonely sojourn among the savages so bemused the *Brooklyn Eagle* its front-page lead story was headlined: "Mrs. Akeley, Quiet and Gray, To Hunt Big Game and Study Baby Life in African Wilds . . . Going Alone into Jungle on Brooklyn Museum Commission and Carries Her Own Table Linen." Accompanied by a photograph of Delia, the story expressed astonishment that such "a soft-voiced,

*Delia at the time of her first expedition to
Africa for the Brooklyn Museum*

sweet-faced woman, so feminine that it is difficult to associate her
with the many acts of prowess with which she is credited," could
be off on such an improbable, unfeminine undertaking.

An article in the *New York World* claimed Delia was going "to
get away from civilization, where she can forget." "Woman to
Forget Marital Woe by Fighting African Jungle Beasts — Mrs.
Akeley Going Alone to Land Where She Saved Husband, Now
Divorced," the headline read.

Despite all the fuss, Delia was not the first Western woman —
nor indeed even the first American woman — to challenge Africa
alone.

The tragic Dutch heiress Alexine Tinné had brought her expeditionary ship up the Nile, hoping to explore the headwaters,
first in 1862 and again in 1863, with the loss of several lives. After
she set out to cross the Sahara to Lake Chad, she was shot to death
by marauding Tauregs. In 1891 May French Seldon, a belligerent
American feminist, entered Africa from the east, put together a

115

caravan, and proceeded to Lake Chala on Mount Kilimanjaro's slopes, exploring the waters in a pontoon. And then there was Mary Kingsley, the English intellectual, who traveled along Africa's West Coast and into the Congo Free State as a trader in the 1890s.

Although arriving in Africa later than these, in the first decade of the twentieth century, Delia and her husband had trod terrain completely unknown to most Westerners. And now, in the mid-twenties, returning alone, she would again penetrate some of the remaining little-explored regions of the globe.

Delia was operating on a shoestring. Although traveling under the Brooklyn Museum's aegis, she was largely financing herself, museums being notoriously short of funds for expeditions in those days. To economize, she planned to do her own outfitting rather than use an agent, purchasing from the government army-navy stores in London, which had long experience in supplying British colonial needs. Besides, she said, she wanted to organize, equip, and carry through to the finish an expedition of her own, utilizing knowledge in selecting canned foods, tents, guns, cameras, and medical supplies gained in her managerial work on the Akeley expeditions.

She had announced her departure date for London to be June 1, 1923. But by mid-June she had still not set forth. She had dreamed up a new angle to help finance her work.

"Daring Big Game Huntress Plans to Bring Back Pair of Gorillas for B'klyn Zoo," the *Brooklyn Eagle* announced on June 15. Delia proposed to capture alive a young male and female gorilla for the Brooklyn Zoo, for which she would need about twenty-five thousand dollars. Although she received instant verbal support from Max Arens, secretary of the Brooklyn Zoological Society, his call for funds from the public was not answered and the matter of live gorillas was dropped. Perhaps it was just as well, for Delia had had no experience with gorillas and would undoubtedly have encountered problems.

These negotiations for funds, and possibly other attempts, delayed Delia's departure. She did not get away until the following year. On August 23, 1924, she sailed for London on the Atlantic liner, *Minnewaska*. After assembling her equipment in London, she shipped on the monthly French Mail line for Mombasa, Kenya, British East Africa.

She was faced with a crisis the moment she landed. She had only five hours to catch the infrequent coastal steamer leaving for Lamu, the island town at the Tana River's mouth, which would be her starting point for the interior. If she missed it, she would be stuck in Mombasa and have to wait days for the next boat. She hastened to the wharf where her gear was being unloaded to arrange a swift transfer, but learned her precious canned goods, purchased in London, had already been consigned to a lighter with tons of freight piled on top. Her only choice was to restock from local merchants. Later she nearly died of ptomaine poisoning from eating these supplies.

The miserable tub for Lamu, locally nicknamed the "Rolling Tuna," pitched and rolled and Delia was violently seasick on the overnight trip. And her send-off from Lamu was ominous. The district commissioner granted her permission to enter the officially closed territory along the Tana River, but he issued dire warnings of dangerous conditions and instructions to turn back instantly upon official request. Somali nomads roamed the region, fiercely hostile to whites, she was told. Indeed, when a superior learned of her permit, an effort was made to retract it. But she slipped away to the mainland before she could be stopped.

At the first habitation Delia assembled her caravan, hiring porters and donkeys. She decided to forgo a donkey for herself in order to save money. She could study the country better on foot, she decided.

Blithely ignoring the forbidding outlook, she departed with her little caravan; while it consisted of only a handful of porters and donkeys, at least it was her very own. She started the trek across the immense, largely undeveloped heartland of Africa on October 16, 1924, only two days before Carl Akeley, back in the United States, married Mary Lee Jobe.

Actually, Delia wasn't quite under way yet. Not hiring a donkey to ride had been unwise. She was soon footsore and exhausted from pushing through particularly tough brush country in melting heat. She sent a porter back to the village to bring another donkey. He returned with an animal, but not with a saddle. Dead tired,

Delia was nonetheless glad to ride bareback. And now she could start in earnest.

This courageous journey across the African continent can be only imperfectly pieced together through Delia's book *Jungle Portraits*, her interviews with magazine and newspaper reporters, and through her diaries, which have recently come to light. These diaries, however, are disjointed accounts, kept irregularly, scribbled in pencil on fading paper, and filled with native words and with place names impossible to find on any map. They give, however, fascinating highlights of her progress.

Several plodding days brought her to the Wafocomo tribe on the Tana River, where she disbanded the donkey caravan and bargained for dugouts. But when the canoes showed up, she reported, her "heart sank"; they were not the substantial craft of her earlier experiences but were small and unstable. How could they avoid being capsized in a river filled with crocodiles and hippos? She lowered herself gingerly into "a sort of rickety steamer chair" that made her canoe top-heavy, and gazed doubtfully at yawning holes in the sides of the hollowed-out trunks that would have to be patched and repatched with mud to prevent sinking.

To her relief, her men proved expert canoers, familiar with the river. Even so, Delia had to help paddle from time to time to avoid sandbars, boulders, and half-submerged trees in the treacherous current. But she gloried in the ever-varying river scenery.

Widening into lakelike spaciousness, the river would then narrow again so trees met overhead, the banks sometimes twenty feet high. On rounding a sandbar, the caravan might startle flocks of pelicans, black and white ibises, terns, cranes, geese, and ducks, all rising with a great flapping of wings and splashing of water. Sometimes the bellow of a hippo sent the boatmen paddling furiously for the shore. Thousands of weaver birds clustered around nests that dangled from trees "like decorations on a Christmas tree," round constructions of woven grass hanging in large colonies. Tropical flowers, brilliant birds, chattering monkeys — it was a marvelous bedlam of sound and color.

"The brighter and hotter grew the sun, the livelier and busier became the life along the river. Strange sounds reached us from all sides, the buzzing of millions of insects filled the air. Baboons barked, small monkeys screeched; doves, woodpeckers, finches, hornbills and hosts of other birds added their quota to the fascinating sounds."

Management of her men soon loomed as an uppermost preoccupation for Delia. "First suspicion of trouble with safari," she scribbled in her diary on November 4, while traveling by dugout. "Ali [her tent boy], trying to be smart, told me the men said camp was close, when it was a long way off. Then Mohammed refused to give Samuel fire for the porters to use. I asked Ali to give him a box of matches, but he had to be urged to comply. Tomorrow I hope they will be in better humor. I hate trouble."

The porters' recalcitrance appears again in her November 10 entry: "The second day we've had rain. I am housed in a Government hostel which leaks in many places. The rain was so heavy that suddenly I looked up to see a river of water rushing in the door and threatening to drive me and my belongings out . . . Called Ali and he and Mohammed worked frantically carrying dirt with their hands to bank up the entrance. They appealed for help from the porters, but they only laughed and remained in their hut. I didn't say anything for if the porters disobeyed my orders there would be real trouble and I might not be able to go on."

Yet at the same time Delia felt a fondness for her men and would write frequently with a mixture of irritation and affection as she crossed Africa. "I gave orders for the men to go along as silently as possible while I looked for game along the shore. It's hard to keep these men silent when they break into song and conversation at unexpected and anxious moments. Perhaps when I'm trying to make a picture and want the canoe to remain perfectly still one will bring his boat up and bump into ours — all for the loan of a pinch of snuff. One's temper gets tried to the limit at times, [but] they are a happy careless lot and when called at four o'clock in the morning to push a heavy dugout against a stiff current for six hours there are few grunts or bad tempers. They are exasperating at times but I love them and appreciate their good qualities."

Food was hard to come by along the Tana. "Food is bad and I have little liking for it," she wrote. Elsewhere she recorded: "We left camp at 5:15 as usual. I had breakfast by the light of the camp fire. I am so sick of eggs that I told Mohammed to serve nothing but coffee and crackers."

Food was constantly in the thoughts of her men and was the

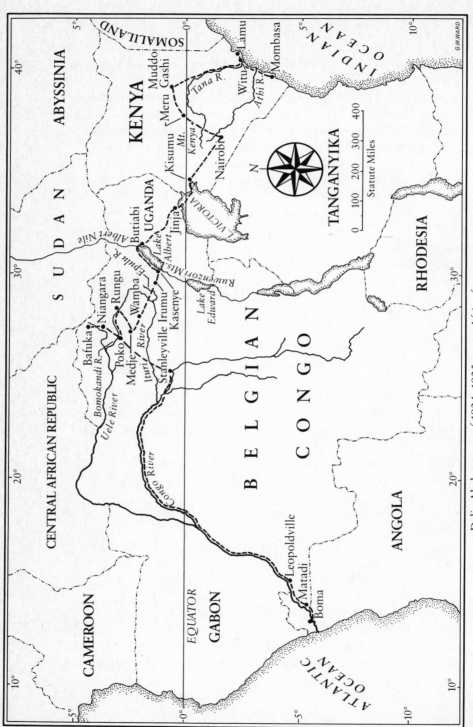

Delia Akeley route of 1924–1925 across Africa from east to west

main topic of their conversation. "These nine men eat thirty pounds of rice between them every day besides corn, sweet potatoes, and meat when they get it, and yet there is not a fat man among them nor have I seen a fat man or woman on the Tana River." Delia was continuously bargaining in hamlets along the river for food supplies for her party.

Hunting was not easy either, more often frustrating.

We remained one day under the acacia trees at our camp above Masabubu to have a hunt . . . Late in the afternoon a man came to camp and said there was plenty of game in the banana trees a half hour away . . . He was so sure there were oryx and gerenuk I decided to stay over and have a try for them. So at five o'clock the next morning, with the man as a guide, five of my men and myself started on a hunt. For five solid hours I hunted under a blistering sun. The sandy bush was blistering hot and there were plenty of tracks but I only saw reedbuck and missed them. I gave it up when my water bottle was almost empty and plodded wearily back to camp.

I felt so sorry for the men who were also tired and discouraged, that I gave them four shillings to buy a sheep. Ali hallowed it so the Mohammedans could have some of the meat, too. They were all so grateful — at least, for the time being, or while they were gorging — that they built three camp fires around my tent because one of them thought he heard a leopard snarl. I nearly roasted for the nights are almost as hot as the days. At three o'clock it began to rain and the men hastily rolled up their sleeping mats and scrambled under the fly of my tent like a lot of chicks under their mother's wing. The rain was a false alarm though, so at half past four we were up and ready to march by five thirty. I bought a snuff box (three shillings) and a knob carry [she means "knobker-rie," a short club with a knobbed end, used as a weapon] for sixty cents from the hunter-guide. I wanted some bead work which they make but they always want too much . . . The water is so dirty and the air is so full of moisture that I cannot develop pictures and I'm afraid they will be failures.

Not only was she photographing and hunting during the day, she was also preserving and caring for any skins, and developing her negatives, at night. Every specimen she successfully brought down and preserved was a treasure. It was particularly heartbreaking, therefore, when she lost a beautiful kudo, a rare species of antelope. She had skinned the animal and placed the skin in the trophy canoe, but while gliding up the river a four-foot lizard dropped from a tree into the boat. "We had to be on the constant alert for these lizards. As large as young alligators, they lay on branches overhanging the river watching for birds." The dugout capsized at a very deep spot, and though some of the trophies were saved, the kudo was not.

Delia's advance up the Tana might have been that of a royal potentate, so noisy and excited were the populace along the banks. They lined the shore at every settlement. Long before her arrival, the singing of her canoemen had given news of the remarkable creature on her way.

> When approaching a village they told in song all they knew about me and some things they did not know, for African natives are past masters in the art of exaggeration; they are anything but the simple children so many travelers seem to think.
>
> My men knew quite well that the more importance they attached to me and my expedition, the greater the reflected glory to themselves . . . and sometimes I would learn with amazement of . . . the great number of lions and elephants that had fallen to my unerring aim . . . of my great wealth and my generosity.

During receptions on shore, the enthusiastic villagers often started dancing from sheer excitement, and the celebration would continue for hours, all giving Delia a sense of intimacy and participation she hugely enjoyed.

She fully understood she was "as much a curiosity to them as a freak in the sideshow of a circus," and for several reasons. "I wasn't always the first white woman they had seen, but they had never seen a woman wearing knickers. The women they occasionally — very rarely — saw were wives of officials. Another thing that made me a being apart, in their eyes, was my white hair. The natives retain the color of their hair until they are on the brink of death. So they gave me a name which means in English, 'the woman-with-an-old-head-in-a-young-body.' "

She tried to travel in both comfort and style and departed each camp only after observing the proper friendly protocol toward the local chief. Bags and boxes were packed the night before striking camp, the canoes patched with mud. Then she called on the nearby chief with gifts of printed cotton cloth and red bandanas to thank him for help on hunting excursions. Her gift for special courtesies was a safety razor fitted into the end of a stick. Frequently her gift was matched by one from the chief, perhaps a handsome carved snuffbox or other example of local craft. Finally she photographed the chief in various poses, which he chose, and then the entire village escorted her back to her camp.

Before daylight next morning, Ali would serve breakfast on a table beside a campfire, the white mists hiding the river. Delia believed in starting on a full stomach, as do all experienced explorers, who never count on what might be available for food later in the day. Papaya, native honey, and white bread toast might be her breakfast menu. She made her own bread with English flour and native banana beer in lieu of yeast, baking it in a covered pan set on stones over a small fire. She baked cakes and pies in the same way on the same primitive "oven." She drank Kenya's native coffee.

She ended a day on the trail with the same attempt at civilized manners. Camp was set up long before dusk while light allowed choice of a good site. By four o'clock her tent boy was preparing her hot bath in her collapsible rubber tub. After a day of mud and dripping swamps or melting heat, this was "the only possible luxury of the jungle."

She was still on the Tana when ptomaine poisoning struck and she lay "sick to death for days." Never ill on her two previous expeditions, she would now have given anything for "a word of English" to comfort her.

"How I managed to recover, I don't know. I was mostly afraid that I wouldn't be able to keep the boys from bringing on a witch doctor," she said. But finally she struggled up from her cot and pressed on.

She ended her "unforgettable canoe journey of ten weeks" on the Tana at the British military post of San Kuri, where she was offered the hospitality of the commanding officer's bungalow in his absence. She immediately ordered camels for her next march, then relaxed amid civilized comforts for a welcomed respite after two and a half months on the trail.

Now rested, with a new corps of porters, Delia set forth across the desolate Somali desert, headed northward toward Abyssinia (Ethiopia, today). Few whites crossed this severely barren strip because of the hostile Somali tribesmen, as she'd been so firmly warned in Lamu. Undaunted, she traveled at night by moonlight to avoid blazing daytime heat, hunting in the evenings and early mornings in cooler hours. No threatening tribesmen or other menace impeded her progress. She was in a particularly happy state of mind when the little caravan at last reached the settlement and military post of Muddo Gashi without incident.

Here she was met by an amazed white officer who regarded her "with horror." " 'For Heaven's sake, how did you ever manage to get through alive?' he exclaimed. 'The natives have just killed one of our officers, and they are on the rampage. We never dream of leaving the settlement without taking thirty-five or forty soldiers with us!' "

Irritated, Delia wanted to respond, "That's why the natives are hostile. They fear and hate white people [because] they resent their intrusion." She had proved that a woman with a friendly approach could go safely among the local Africans. But these men were all soldiers! No wonder the Africans were unreconciled. But she was forbidden to proceed. It was far too dangerous, the officials declared. Regretfully, she turned southward for the Isiolo plains and Meru, a town just northeast of Mount Kenya. In Meru she hired a large motor truck to carry her collection of specimens, two Swahili servants, and her equipment to Kenya's capital, Nairobi. During her first visit to Nairobi during the 1905–1906 Akeley expedition, she had seen wild game grazing on the outskirts of the settlement. Now she was greeted by a prospering town, more modern than she really liked. She shipped her prized specimens to the Brooklyn Museum and looked up old friends, who immediately set in to dissuade her from her proposed journey across the Congo, dangerous for a man and unthinkable for a lone woman.

She listened but paid little heed. She had set her heart on searching for the possibly least known of all African tribes, the Pygmies of the Congo. She admitted she had read far too much about the Congo's vast forests, "deadly climate," cannibals, witch doctors, and the "elusive" Pygmies to hold any illusions "about the seriousness of my self-imposed task or the dangers that awaited me in the jungle depths." But she was stubbornly determined.

She was in high spirits when she took the Kenya-Uganda Railway for Kisumu, the rail terminus and Kenyan port on Lake Victoria Nyanza, to cross by boat to Uganda. She planned on entering the Belgian Congo after a slight detour to the Ruwenzori, the great mountain massif between Lakes Albert and Edward whose crowning peak is the 16,763-foot Mount Stanley, long thought to be Ptolemy's mystic "Mountains of the Moon" and the source of the Nile River. Delia had never viewed the glorious mist-hung peaks, and thought a glimpse of their famed beauty would be a deserved reward for work well done in the strenuous months since her arrival in Africa.

From Kisumu she cabled dispatches to the *New York World* and the North American Newspaper Alliance, dated April 27, 1925, describing her Tana and Somali Desert expeditions and detailing her further itinerary: "I plan to go north to Kilo and from there to pygmy country, then northwest into the French Congo, then northeast to Nigeria and Lake Chad. From there, I shall either cut across to the railway or come out by way of the Niger River." The French Congo, or French Equatorial Africa, as it was then named, is the Central African Republic today. A hazardous itinerary indeed!

These cables brought relief to American friends who only a few weeks earlier had read in the *Brooklyn Eagle* that "for more than two months there has been no word from Mrs. Delia Akeley, noted big-game hunter and explorer, who sailed from Brooklyn on August 24 . . . under the auspices of The Brooklyn Museum and expected to travel over country which had been practically unexplored by any white man." Dr. Englehardt was quoted to be of the opinion that although nothing had been heard from her since November or December, "no special anxiety was felt for her safety" because she was known to be out of touch with civilization.

Englehardt presently also received a letter with a Kisumu date-line reporting that she had shipped "most of the specimens asked for by the Museum" and hinting strongly at stringent finances. "Everything very expensive here and without my former experiences I would never be able to carry on. I only regret that I haven't the means to make a really fine collection for the Museum now. The country is being settled so fast that in a few years, *a very few years,* it will be too late." Her prize catch was something she called a "hairless mole," of which she had several examples. The "hairless mole" was later pronounced rather a rare small rodent, *Heterocephalus phillipsii,* which had not reached the United States before.

Englehardt would later report approvingly in the *Brooklyn Museum Quarterly* on receiving her shipment: "Her collections of big game mammals obtained there [Kenya Colony and Somaliland], including many fine specimens of antelopes, gazelles, a lion, hyaenas, and other animals of interest, reached the Museum in excellent condition and all the skins after going through the process of tanning, are now ready for mounting."

Aboard the Lake Victoria steamer, on the enormous body of water that is almost like a sea, Delia encountered a Swedish official from the lower and central Belgian Congo districts who urged her to take a northerly route into the Congo rather than the Ruwenzori route. He advised her that Pygmy groups of the most undefiled sort lived in the exceedingly wild, undisturbed region north of the Aruwimi and Ituri rivers and south of the Uele River, in the northeastern districts of De Litur and Bas Uele — some of the most remote country in all the Congo.

With the flexibility of the true explorer, Delia abandoned her cherished dream of seeing the glories of the Ruwenzori, and instead of continuing to Kampala on the western shore she disembarked at Jinja at the lake's northern extremity, then headed, probably by bus or lorry, for Butiaba on Lake Albert. Here she discovered that in the Jinja transfer some of her ammunition had been lost or stolen, a crippling blow for one preparing to trek across the remainder of the African continent.

Awaiting word of her missing equipment, she took time for a short tourist trip to the Murchison Falls to view the spectacle of the

Victoria Nile cascading four hundred feet through its narrow gorge into Lake Albert. In the briskly developed, tourist-oriented Murchison area, she was shocked at the changes from the old days, when she had hunted elephants in the great Budongo Forest and camped on the escarpment high above Lake Albert. "My route lay over some of the old elephant country where we had hunted specimens for the New York Museum group. I marveled at the change. On both sides of the well made road over which we traveled in a comfortable motor car, were gardens surrounded by thriving fields of cotton. Babies, chickens, and goats fled from the road and disappeared into the shady banana groves as we approached. In place of the great herds of elephants that once frightened and thrilled me, we met prosperous, white-robed natives with books under their arms."

She faced a different Africa, though, once she had crossed Lake Albert for Kasenye, at the portals of the Belgian Congo. Here savage areas had been little penetrated since Henry Morton Stanley's explorations in the 1870s except by random hunters, traders, a few settlers, miners, and missionaries. And government officials. She would encounter in lonely places, not always too agreeably, an assortment of officials of the Belgian administration. The Congo was still under Belgian rule, as it had been since 1910. (It would continue under Belgian rule until it became the Democratic Republic of the Congo in 1960; in 1971 it was renamed Zaire.)

The implacable reality of the Congo seized Delia when a motor truck dumped her and her belongings at the Epulu River, at the terminus of a new highway somewhere west of Irumu. The wretched two-room rest house here was the jumping off point for the endless Ituri Forest extending west and north. This was the beginning of her suffering through a succession of miserable Congo rest houses that would color her entire experience of this land.

Erected by local officials at comfortable marching distances for travelers and government officials, the typical rest house consisted of two rooms separated by a broad corridor open at both ends. But in the remoter areas it might be merely a "glorified edition of a native hut, built after the local design." She refers to their filth time and again in her diary, to the bats, snakes, and vermin, to the leaky roofs, and to the depressing environment, particularly in a dismal rainy season. For some reason, tents were not welcomed in the Congo so she was forced to use the government-built structures. Describing one in her diary, she says: "The rest house is dirty and there are big cracks in the floor where the fleas and dudus [vermin?] live. I could see the fleas jumping on my shirt and trousers and they swarmed over my hands and face. The porters as usual were sleeping in these rooms. There is no way to prevent them I suppose. How I hate the Congo rest house with its dark uninviting high walls and dark and overhanging roof. I cannot use cold cream on my face or hands for the wasps, bees, and other insects that swarm around me. The mosquitoes and fleas are so bad here that I look as if I had the measles. I am covered with red spots."

Frequently she found the place too hot for sleep. "Not a bit of air gets into these ant and spider infested dungeons," she complained. "A native hut has nothing on the Belgian's idea of a safe place to stay." In the Congo's steaming heat and teeming rainfalls, these huts quickly fell into decay. "The roof leaks, the supports rot and become insecure and wobbly and ready to topple over at the slightest encouragement."

The houses were completely unfurnished, and the occupant supplied food, bed, bedding, bathtub, and servants. Sanitary conditions and upkeep depended upon the local white official in charge. The traveler never knew what tropical disease might be picked up from the former occupants. In *Jungle Portraits* she humorously described how disconcerting it was "to receive a visit from a loquacious Sultan just after you are installed in a rest house and have him describe, with gruesome detail, how the last occupant died, a victim of some jungle disease, possibly contagious; or to call your attention to the new roof, which he assures you he was obliged to put on the house to replace the old one which a few nights before a band of marauding elephants had carried away."

Around the last day of March 1925, she was ferried across the Epulu with her porters in a huge dugout, acutely aware that she was plunging into country more remote and untouched than any she had yet traversed. "With my little band of untrained men, whose language I did not speak, I set out on this last lap of my journey in quest of the pygmies," she recalled. Twenty-five porters to carry her loads and eight more to take turns at bearing the litter, or *tepoi,* made up this safari.

Right off, she encountered trouble in disciplining her men. "They are not at all friendly like the East African natives," she wrote in her journal of the local population, as well as of her porters. Soon after crossing the Ituri River in early April, headed for the habitation of Wamba, she reported, "We came to some *shambas* [village gardens] where my men and my loads were scattered in all directions. I got out of the *tepoi* and after a wild time of yelling and calling and pushing, I got them started again." A few days later, she said: "Porters threatened to leave. Wanted to be paid off. Headman very bad. He had two women whom the tent boy says he is 'renting out' to the men."

Troubles continued. "The men were rebellious as usual," according to her April 18 entry, "and it was a struggle to get on. They stopped at every village to smoke or eat bananas. They are eating constantly, and yesterday the chief said they all ate so much they were all belly. As we passed through the different villages friends of the porters carried their loads and when I reached camp I had forty porters instead of twenty-five."

More annoyed than fearful, however, she could administer a slap if needed. Catching a cook's boy stealing bananas, she "boxed his ears." She struck another porter with a knife. She was hunting in very difficult high-grass country but, delayed by a tropical storm, sought cover in a native hut, her men crowding into another. They sang and talked and laughed loudly; but during a lull in the storm one came after her, reporting that one of the porters was very sick. "I went over and he was shivering and shaking. I realized at once that it was a fake, so I told the men to rub him and they began in a half-hearted way. I saw the man open his eyes to look at me. He closed them quickly and pretended to fall over. I had a flat knife in my hand which I had just bought off a native and I struck him a blow on his stomach. He bounced up immediately and I laughed and went back to my shelter. The men began to yell and laugh when they realized they couldn't fool me that way."

But when there was genuine distress she was kindly. "The tent boy made a great fuss over a man who had bad feet yesterday so I paid the man and ordered him back to his home." In another

129

instance: "The porters hadn't been on the road long before we came to the men who were carrying part of my tent. One of them had a hernia and could not walk. He was in great pain, so I bandaged his abdomen and put him in the *tepoi* and sent him back to a *shamba* and I walked."

She was sensitive also to Belgian cruelty toward the natives. At Poko on the Bomakana River she wrote feelingly of the brutality of the Belgian administrators and their minions.

Poko is not a pretty station. The Government office is near the river. Roads cut across the place in all directions. It is in a valley and one feels shut in. To me it is not as pleasant as a clearing in the forest. It is very damp and the air is heavy. There is no life in the natives. They seldom sing as they work and there is no beating of drums. There are many poor wretches in chains carrying dirt to build the roads and sometimes one hears the poor devils screaming when they are being beaten by the black *askaris* [foreman or local soldier]. The "Congo Free State" [she means the Belgian Congo] is building amazingly good roads across vast stretches of country, bridging innumerable streams. She has discovered, and is developing, rich gold, copper, diamond, radium, platinum mines and she is clearing and cultivating vast tracts for cotton and grains which promise to be a veritable gold mine in themselves. The country as far west as Medje is sacked to supply the Kilo gold mines with food and palm oil and labor. The work is all done by the black man who everyone says is lazy. [But] the white man never does any manual labor. It is true the black man is a slow worker. All labor is performed to the accompaniment of song and the tune is not often lively as it is when they dance and play about their *shambas*. Men are arrested or jailed for any slight offense, an iron collar put about the neck and this is fastened to the iron collar on the neck of another helpless soul like himself by means of an eight foot iron chain. Sometimes eight or ten men are fastened one to the other in this way. They work, eat, and sleep with these devices of civilization upon them. Their black gaolers are sometimes more cruel and if a man falls by the wayside while performing his labor he is beaten and kicked because he hinders the others. I once saw at Kasenya an old man in chains fall when coming up the steep ascent from Lake Albert with a barrel of water. It was the third time he had made the journey that morning. When he was almost at the top his strength failed and he fell to the ground. The *askari* took his gun and pounded the old man until he screamed. The white postmaster and his wife were looking on and they laughed. The *askari* thinking he was gaining favor or giving amusement beat the man harder until he screamed with pain. I finally could stand it no longer and stepped to the door of the rest house and shouted . . . [African words meaning "stop"].

Another journal passage describes the treatment of men who resisted being conscripted for labor. They had fought off their would-be captors with spears. "Consequently, they must pay the price," she wrote from her rest house.

As I sit here on the veranda, I can see poor helpless devils being kicked as the *askaris* drive them before them to prison. One *askari* had two men by the scruff of the neck and every few steps he knocked their heads together. Another *askari* had one he was dragging back and forth and hitting over the head. Four times they raced across the open space with four and five helpless devils at a time. I can hear the shrieks and the thud of the whip on their bare bodies. Tomorrow they will be in chains. But from daylight until dark their bruised and cut bodies will bend over the task of road building so that the wheels of civilization may pass. It is an inexpensive way as far as money is concerned to develop a country. But on the other hand, isn't it expensive after all!

History would prove her prophetic insight correct when the hated Belgian rule ended in 1960, thrown off by tribal demand for independence.

Delia's path through the Upper Congo must be gleaned from her diaries, as she never published a detailed report of her exact route. These journals, unfortunately, could be kept only intermittently, and at one point entries ceased altogether. She bewailed the constant difficulties of writing because of interference by natives and noise, interruptions, and the attacks of insects about her lantern, which made work after dark almost impossible.

Her entries indicate that leaving the Epulu River she headed northwest toward Wamba, today a modest town but then a mere way station; but in any case a known goal. She crossed the Ituri River probably at present-day Nduye.

Her progress in the Congo was accompanied by the same noisy hubbub as on the Tana. "The natives rushed out of the villages when they heard the *tepoi* boys singing that I was a woman, and they followed us and shouted." Although they hated and hid from the white man, they were burning with curiosity about a white woman, traveling alone, without military escort, and wearing pants. And always that freakish white hair!

The sultan, or sultans, as the case might be, met her miles before the village, clogging the roads with their retinues. The crowd followed her to the village, settling around the rest house and remaining for hours. Sometimes the sultan held court on her very veranda, disposing of community disputes the whole day.

"It has been impossible to get rid of the Sultans and their wives and followers," she wrote desperately in one village. "They brought their chairs, their food, and their family and some of their friends. They also brought bad eggs to sell and sick chickens, ivory hatpins, knives, etc. I had to take my table into the bedroom so I could have my dinner without watching them scratch. The old Sultan smoked a stinking pipe. There were wives and slaves ready to pick up his flybrush or pick the lice off his old black cotton coat. There were dozens of *askaris* running his errands and they all carried guns and saluted him when they approached. When peasants came to offer anything they were most servile, almost getting on their knees, and always offering it with both hands; a peasant does not think of speaking before he is spoken to."

Delia's African vocabulary, though limited, was actually quite strong in useful words and phrases. The women wanted to know why Delia was so flat in front, why she had no milk. When she realized that having a family was so prestigious, she made one up on the spot. "Oh, but I have five children," she said, holding up five fingers. Respect advanced so noticeably that she wished she had claimed ten. Her porters now bragged about her five children, and women with large families lined up their offspring before her as though expecting some kind of prize. In one village every woman was pregnant. One porter ran his hand over the protruding abdomen of several mothers-to-be, saying he wished the babies were to be his. Delia noted that the women did not object to the intimacy.

Rising at dawn and setting forth no later than 6:30, Delia pressed northward through "good elephant country" with "elephant paths everywhere" and through "some lovely bits of forest." A great crashing and trumpeting close to the road at one moment caused panic. "The men dropped the *tepoi* and ran for their lives. I landed on my feet but my leg is terribly bruised and awfully sore tonight," she complained. "The elephants had been crossing, recrossing and feeding along the road all night for trees were lying across the path and in some places the droppings were still steaming."

But she was not hunting elephants, and the kind of animals she sought were scarce. The forest had grown denser and the ground was often so swampy she sank to her knees in mud. Moreover, the local peole were unhelpful. "They invariably say that at the next camp I will find plenty of game." The same reluctance to part with their "curios" thwarted her collecting. "If I try to buy a knife or anything else they say at the next camp I will find better ones."

Even before reaching Wamba, Delia encountered Pygmies when she plunged into the deep forest at a place known to lead to their camp. "The huts were made of leaves, but in the forest when they are hunting or getting away from officials or white people they sleep under a few bushes or vines like the Wanderobo of East Africa," she reported. "They (pig) [her abbreviation for Pygmies] were not as small as I thought they would be. Some of the women were tiny but the men were huskies with a great deal of hair on their bodies . . . They all wore the usual covering, a bit of bark cloth. One man had a belt made of okapi skin and they all carried their elephant spears and little bows and arrows. I tried to buy some but they did not want to part with them." She decided that although locally they were called M'Butes, they had intermarried with other tribes. She was not particularly impressed with these examples of Pygmy types.

In another village, a Walese sultan brought her a Pygmy family, a father, mother, and tiny child, who seemed to be a purer strain. To befriend them so that they would sit for photographs, Delia presented salt and tobacco, among the jungle's most coveted luxuries, to the adults, then sought a present for the baby perched on its mother's hip. From her store of gifts she chose a red balloon, which she inflated before emerging from her doorway, holding it by a string.

The effect was electrifying. Not only for the Pygmies, but for the villagers and her own porters. No one had ever seen such an apparition before. She tied the string to the baby's wrist, to the astonishment of the onlookers. "Wild with curiosity," they all surged forward to get a closer look.

But quickly they were ordered back. The sultan and the old witch doctor were alert to the protection of their flock. "First the Sultan and then the witch doctor harangued the crowd," Delia recounted years later, still laughing at the scene. For the safety of everyone, they would be the first to inspect the curious thing that, they said, "had neither head nor tail, hands nor feet nor wings. Yet it had to be tied like a bird to keep it from getting away."

Amid an "intense hush," the two brave men crept cautiously forward. Suddenly a gust of wind whipped the balloon straight at them. Terrified, the two hastily retreated. The witch doctor stumbled over a stool and fell. But he recovered himself quickly and announced in "sepulchral tones" that this object imprisoned a spirit that sought release.

At this point the Pygmy mother, recognizing that a treasure had fallen to her family, snatched the balloon from the baby's arm and dashed off toward the forest, clutching the string. The entire village let out a furious whoop and set off after her. However, they were all in for a new surprise, even Delia, who must have been thoroughly enjoying this episode. A strong breeze yanked the string out of the mother's hand and the red sphere rose toward the sky. Then, of all oddities, two hawks flying by zeroed in on the balloon, attacking it and causing it to burst. The amazed villagers were left gaping at the empty air, waiting for the released spirit to make its appearance.

Delia, who must have suppressed her laughter only with great effort, seized the chance to teach a lesson in honesty. This was the kind of "miracle" that punished persons who stole, she said. The mother should not have taken the balloon from the baby. Delia's porters would later spread this cautionary tale around the camp-fires along the trail, a deterrent, Delia believed, that saved her from heavy pilfering in the Congo.

The balloon out of the way, Delia began setting up her tripod for photographs. When she saw that the Pygmy couple were already posing for her shot, her enthusiasm collapsed as completely as had the balloon. Obviously these Pygmies had already had contact with the outside world and were not the undefiled specimens she sought.

So she pushed yet deeper into the forest, always heading north-ward. One day she came across a tiny village where a group of small women, apparently Pygmies, were dancing, "stupidly drunk" and sweating heavily as they circled and stamped their bare feet. They did not notice her setting up her camera until one of them caught sight of the queer object. Shrieking, they bolted "like antelopes" into the forest. Delia's porters finally coaxed them back.

They were from a village two days' march distant. Delia gave them salt, beguiled them with a mirror — their first glimpse of themselves — and sent a porter with them to announce she would be visiting the sultan with gifts of tobacco and salt. These people at last seemed to be the real thing.

In due time the sultan sent her a guide. She now faced a forest truly primeval, where there would be no missionary or official to note her disappearance. She left most of her men and simplified her equipment before proceeding.

"It would be difficult to describe my feelings of mixed fear and determination as I followed my little guide into the dripping, rain-soaked forest the next morning," she wrote in *Jungle Portraits*. No diary covers this foray, where the protocols of her regular safari must of necessity have been abandoned. "Wet to the skin, almost as soon as we started, I followed mile after mile through the tangled undergrowth. It was so dense that the trail was hardly distinguishable."

Every step was a struggle to keep up with the "gnome-like little man" sent by the sultan. Her eyeglasses steamed in the sweltering humidity. She stumbled over roots, fought off thorny vines. Swift, sure, and evanescent, the small figure moved ahead "like a shadow." At first she managed to follow his trail through the wet early morning foliage. But as the sun rose higher, the dried vegetation closed over his head, and her only clue was the acrid odor of his unwashed body lingering in his wake. He was also constantly darting from side to side to gather and consume slugs, snails, caterpillars, and other edibles, and this also threw her off. That night her mosquito net was ineffective against hoards of flies, midges, and mosquitoes, making sleep impossible.

A shrill whistle sometime the next day and an answering drum heralded the Pygmy village. Her guide pointed to a small man stretched out on the limb of a high tree, the sentinel who had given the whistle signal.

As she entered the village clearing, she sensed a mood that was something between indifference and hostility. No excited throngs pouring out to sing and shout, no sultan with his retinue to meet her. This sultan sat on an ebony stool before a small fire, drinking palm wine dipped from a big black pot. The entire village, some twenty to thirty souls, stood with spears and clubs. Even small boys held bows and arrows.

Delia recoiled at the menacing sight. "As I gazed at the fearsome group of little dwarfs standing in the dim light under the towering trees, my inclination was to turn and run. It took real effort of will power to go forward to the fire."

The lounging monarch did not rise. After a deadly interval he extended a hairy hand and touched her fingers, pointing to the stool beside him. Filling a broken gourd from the black pot, he offered her wine, first drinking to show it wasn't poisoned. Delia pretended to sip, then handed the gourd to her porter, who emptied it with relish.

She now presented the sultan with his first cigarette. He watched carefully as she smoked hers, then did the same with his. Delia grew more certain these Pygmies had had little if any outside contact. Their lack of servility and ceremony was a refreshing contrast to the cringing attitudes of natives who had come under white rule. She settled in for a stay, having her tent pitched near the small beehive-like shelters constructed of a few saplings tied with vines and covered with phrynium leaves, which were the village shelters for sleeping and cover from rain. All other activities took place in the cleared space in front of the huts.

Arriving as an observer, Delia found she was the observed, the "human riddle that had come so suddenly and mysteriously . . . My long, straight, white hair, which I brushed frequently to impress them, was often the subject of warm debates. They also wanted to know if my body was the color of my hands and face. To convince them that it was, I rolled up my sleeves and exposed my bare arms. But this did not satisfy them, so they asked me to remove my clothes."

She refused, but they persisted. "When I bathed, in spite of the vigilance of my boys, both the men and women crawled through the bush and poked their woolly heads under the canvas of my tent." She threw soapy water in their faces. One old man very early one morning crept to her tent, slit the canvas, and would have slit her mosquito net had she not awakened, jumped up, and doused him.

The origin of the Pygmy race and the cause of their diminutive stature are questions that have perplexed civilized society since ancient times. To the ancient Egyptians and Greeks from the time of Homer, the Pygmies were half fact, half myth. The Greeks believed these small people battled with the cranes that migrated to their lands each year, and they recorded these supposed encounters on vases and in poetry. Prince Herkhuf of Egypt's sixth dynasty traveled into equatorial regions and his meeting with the Pygmies was recorded on his tomb. The "dwarfs," as they were frequently called, remained undisturbed for four centuries after Herkhuf, until Georg Schweinfurth "rediscovered" them in the Ituri Forest in 1870 and reported them to the modern world. Henry Morton Stanley, the explorer, encountered them in the Ituri fastness and termed them "the oldest type of primordial man," in his *In Darkest Africa* in 1890.

Delia Akeley, arriving in the Ituri in the mid-1920s, was certainly one of the earliest twentieth-century students of the Congo Pygmies. Although their general habitat had been more or less outlined by now, and many groups had had some contact with whites, many more were still elusive. An airplane had yet to fly over the Congo, and the jungle had not been crisscrossed with roads.

Delia probably arrived at the final moments of their eons of privacy. On her heels would come the French anthropologist Paul Schebesta, the first modern scholar to engage in scientific study of the Bambutes, as the Congo Pygmies were called. (Schebesta later used the term to include all African Pygmy groups, including the Bushmen of South Africa.) Another student who nearly over-lapped Delia's time was Jean-Pierre Hallet, the contemporary writer who grew up on the edge of the Ituri Forest in the 1930s and today crusades to prevent the extinction of all Pygmy groups in the Congo.

Delia's conclusions about the stunted growth of Pygmies, whom she also called Bambutes, is much in harmony with current scientific explanations that attribute dwarfism to a deficiency of a certain growth hormone. She was convinced they started life as humans of normal stature and that some factor or deficiency, which she could not determine in such a short visit, intervened to inhibit growth as they developed. Being allowed to witness a birth helped confirm her theory that the Pygmy newborn was of normal size. Observation of Pygmy children in the villages also indicated this conclusion. For a few years the children grew tall and thin, "like the light-starved vegetation around them," then at a certain age they began to broaden out and develop heavy shoulders and torsos, she found.

Malnutrition and sun starvation, favored explanations of her day for the Pygmy stature, she rejected. "However true . . . with many pygmies in other parts of the world, these reasons certainly have nothing to do with the growth of the Bambute pygmies whom I visited. I found them a healthy, happy, well-nourished people, amazingly free from the awful diseases which are so common and so decimating to other Congo tribes." They spent hours basking in the sunlight that knifed through the forest canopy. And they ate anything that walked or crawled, consuming a great variety of vegetable and animal food. Into the large stew pot brewing on the fire they dropped anything picked up in the forest: bush rats, lizards, grubs, snails, slugs, winged ants, monkeys, edible roots, leaves, and caterpillars. They ate meat in any form, raw, half-

Delia with Pygmies in the Belgian Congo

With a Pygmy mother and baby

cooked, or decayed, and gorged themselves when a large animal was killed. Though unorthodox by white standards, their diet seemed reasonably balanced to Delia.

They pursued no agriculture, no crafts. (Today they would be called "hunter/gatherers" by anthropologists.) They had no furniture except ebony stools, no cooking utensils of their own manufacture, did not make even their spears or bows and arrows. They exchanged meat, ivory, or animal skins for weapons made by blacksmiths of other tribes. They wore practically no clothing except when celebrating; then they tied leaves or bark cloth around the waist with a cord of okapi skin or grass and painted their faces and bodies with clay or soot mixed with fat. Talismans made of chopped elephant eyelashes and huge beetles, sanctified by the witch doctor, were the sole ornaments. The small wooden whistles hung about the neck by a leather string and worn by the men astonished Delia with their piercing sound that carried great distances. Unlike certain other Congo tribes, they did not mutilate their bodies, but from their strong body odor Delia concluded they never bathed.

She took body measurements and reported to the Brooklyn Museum *Bulletin* an average height of about four feet, with a range from three to five feet and a few individuals measuring over five feet — the offspring of intermarriage, she thought. Skin color ranged from coal black to yellowish brown. She studied facial and cranial configurations and described bullet-shaped heads, large piercing eyes, and broad flat noses. Beards and hirsute bodies gave some of the men, with their heavy shoulders, a feral appearance, she said. The men climbed trees and ropelike vines like monkeys, clinging with great agility with arms and legs. They could aim a spear with perfect accuracy from thirty feet above the ground.

They spoke a language "of their own" which she did not attempt to classify linguistically; nor was she able to comprehend it. Yet she came close to rupturing the harmonious relation she had so carefully established by yelling at the sultan one day in Kingwana, a tribal tongue she spoke a little.

A piece of meat the sultan's wife was roasting for his meal fell from a sharp stick and caught fire. With a furious yell, the sultan sprang to his feet and knocked the woman flat on her face. A roar of laughter from the others around the fire encouraged the potentate to further punishment, and he started for the prone woman. Delia rushed toward him, shrieking in Kingwana, *"Toka, toka"* ("get out").

At this astonishing impertinence, the sultan forgot his wife, leapt over her prostrate body, and confronted Delia "with rage-filled eyes." He actually rocked his heavy body from side to side and beat his chest. His appearance so absolutely terrified her, she recalled, her hair and clothing were drenched with perspiration.

Although Delia was paralyzed with fear, the sultan's "sizzling" fury nevertheless struck her as funny, and she burst into laughter. He stared at her in amazement, then his anger subsided and the terrible moment passed. But Delia was still shaking like a leaf, for she well knew it would have been a simple matter for the tribe to "blot me and my little caravan off the map and shift their habitation to another part of the forest."

Relations were perilously strained again when Delia started out with the Pygmy men on what she supposed was a routine hunt; but she soon learned they were stalking an elephant wounded by poisoned stakes in a Pygmy trap. With no interest in such a dangerous expedition, she tried to bribe one man to guide her back to her camp, but he refused. She was caught. The men were on a feverish drive for food.

Impatient with her cumbersome, noisy progress, the sultan angrily motioned her to remove her clothes and travel in the nude as they did. They were annoyed by even the slight noise made when a thorn snagged her garments. They were pitiless when she floundered into a bog and was bitten by swarms of tiny black flies. ("The red blotches did not disappear for weeks," she said.)

Delia managed to keep up with the party, however, until that afternoon, when a major crisis arose. The Pygmies had run nimbly across a natural bridge of vines, but Delia, trying to follow, was soon teetering in midair, much to the Pygmies' amusement. They were laughing and jeering at her when suddenly an elephant's trumpeting shattered the air close by.

The Pygmies vanished instantly into the forest. Delia was left alone, exposed to view high above the heads of a herd of elephants.

She had handed her gun to one of the Pygmy men to hold while she negotiated the difficult crossing, so she had no weapon.

Breathlessly she watched the bushes part and saw a pair of huge tusks appear and a raised trunk sniffing the air. But the wind was in her favor. The immense head backed slowly away and disappeared. The herd moved on and Delia somehow descended, dismayed by the unchivalrous behavior of her friends.

The hunt continued and the dead elephant was soon found, poisoned from his wounds. The Pygmies threw themselves on the carcass in joy, "tears streaming from their eyes." Then they blew whistles to call the tribe. After they had collected the eyelashes and hairs from the ear opening and the tail for fetishes or trading, the orgy began.

As darkness fell, Delia was left to gather firewood alone. Her thin pongee shirt was ragged and dripping, her khaki trousers caked with mud, and the chill jungle night was closing in. A fire was also needed to keep off wild animals. After gorging themselves, the hunters crawled inside the elephant's body cavity and went to sleep.

As the night dragged on, Delia threw sticks at the elephant to awaken the men, then, when this had no effect, she screamed and pretended she had seen a leopard. This brought some of the men to the fireside with spears and they stayed there until daylight. Meat had been sent to a nearby village to be exchanged for palm wine and banana beer, and by midday the bivouac was thronged with Pygmies deliriously feasting and drinking. Delia guessed the orgy would last five days, but she somehow managed to get back to her porters and tent before that, and soon was on her way.

Pushing hard through the steaming forest and scrub bush, she reached Wamba on May 4, 1925, to the astonishment of two missionary couples living there. By a freakish coincidence, a copy of the *Brooklyn Eagle* of March 1, 1925, had found its way to far-off Wamba just one day before, carrying the news that Delia Akeley was "missing" somewhere in Africa. One of the missionaries hastened to write the *Eagle* reassuringly that Mrs. Akeley had arrived in Wamba "practically in the middle of Africa, safe and well and looking the picture of health . . . To us it is a wonder that she is able to cross Africa alone, knowing only a few words of

*Delia's safari at times counted twenty-five porters and eight
carriers for her litter chair, four carriers at at time.*

the dialect of these parts and speaking French, the official language
of the Belgian Congo . . . However, she gets her work done . . . She
has made a wonderful collection of photographs chiefly relating to
the life and customs of women and their babies."

Delia tarried only four days in Wamba, long enough to photograph a great gathering of chiefs for a tribunal, catching the pomp
and ceremony of sultans decked out with spears, shields, guns, and
hats decorated with parrot feathers. Then she set forth on the hilly
road for Medje, a seven-day journey.

In Medje, "just a great clearing in the Ituri Forest," she paid off
her porters and asked the sultan for new ones. The customary
summons was sent forth. "The drums began booming out their call
for porters again this morning, and it is wonderful to think the
sound carries its message so far," she observed.

The code drums, the marvelous communication system of the
Congo, had pursued her steps throughout the trek. Made of hollow
logs, the wooden drums were an institution in every village. They
transmitted over great distances messages of all kinds in codes
older than anyone knew. Before Delia's arrival in a village, a message would already have been relayed announcing who she was,
where she was going, the number of her porters, and how much

143

food the local population would be expected to deliver to her camp for the caravan — the expected courtesy of the area. The singing of her *tepoi* boys and porters only confirmed what the populace ahead already knew.

The drums so intrigued Delia that when in an encampment for several days she organized drummer contests. Offer of a prize inspired contestants from nearby villages to drag their huge drums by lianas over the forest trails to compete. The contests by the campfire usually turned into dancing revels that might last until dawn. Delia learned not to ask sultans to judge; they always gave the prize to themselves!

Delia's increasingly somber mood as she pressed northward toward Rungu, her next identifiable destination, is reflected in a letter written May 24, 1925, from a place she calls Nakabu, to the editor of the magazine *The Woman's Viewpoint.*

> Tomorrow, if nothing happens, I will reach Rungu, a station on the Bomokandi River, where there is a white official and where I can post this scribble and get it started on the long journey to you . . . I have now been in the great Ituri Forest for three months, camping in the little clearings where the natives have their village, and I am beginning to feel that I have had enough of the high trees and the awful tangle of twisted, twining, clinging things that grow in positive nightmare fashion beneath the trees . . . The jungle is morbid, unwholesome, and is beginning to get on my nerves, I fear. I suffer most at night, for we do not use tents here, as we do on the plains, but little mud huts. The ants, spiders, rats, bats, and snakes take possession of these rest houses as soon as they are built. Consequently live things, as well as a fine dust created by the boring of insects, keep dropping on one's head. Fleas, jiggers, and ticks await each new arrival. I keep a light burning all night in my little mud hut, and even then the rats will run up the legs of my folding cot and wake me up. If I try to work at night, either writing or sorting out my specimens obtained during the day, the bats fly about and swoop around my towel-covered head . . . But I am not sorry I came, and I am far from ready to quit.

And quit she did not. She now trekked westward along the "dirty brown" Bomokandi River toward Poko. Relentlessly she pursued her task of photographing the native peoples. She devoted hours in camp developing her negatives, enduring every adversity that could break a photographer's heart. Torrential rains filled the air with moisture that kept negatives from drying. Sudden winds swept through the rest house, soiling the wet negatives. Weak or bad developing chemicals ruined the work of hours of photographing.

Somewhere out of Rungu she ran into the unusual Wazanda tribe. "All the women have front teeth filed so there is an inverted v-shaped opening. Their language is quite different from the other tribes. Very little body decoration like tattooing done here," she recorded. It was customary to bind the heads of children. Delia sketched the distorted head shape typical of the men whose heads had been bound.

Frequent swamps and high grass now impeded her progress. Traveling grew more difficult. "Trail very bad," she wrote. At one place, it took twenty men to get the *tepoi* across a swamp where water was waist high. About a week's march out of Rungu, they encountered a rest house so awful that the porters put up her tent without even consulting her. She was delighted when she arrived. "It was like getting home after a long absence to get into a clean tent again."

To reach Poko, the caravan crossed the Bomokandi River in small boats; slippery from muddy feet and overcrowded with natives, the boats almost overturned. Delia found Poko detestable: built "in the bottom of a bowl" along the Bomokandi River and shut in by surrounding hills, its air was "dead and heavy," and a heavy white fog each morning when the native prisoners started to work made them seem "like shadows." But it had attracted her because it was located on the handsome new road built by the Belgians. By a bus almost as dirty as the boats, she was able to motor from Poko to Niangara on the Uele River. In Niangara she managed, with difficulty, to arrange for permits to import ammunition and developing chemicals from Khartoum in Egypt, a transaction that would entail a six-week wait.

Evidently expecting to return to Niangara for her supplies, she left its decided discomforts until they should arrive there and pressed northward to Bafuka. Bafuka turned out to be "a big village, nice and clean," where her veranda faced the "main street"

— a path across a wide sand-covered space surrounded by native huts and granaries built on poles. She had been promised good hunting in this area. The sultan, although old and ill, was friendly, and offered a competent hunting guide and food. Things looked promising.

Then one evening Delia learned she was in cannibal country. Her cook and tent boy declared that had they come alone to this place without the company of a white person they would have been killed and eaten. "They claim that most of the tribes eat human flesh," she confided in her journal, and they said that six tribes eat raw flesh. They also told her how the Belgians subdued the natives. "They talked until almost nine. I let them ramble on for they have both traveled with officials and are well informed on affairs in the country," she recounted.

> While we were talking, two black men suddenly appeared at the door and deposited a black pot and a bundle of something wrapped in banana leaf. They said the Sultan had sent food for my boys. I went over with the lantern to see what was in the pot for it was still hot and steaming. The man stooped down and lifted up a well-cooked forearm. The natives in the forest regularly all eat monkeys and I thought ho! here is a young chimpanzee or gorilla feast. But to my horror the next piece he picked up to show me was a good sized hand, and the long thumb told me that it did not belong to a monkey. It made me quite sick and the awful thing is that the two boys who are with me constantly are eaters of human flesh and even now I can hear them laughing and talking over their feast. The Sultan also sent women for my boys as they are in the habit of doing for the white men. No wonder the sky sheds tears at night and the thunder booms and the lightning threatens. The Congo is cruel.

Although her personal revulsion for cannibalism is revealed in her journal, she never published an account of this incident nor leveled judgment about the subject in later interviews. Her tent boy caught flying ants swarming about her lantern at night and plopped them into his mouth. As a seasoned traveler, she pragmatically accepted the fact that dietary differences existed. She found cannibalism here to be simply another dietary custom, and for her that was that.

For the next month, headquartered in Bafuka, Delia devoted herself fully to hunting, attempting to augment her slender specimen collection of Congo game. The heavy cover of high grass because of the rainy season foiled her efforts. Day after day she struck out with the sultan's hunter, seeking waterbuck and other game, only to track futilely for long, exhausting hours and to return to her camp empty-handed. Mounting discouragement is reflected in her diary entry of Friday, July 10:

> Tossed a coin last night to see if I would have another try for waterbuck. To "stay" won. So I went out at six o'clock. Mocambo [the sultan's tracker] led the way and we went to a new hunting ground where the grass was so coarse it cut my trousers to ribbons and the legs of the men were bleeding. Jumped a family of three [waterbuck] five times and only got one shot at them. Then with the steam rising from the rain-soaked grass and from my perspiring body, my glasses fogged as usual and the perspiration dripped off my eyelashes into my eyes and made them smart like the mischief. We worked hard until both boys wanted to give up the chase. They were tired and so was I dead tired after days of hopeless hard work. The only time I have worked harder was when I was following elephants in Uganda. I have only two cartridges left for my Mannlicher . . . and I am going back with few animals.
>
> The range of empty swamp lands, grasslands, and bush which the animals have is tremendous and it is not strange that during the . . . weeks I have hunted here, I have seen only the animals I was tracking. I saw no snakes although I waded across swamps, rivers, and small streams. My clothes were soaked from the time I left the *tepoi* in a *shamba* until I returned to camp. Three times we were caught in the terrific rain storm and in two minutes after the rain started my teeth were chattering with the cold. The sudden change from terrific heat to icy cold rain gave me a chill and a hot brandy was the only thing which saved me from the fever which one usually has on such occasions here.
>
> When I returned home today I found the Belgian flags flying

and the Italian official from Doruma here to collect the tax . . .
Official very nice, more like a real man than the other officials
whom I have met. He said there were lots of animals three days
away from here, but the grass is high now. Had I been able to
come through Kilo as I had planned I would have gotten just what
I wanted for the grass was short then.

Each night when the bugle sounds at six o'clock the village
dogs begin to howl, chickens run around looking for a place to
roost, and all stop work. It sounded very uncanny tonight when I
knew the old Sultan was so ill and lying on his skin-covered couch
panting and fighting for his very life with each breath. He must be
about seventy or seventy-five years old. There was a fire and the
air was stifling. Perspiration rolled off his face . . . A woman and a
boy were the only ones in the hut with him.

This forlorn report is the last entry made in her traveler's log.
For some time she had mentioned having a cold, or written of
doubling her doses of quinine. The buoyancy that had led her into
this adventure was subsiding. At some point after the July 10
notes, she came down with a bout of fever, which caused her to
decide she had had enough of the Congo.

"I was delirious half the time," she told a reporter for the *Brooklyn Eagle* on her return home. "When I wasn't I could hear the
cook and my personal boy . . . discussing how they would prepare
my body and arguing over how they would divide up my clothes.
Each morning one of them would come in and ask politely if I was
going to die that day. I always replied I didn't think so.

"Eventually, I recovered. But I had fever twice after that. The last
time . . . I slept in the mud. The legs of my bed just went right down
into it. When I finally could get up I made tracks straight for
home."

"Tracks straight for home" means she abandoned her original
plan of crossing French Equatorial Africa to Lake Chad, then
crossing Nigeria to the Niger River, by which she planned to reach
Africa's west coast, a journey mostly overland and of many hundreds of miles. Instead she chose the quickest exit route. She probably took a bus from Niangara to Stanleyville (Kisangani today), a
riverboat at Stanleyville, and a train at Leopoldville. She reached
Boma near the Congo River's mouth on September 3, 1925, nearly

two months after her last diary entry on July 10, an interval about which we have few details. It was almost eleven months since she had set out from Lamu, Kenya, on the east coast on her remarkable east-west traverse. Crossing the Belgian Congo from Lake Albert to the Atlantic Ocean had taken five months, twenty-six days. She had lost thirty pounds en route.

In addition to valuable artifacts, she supplied the Brooklyn Museum with more than thirty specimens of game animals, including waterbuck, duiker, cob, and the dainty dik-dik, smallest of the antelopes. She also sold 190 objects of scientific or cultural interest to the Newark Museum in New Jersey.

At a press conference in Dr. Englehardt's Brooklyn Museum office, she regaled reporters with adventure tales, including the story of a daring visit to a witch doctor while blackened and clothed as a native woman.

During the next four years Delia wrote for publication for the first time, producing two books and several articles for *The Saturday Evening Post, Collier's,* and *Century.* The *New York Times* described her as "the lovely, slim woman with gentle voice and pale face who hunts lions and looks like a duchess." She dedicated the biography of her "favorite monkey": "To the memory of Carl Ethan Akeley whose life and work I shared for many years and who understood and loved 'J.T., Jr.' as I did."

One of Delia's women friends thought her too charitable toward her former husband. "I know how much you appreciate his great work apart from his failure on the personal side," she wrote. "But few women would be capable of separating the two things and giving such whole-hearted praise to what was good." Then, more snippily, she inquired, "And what about No. 2, is she still seeking the limelight?"

Her opinion of Akeley's second wife was shared by many. After only two years of marriage and a few months in Africa, the widow overnight had become *the* authority on Akeley and a prolific author on his work. Her first book was loaded with references to "my husband" and to "long-held dreams and heart's desires" which must have sounded hollow to Delia, who had stood by Akeley through his earliest, most strenuous career years. Mary Jobe obliterated Delia's contributions, even the epic rescue after the elephant's mauling, attributing it to Bill the tent boy who, in fact, was not even with Akeley but with Delia at the time of the accident.

The scientific community was even more unjust. Her role in Akeley's career was well known, yet when commemorative articles were published in scientific journals after his death it was Mary Jobe's bravery that was extolled and not a word mentioned about Delia. Her status as a divorced woman in a day when divorce was a scandal made such references much too awkward.

Delia was soon off on a new expedition for the Brooklyn Museum. When her plan to study Pygmies again was made public, she was besieged by other women, most of them strangers, asking to come along as members of the expedition. She decided to retain her solo role rather than expose another person to the trials she expected to undergo.

This time she entered Africa at Port Sudan on the Red Sea in November 1929, traveled by rail to Khartoum, then by steamer up the Nile to Rejaf, and from there entered the Belgian Congo by bus. She kept no chronicle of this return to the Congo, at least none that has been located. But it is known she made her headquarters at Avakubi, an active rubber center on the Ituri River, branching out into the surrounding jungle.

After five months in the Pygmy realm, she had to give up — not by choice, but because of continuous torrential rains. "It was a season of terrific storms and abnormal rainfall, and life in the forest was distressingly unpleasant," she explained afterward. "But I learned more about pygmies and forest-dwelling animals than I did on all my other expeditions combined."

She also amassed five thousand feet of film and over fifteen hundred photographs of Pygmies and other native peoples, as well as a collection of tools, ornaments, and weapons, in return for some of which she had only had to comb her long white hair, still a talisman of potent allure. On her return, the *New York Times* ran a full-page sepia spread of her photographs, one showing Delia towering over a Pygmy man, "almost a foot shorter than Mrs. Akeley, who is five feet five inches in height."

Afterward Delia lectured, began a book on the Pygmies, and talked of visiting Pygmies in other parts of the world. But instead, at sixty-four, still stylish and charming looking, she remarried. In

The New York Times *ran this full-page layout of Delia Akeley's Pygmy photographs.*

1939 she was wed to Dr. Warren D. Howe, an old neighbor and friend, now a widower, whom she and Carl Akeley had known in their Chicago days. The family friendship had survived the years. Howe's grandchildren already called her "Aunt Mickey." Now the daredevil adventurer eased into the leisurely, protected life of a well-heeled wife, dividing the year between Howe's beautiful old New England farm in Dorset, Vermont, and his winter home in Captiva, Florida. When Dr. Howe died in 1951, Delia remained in Florida, living in a Daytona Beach hotel.

Two years before her death, she relented in her silence toward her family and invited a nephew and his two daughters to visit, although they were virtual strangers. They found a frail, slender old lady with a cane — some trouble related to J.T.'s bite — who was eager to fill in the missing decades. They, in turn, were curious about a career they had followed only through newspapers.

Delia died quietly on May 22, 1970, at age ninety-five, not from some terrible tropical fever, not gored to death by an elephant, nor squashed in a buffalo stampede, but simply from old age. The little farm girl who had run away when she was thirteen left an estate of one and a half million dollars. Each of the relatives received a generous bequest.

Thus an indomitable spirit passed, an extraordinary and wholly untypical life ended. Delia Akeley had brought the picturesque aura and glamour of nineteenth-century colonial African exploration into the twentieth century. Not a scientist, she approached Africa respectfully as a student, observer, even participant, for she enjoyed intimate contact with tribal people. Her sympathetic bearing made possible her invaluable harvest of native objects from East and Central Africa at a time when museum acquisitions of such materials came largely from Africa's more accessible west coast. These and her specimens of African mammals and birds were all channeled for posterity to splendid museums. She is today represented in the Chicago, New York, Brooklyn, and Newark museums, a phenomenal achievement for a woman of her day.

Yet her greatest legacy may be her faith in the power of a friendly approach to an alien people. She proved over and over that a woman alone, without armed escort, could travel through the most remote areas of Africa, live in the villages, mingle with different tribes, take part in daily affairs, make friends, particularly with the women, and remain safe. Her most powerful weapon was not the revolver always at her bedside but her belief in simple human understanding. She utilized this capacity to win acceptance, together with her remarkable abilities as a hunter, her knowledge of taxidermy, and her skill as a collector, to contribute enormously to our knowledge of Africa.

With spunk, resilience, curiosity, and tenacity she slogged her way through hazards, discomforts, and discouragements that might well have caused many a man to quail. And yet she did not travel without fear. "I'm always frightened in the jungle — always prepared for a violent death," she said. "I never go without taking along the means to end it quickly if I am mortally hurt. But I love it."

MARGUERITE HARRISON

1879–1967

ON WHAT MUST HAVE BEEN a whimsical impulse, Marguerite Harrison decided one day in 1915 to apply for a job at the *Baltimore Sun*. Not that she didn't acutely need more income. A widow at thirty-six with a thirteen-year-old son, she had been left almost penniless by her husband's death. At first she turned to the course most often chosen by women of gentility in those days: she converted her large home on Charles Street in Baltimore into a boarding house and took in roomers. But it was soon clear that boarders did not bring in enough money.

Marguerite had no training in the usual careers open to women of her day, those of teacher, nurse, librarian, and secretary. But for that matter she was equally unequipped to be a reporter. She had never written a news story in her life, didn't type, and had had only a single semester of college.

Nevertheless, without the slightest notion of how she might fit in, she applied to the *Baltimore Sun*, a virtually all-male preserve. Whether it was the letter of introduction she carried from her powerful brother-in-law, Albert Ritchie, who would serve several terms as Maryland's governor, or her own wide social connections as a member of a prominent Baltimore family that swung the decision, Frank Kent, the managing editor, hired her as assistant society editor.

Whatever the motivation on either side, it was a decision that led to an astonishing career as a journalist, author, spy, documentary filmmaker, and explorer of exotic shores.

Although on her first day at the *Sun*, Marguerite did not even know how to flip up the lid of the office desk to bring out the typewriter, she was a fast learner. Very soon she was turning out good copy and with a swiftness that before long netted her the assignment of music and drama critic; in addition, she began a weekly column called "Overheard in the Wings" that featured interviews with visiting artists, frequently leading names of the day. Before many months she was earning twenty dollars a week, later raised to thirty. This was augmented, with Governor Ritchie's help, by an appointment to the State Board of Motion Picture Censors which paid twenty-five hundred dollars yearly.

After the United States entered World War I in 1917, Marguerite was assigned to cover women's role in the war effort. She donned a conductor's uniform to run streetcars, and worked as a skilled laborer in Bethlehem Steel Company's Sparrows Point plant near Baltimore, where she discovered women functioned as effectively as men. Her extraordinary facility with languages, learned through European travel with her family, opened doors to interviews others could not handle.

She was now working fourteen-hour days, stumbling back late in the evening to the boarding house, which was run by a house-keeper and cook. She could spend only Sundays with her son. But this "orgy of intensive work with neither time nor thought for any human relationships or relaxation" also left her little leisure for self-pity in her struggle to restore her shattered life and identity.

Her comfortable world had fallen apart in the spring of 1915. Her blissful fourteen-year marriage had ended with her husband's swift death from a brain tumor. Her mother had died only weeks earlier. And her father, whom she idolized, had undergone cata-strophic financial reverses in the loss of the steamship line he had founded, a tragic dénouement to his life's work.

At birth Marguerite's life seemed assured of security and luxury. She was born Marguerite Elton Baker in October 1879 to parents of venerable and moneyed lineage, both sides long settled in Mary-land and distinguished from colonial days. Grandfather Baker, her father's father, a bank president and owner of prosperous glass factories, had created Atholl, a magnificent estate near Baltimore, whose grounds were surmounted by a huge granite house with a towering cupola and stained glass windows. As each of the seven Baker sons married, the father built a new house for him on the Atholl grounds. When Marguerite's father, Bernard Nadal Baker, just graduated from Yale at twenty-two, married her mother, aged eighteen, he was given Olden, Marguerite's first home.

The storage and lighterage business founded by Marguerite's father prospered in Baltimore's brisk shipping trade and grew into the lucrative and prestigious Atlantic Transport Lines, for years one of the important transatlantic lines. Success inspired him to build a new home even grander than Olden or Atholl. Marguerite's mother had been bequeathed a large, historic estate near Baltimore called Ingleside, and here Baker built a Georgian-style twenty-two-room mansion, patterned after one he had admired in England, and acquired three or four hundred additional acres for stables, overseer's cottage, tenant houses, barns, gatehouse, and farm buildings. Marguerite's mother furnished this beautiful house with fine eighteenth-century English and American furniture and made the gardens into a horticultural show place.

Amid this opulence, Marguerite and her younger sister, Elizabeth, were reared like royalty, with nurses, governesses, exquisite imported clothes, summers in England. The crossings were aboard one of her father's ships, where Marguerite had the run of the decks and access to the entire crew. By the age of ten, she wrote in her memoirs, she knew more about ships than many an older landlubber.

In London, Baker's position in shipping circles brought his family into social contact with highly placed English families, including invitations to English country estates. As a young girl, Marguerite met not only all the British shipping magnates but also such international personalities as Sir Robert Baden-Powell, founder of the Boy Scouts, the actress Ellen Terry, J. Pierpont Morgan, the financier, Sir Henry Lucy, editor of *Punch,* Sir Henry Irving of the theater, the artist Sir Laurence Alma-Tadema, and many others. Her father's loan of the S.S. *Maine* as a hospital ship during the Boer War brought them to the notice of Lady Randolph Churchill and members of the British royal family. Tea at Kensington Palace, races at Ascot, and, at last, a presentation at the court of Victoria followed.

Marguerite was twelve when she was entered as a day pupil at the exclusive St. Timothy's School for Girls, in Cantonsville on Baltimore's outskirts. She lived nearby with relatives at Elton Park, another splendid residence, where Grandfather Elton's Quaker liberalism and independence of opinion, and his library rich in books on travel, exploration, and history, were, she later believed, strong influences in shaping her own thinking.

All these elements of a fairytale youth, surprisingly, did not add up to a happy childhood. In retrospect Marguerite felt that in these early years she was pent up, stifled, lonely. Estranged from her mother virtually from birth, according to her autobiography, she felt that her arrival was as rude a shock to her unready mother as the violent hurricane that hit Baltimore at the same time. At nineteen and newly wed, her mother did not welcome a child. An intimacy never developed, and ultimately they became totally alienated. Marguerite and her sister Elizabeth, two years younger, likewise remained strangers. They differed in almost every respect, from physical appearance to temperament. Lively, curious, adventurous, Marguerite was the one who could climb anything, Elizabeth the timorous one who wouldn't follow. As an adult, Marguerite became an unwilling rival of her sister in a serious affair of the heart, which permanently severed their ties. Marguerite wrote of this sister she hardly knew, "When I dally with the doctrine of reincarnation, which has always had a tremendous fascination for me, I imagine that we must have lived our previous lives in different periods and among peoples alien in blood and civilization. She was never a part of my life."

Sadly, Marguerite admitted, "my father was the only person in the world for whom I felt any great affection, and I loved him with a passionate devotion that amounted to adoration." She had been separated even from her peers, she said. Hovering governesses and the formality of her home discouraged playmates, and her mother feared that the girls would "catch something" if they fraternized too freely with other children. Her mother's hypochondriacal concern for Marguerite's health, which she considered "delicate," kept her out of sports and even of dance classes. Moreover, her mother gradually alienated her husband's six brothers and thus separated the girls from a large brood of cousins they might have known.

At St. Timothy's, in close contact with girls of her own age for the first time, Marguerite felt "different," "awkward," that the other girls were unfathomably mysterious. An avid reader, adept at languages, and encouraged by her mother to parade her learning, she became an irritating bluestocking and pedant — or so she later thought. Her memoirs poignantly reflect the isolation of the brilliant, sensitive child, an isolation so often the lot of the precocious.

After five years at St. Timothy's, Marguerite's parents placed her in Radcliffe College for a year. Her mother's purpose was not education but to prepare her daughter for her society debut and a brilliant marriage. She accompanied Marguerite to Cambridge, chose a suitable, properly chaperoned boarding house, and left her daughter on her own for the first time in her life.

Marguerite reacted by getting herself secretly engaged almost overnight to the landlady's son, an affair that flourished only until the Christmas holidays, when her suspicious mother discovered their letters. Marguerite was yanked from college and whisked off to Italy to forget the whole business, which, she recalled, she did rather promptly. The unfinished Radcliffe semester, her only college experience, became grounds in later years after her various international escapades for frequent references in the press to her as "the Radcliffe girl" who had done this or that, misleadingly implying that she was an atypical alumna, who had wandered far from the mainstream of the usual Radcliffe career.

Even before her debut, the winter after leaving Radcliffe she had set herself to become engaged to a certain Thomas Bullitt Harrison, a handsome, charming man, slightly older, but nonetheless a "catch." Despite the unremitting chaperonage at Baltimore's lavish debutante cotillions, Marguerite managed by deliberate flirting to make him fall in love with her, only, as she later admitted, to discover she had fallen in love with him.

When they announced their plan to marry, Marguerite's mother "ranted, raved, stormed, and had hysterics," then snatched her away for the usual cure, two months in Italy. Tom was not the princeling, the top-flight diplomat, the member of the British peerage envisioned by her mother for her daughter. This time the cure didn't take; Marguerite returned still pledged to Tom. He might be poor, but he came of a good family, son of a charming woman whom Marguerite grew to love, with an equally charming stepfather, Dr. Joseph S. Ames, who would one day become president of The Johns Hopkins University.

161

Mrs. Baker compensated for her lost social aspirations by staging a wedding Marguerite described as "one of the most splendid ever seen in Baltimore." Her trousseau — "more fit for a princess than for the wife of a poor man" — included forty custom-made gowns, twenty-four hats, nineteen pairs of shoes, and infinite varieties of gloves and accessories. Two reverends and a bishop officiated, with ten bridesmaids and ten groomsmen in the wedding party. Afterward, Mrs. Baker sank into bitter, unforgiving invalidism. "She never openly showed any signs of affection for me and she hated Tom," Marguerite said. She died fourteen years later still unreconciled, although devoted to Marguerite's son, Thomas Bullitt Harrison II.

Marguerite gave birth to "Tommy" in March 1902, a scant nine months from her wedding date, and settled happily into contented homemaking, "forever making curtains, cushions, and lamp shades." Through her husband's mother and stepfather, she gained her first experience of a united family. This happy life, so different from her internationally oriented youth, lasted the full fourteen years until her husband's death. Not only was she then penniless, but her husband had incurred a debt of nearly seventy thousand dollars during his last months of ill health. Though not legally obligated, she swore to repay this debt, and also vowed never to love so intensely again, not even to grow too attached to her young son.

By early 1918, with the war raging in Europe, Marguerite began wishing for a more active role than that of mere reporter on the home front. She was especially curious about conditions in Germany, a country she had visited in peacetime with her family. A restless urge to return to Germany, to see what it had become, seized her — a strange fantasy for an American civilian in 1918, particularly a woman, and an all but impossible one to fulfill. All normal communication and traffic between the United States and Europe had been disrupted by the movement of armies and military supplies. Europe itself was one vast battlefield, with Germany the focus of surging armies hoping to overrun it.

Marguerite chose a remarkable path of entry. She decided to become a spy, and, with an evident minimum of soul-searching debate, lost no time in communicating her willingness to serve her country (and satisfy her own wanderlust) to the chief of the army's Military Intelligence Division, General Marlborough Churchill. Dr. Ames, her stepfather-in-law and a personal friend of General Churchill, wrote a letter of introduction.

On the official information blank, Marguerite described herself as five feet six inches tall, weighing 125 pounds, using no stimulants, tobacco, or drugs, and without physical defects. Answering the question "With what foreign countries and localities are you familiar," she stated: "The British Isles, France, Holland, Germany, Italy, Austria, Switzerland, Northern Italy, Rome, Naples, Tyrol. I have absolute command of French and German, am very fluent and have a good accent in Italian and speak a little Spanish. Without any trouble I could pass as a French woman, and after a little practice, as German-Swiss . . . I have been in Europe fourteen times . . . I have been much on steamers and am familiar in a general way with ships of the merchant marine."

These two documents, Dr. Ames's letter and Marguerite's résumé, form part of two large packets of data relating to Marguerite's service as a spy for the Military Intelligence Division, or MID, of the United States War Department. The considerable materials make up File #PF-39205, the Marguerite Harrison personnel file, which is catalogued in the United States National Archives. The collection of letters, cables, reports, clippings, and memoranda trace Marguerite's career as a spy from its first moments, through its exciting and dangerous course that would make her an international figure.

Marguerite's overture to the MID was presently answered with instructions suitably arcane to foreshadow the covert world she was about to enter. She was told to meet an anonymous man wearing civilian clothing in the lobby of a Baltimore hotel. His report of this meeting would have pleased Marguerite.

I met Mrs. Harrison by appointment at the Hotel Emerson, Baltimore, 3 P.M., September 28th, and discussed with her the subject of representing us abroad . . . Mrs. Harrison is a cultured lady, a widow, 39 years of age, of very attractive personality and of high intelligence . . . She is an accomplished linguist and speaks

German and French fluently, Italian quite well and some Spanish. She spoke German with such fluency that I questioned her as to where she learned it, etc. She said she had always had a talent for language and remarked her family had been American for eight generations.

Mrs. Harrison said she would say she is German-Swiss and I have no doubt she could readily deceive the average person. She remarked she is fearless, fond of adventure, and has an intense desire to do something for her country. She also said she is "callous" as to love affairs and that with her years, she had passed the foolish stage. She could easily be considered ten years younger. She has a son fifteen years of age . . . I believe she would be discreet; she impressed me most favorably . . . She said she would be ready to start December 1st.

A salary of $250 a month with another $250 for expenses was tentatively suggested, but before she could get away, Armistice was declared, on November 11, 1918. Marguerite thought her career as a spy was aborted. However, within hours she was notified that the MID still planned to send her to Europe, but with a new assignment. She would report political and economic matters of possible interest to the United States delegation at the forthcoming peace conference. Although the element of danger had lessened now that war had ceased, the assignment was still not without peril. Marguerite welcomed it with excitement.

Outside of the War Department, only her immediate family and the managing editor of the *Baltimore Sun* knew she was bound for Germany as a secret agent when she sailed for Bordeaux, France, on the French liner *Espagne* in December 1918. She was assigned the signature "B" for the transmission of messages, given her code name and cipher tables (still in her file), and reminded of "the absolute necessity of the most extraordinary care as to secrecy."

She was traveling under the cover of a correspondent on special assignment to the *Baltimore Sun,* and would write feature articles for the paper while carrying out her intelligence collecting. She was not to be involved in strategic or military intelligence, only political, social, and economic reporting.

War-wracked France was a sea of mud, and Marguerite's trip

northward from the south of France was a long, slogging journey. Despite her official letters, transport was difficult to arrange, roads terrible, camps often wretched. Billeted like the soldiers, she slept mostly in makeshift huts and sheds, frequently in the heavy dampness and cold of early winter, for there was no firewood. She slept on her pack when beds were too dirty or wet, or were entirely lacking. Paris was still sandbagged and camouflaged.

In Paris on Christmas Eve she received the news of her father's unexpected death following an operation. Another link with her past was gone.

Coblenz, Germany, headquarters of the American Army of Occupation, was her first major destination. It took her several weeks to work her way up to the Rhineland, hitchhiking rides on military transports. But after Coblenz, she would have to devise her own means of getting on to Berlin, her final goal.

In Coblenz at last, she was able to obtain a laissez-passer from the French authorities for travel on to Mainz, Germany, headquarters of the French Army of Occupation. From Coblenz to Mainz was therefore no problem. But beyond Mainz lay unoccupied Germany, only a few weeks earlier the unconquered enemy, still cut off from communication with the outside world, since international news coverage had not yet been reestablished. It was from Mainz to Berlin that she must elude the authorities.

At five o'clock on a frigid January morning, she crossed the French bridgehead at Mainz aboard a slow train bound for Frankfurt. It was filled with sleepy German workmen going from their homes in the occupied zone to jobs in industrial plants in Frankfurt, a movement permitted by the French military. No one seemed to notice that she was an American.

Day had still not broken when she disembarked at Frankfurt. There were almost no street lights. She was now alone, now on "enemy" soil, now vulnerable. She set out on foot for a hotel she had stayed at as a child, the Frankfurter Hof. There were no cabs and she had no choice but to walk. To her relief the hotel was still there, and open. Lugging her two suitcases and typewriter, she walked into the lobby, startling the night clerk nearly out of his wits. An American woman traveler appearing at that spectral hour after four years of war seemed an apparition indeed. Identifying herself as an American newspaper correspondent, she was given a comfortable room.

Left-wing Workmen's and Soldiers' Councils had taken over local governments all over the country, and it was to one of their offices Marguerite went later that day to seek a travel permit for further movement. Her newspaper credentials and American passport made it easy to obtain, but only as far as Kassel, for beyond Kassel, she learned, the railroad was still in the hands of "the remnants of von Hindenburg's army, which was loyal to the new Republican government and no civilians were permitted to reach the capital."

The train to Kassel was packed with demobilized German soldiers, and she wedged into a compartment designed for eight but jammed with fourteen. In Kassel she hired a droshky and drove to General von Hindenburg's headquarters, seeking the officer in charge of transportation. He protested that her entrance into Germany was highly "irregular," but she must have charmed him as she had others, for he granted her a travel permit for a troop train leaving for Berlin the following morning. Again there were no cabs when she reached the Berlin station toward midnight, so she sat on her baggage and waited. At length she secured an old droshky driver and boldly ordered him to take her to the only hotel she had ever stayed in there, the Bristol. For all she knew, it might have vanished in the intervening years. She did know, however, that internal conflict was still going on in the capital between members of the Spartacist movement, fighting for a German Soviet Republic, and supporters of the existing provisional government. She later described this arrival in Berlin, climaxing her audacious dash into a Germany not yet occupied by Allied troops.

"Hotel Bristol," I said in a commanding tone.

"What!" the cabby almost shouted. "The Hotel Bristol is *abgesperrt!* Only the *Militär* can pass through the Brandenburger Thor at this hour of the night, *Gnädige.*"

"I belong to the *Militär,*" I said grandly, displaying my pass from Cassel, and at the same time beginning to throw my luggage in the front seat.

I knew that Berlin was in a state of siege but I did not anticipate that I would have any more difficulty in getting to the Bristol than to any other hotel. What I did not realize was that the Wilhelmstrasse, where fighting was even then taking place, opened into the Unter den Linden where the Bristol was situated.

The driver muttered something about shooting, but he was of the old school and deeply impressed by my official pass. So he started off, albeit unwillingly . . .

As we drove down the Budapesther Strasse toward the Brandenburger Thor I began to hear the barking of rifles and the sharp put-put of machine guns in the distance.

"Shall I go on, *Fräulein?*" the driver asked respectfully, but anxiously.

"*Gewiss,*" I answered sternly . . .

To this day I have never known why the patrol on duty at the Brandenburger Thor let me through. I think it was due as much to sheer astonishment at seeing a lone woman under such circumstances as to my military pass . . . As we approached the entrance to the Wilhelmstrasse there was a sharp fusillade quite close to us, followed by the rattle of a "sewing machine," as the Germans called their machine guns. Bullets bounced on the pavement and ricocheted from the walls of buildings around us . . . In another minute we drew up in front of the Bristol. Every curtain was drawn, shutters were fastened, and the heavy wrought-iron doors were bolted and barred. I paid the driver, who dumped my bags on the sidewalk and vanished at a gallop, without saying a word. Then I rang the night bell and stood waiting, pressed as close as possible against the door. Presently I heard the key turn in the lock and a night porter, looking almost as frightened as I felt, poked his head through a crack in the door.

"*Um Gottes Willen, Fräulein,*" was all he said as he grabbed me with one hand and my bags with the other, literally dragging me into the vestibule.

Marguerite had already scored a mark by becoming one of her country's earliest women correspondents by virtue of her assignment from the *Baltimore Sun.* Now she would be credited as being the first English-speaking woman correspondent to reach Berlin after the armistice.

Her newspaper credentials and letters of introduction to members of Berlin's elite quickly opened inner circles of Berlin society to the beautiful American woman so fluent in German, so interesting a conversationalist. She was soon a dinner guest in the homes of some of the most highly placed of the old aristocracy.

But she knew that in order to gain a sense of the political climate of the country she would have to mingle with all strata of society. She circulated among the old Prussian Pan-Germanists who talked of the monarchy's return, the dissidents of the radical left, the lower-middle-class families now almost starving, and the people of the street who were in abject need. She walked from elegant shops where Parisian dresses sold for fortunes into public markets where lines of waiting people were finally turned away empty-handed.

"I rarely had a half-hour to myself during the day. My life was one of continual activity and tension. I was obliged to make and maintain contacts with every political party. I could not afford to overlook any happening great or small that would throw light on conditions in Germany or the secret machinations of this faction or that."

Voluminous reports to the MID were written in the dead of night, after a theater performance, a dinner party, or some political meeting. They were discreetly dropped off at the Hotel Adlon for her Berlin contact, a Colonel Bouvier, whom she rarely saw, lest she arouse suspicion. She also regularly had to file interesting stories for the *Baltimore Sun*.

It was a disciplined, hard-working regime, bird-dogging rumors and leads, a distant shadow of the life of the female spy of legend. Marguerite wrote of this contrast with amusement: "I had from the first made up my mind that I would not pose as either a Socialist or a reactionary and thus get better information under false pretenses, nor would I trade on any such thing as sex appeal. So far as possible I made myself absolutely sexless and impersonal, partly as a measure of self-protection in an atmosphere fraught with dangers of this description and partly because I had a contempt for such tactics. I often used to smile when I compared my own life with that of the beautiful and baleful spies of popular fiction and movies, who stole secret documents from drunken diplomats and officers after champagne suppers or cajoled their lovers into revealing state secrets."

168

Marguerite Harrison in the mid-1920s

Whether she utilized them or not, Marguerite was endowed with the attributes of a femme fatale, according to others who viewed her in later knowledge of her double role as spy and journalist. A British journalist, S. K. Ratcliffe, writing a review of her autobiography published years later, sharply etched her in her Berlin days.

"For the astonishing role she played . . . during the first wild stage soon after the war, Marguerite Harrison possessed all the qualifications, as her journalist colleagues and enemies were alike ready to admit. She was brilliantly attractive in appearance, and assured in manner; she had a steely intelligence, and she was everywhere at home. Language had few difficulties for her. In public speech she was swift and pointed . . . Hers has been an amazing career."

Marguerite worked under the constant strain of possible discovery. Although her cover as a journalist appeared to be successful, she could never be certain. If exposed she could be repudiated by her own government, she knew, and at the very least viewed as an unwelcome illegal by the Germans, perhaps worse. She certainly was aware of the all-too-recent wartime treatment of spies, even women. Edith Louisa Cavell, the British nurse who aided the escape of Allied soldiers out of Belgium, had been shot by the Germans in October 1915. Gertrud Margarete Zelle, the infamous

Mata Hari, had been executed by a French firing squad at Vin-
cennes only two years later, in October 1917, although she was in
reality a dance-hall girl whose spying was probably a myth.

Ironically it was a journalist colleague, a Mrs. Stan Harding, a
British newspaperwoman, lately arrived in Berlin, who suspected
Marguerite's cover. Finding her a congenial companion, Marguerite invited her to share her hotel room. But Mrs. Harding pieced
together scraps of a written report Marguerite hastily threw into a
wastebasket and surmised the information was of an intelligence
character. The Britisher boldly proposed that they work together,
Marguerite paying her for her information. Concealing her astonishment and perturbation, Marguerite calmly answered that she
would consult her superior.

Marguerite was advised to accept the offer, and thereafter she
acknowledged Mrs. Harding's contributions to her reports — an
involvement later to destroy the friendship and to grow into an
international fracas.

Signing of the Versailles peace treaty in June 1919 ended Marguerite's intelligence work in Berlin, and she departed appalled at
the severity of the peace terms. Her intelligence reports had pre-
dicted that heavy reprisals by the Allies would drive the Germans
to the Soviets or into a reactionary camp. She foresaw trends that
would provoke World War II years later, including the rising anti-
Semitic sentiments that foreshadowed the future Nazi movement.

Her departure from Europe, on a transport loaded with army
officers and war workers exuberant with the promise of peace,
evoked dismay among intelligence officers in several American em-
bassies in Europe. Correspondence in her MID file reflects the
respect she had gained. Only three months after she had arrived in
Berlin, in March 1919, General Headquarters of the American
Expeditionary Forces was expressing admiration for her reports:
Mrs. Harrison "has proved to be a most valuable agent. Her reports are full of information derived by conversation with officials
of the German government," one comment stated. The consensus
was that she was too good to lose. The American military attaché
in The Hague was particularly vehement in urging that she be
returned to Europe, not sent to Mexico as had evidently been
considered.

But Marguerite was already back in Baltimore, working at the *Baltimore Sun* and trying to drop back into the local scene. She quickly realized that Baltimore had become too parochial for her international appetite. This time Russia and its Bolshevik experiment of transforming the formerly imperialist society aroused her curiosity. At the time, the West knew almost nothing about what had gone on inside Russia after the Communist revolution had cut if off from the outside world. How could she enter Russia, still in the throes of change and hostile to all capitalistic outsiders?

Without a word to friends, she quietly sought an audience with her former MID employer, General Marlborough Churchill. She proposed to operate similarly in Russia as she had in Germany, supplying information of a nonmilitary nature under the cover of a journalistic assignment. Despite the peace, such reportage was still useful, and General Churchill welcomed her back into the fold. He cautioned that she "might be exposed to considerable risks and many hardships," she said.

These seem hardly adequate words of warning to one then bound for Russia as a secret agent. The country was still rocked by violence, terror, and executions. Her acceptance of such an assignment seems as improbable as her being hired by the MID to undertake it. She had never been to Russia and did not speak the language. She carried no visa and would have to enter clandestinely by whatever route she could devise.

She sailed for England early in November 1919. Her assignment: to enter Russia, sum up conditions in Moscow and other key cities, and return in a few months "with firsthand information that might help our government determine its attitude toward the new regime." It was straightforward political reporting.

Carrying credentials from the *Sun* and assignments from the *New York Evening Post,* she would be given assignments as a temporary Moscow correspondent by the London bureau of the Associated Press. In Baltimore only her editor at the *Sun* and Dr. Ames knew her true purpose. Before leaving, she paid off her husband's debt with a legacy bequeathed by her father.

Her son Tommy was with her to be placed in school in Lausanne, Switzerland. On shipboard, Marguerite found herself the object of warm attention by a Russian gentleman who said he lived in Lausanne. She withdrew, suspicious of his motives. After his mother had left him at the school, Tommy also repulsed overtures of friendship from the man. In view of later events, Marguerite would always speculate on the role of this figure.

When she bade Tommy good-by, she promised to see him again at Easter time when they would return home together. She did not dream it would be nearly two years before she would be reunited with her son.

The Polish frontier was reputed to provide the easiest approach for an undercover entrance into Russia. Russia and Poland were still at war and contraband traffic moved across the no man's land between with some regularity. Marguerite therefore directed her steps to Warsaw. But orders awaiting her in Warsaw advised a delay because of civil disorders in Russia. During the six-week holding period, she busily collected political information for the American military attaché there and also supplied information to Poles associated with this office, a breach later held against her by the Soviets.

At a Red Cross dance, she was introduced to a Captain Merian C. Cooper, a former *New York Times* reporter. Short, muscular, aggressive, he came from Jacksonville, Florida. He was wearing a Polish aviator's uniform as a member of the Kosciusko Squadron, a group of American flyers aiding the Poles against the Russians. During the war he had been with the Lafayette Escadrille in France, shot down over German lines, made a prisoner, and released after the armistice. He and Marguerite shared a few dances and some small talk, and the next day he returned to his squadron. Neither then imagined how and under what varied circumstances their lives would become intertwined.

With hostilities still active, Marguerite decided a solo dash across the Polish-Russian frontier would be extremely risky, especially since two languages would be involved. A companion-interpreter was essential. She found a Russian Jew named Dr. Anna Karlin who was trying to return to Russia after living in the United States. Fat, dumpy, red-faced, she proved trustworthy and staunch. Marguerite promised to assist her through the Polish lines in return for her assistance once they were in Russia.

On a raw winter morning in January 1920, the two women

slipped out of Warsaw without good-bys. Only the American minister to Poland, Hugh Gibson, and the American military attaché to Warsaw had been alerted to the fact and time of their departure.

Minsk, in the quiet Beresina sector on the frontier, would be the crossing point. In Polish hands at the time, it lay four hundred miles southwest of Moscow. But frequent skirmishes, even in the winter, made crossing dangerous at any point of the front. The commanding general in Minsk adamantly refused a safe-conduct pass through Polish lines. They would be shot down by Red patrols, he said, or, once in Russian territory, as Polish spies. Marguerite gave up trying to persuade him and, leaving Dr. Karlin in the war-blighted city, took a train to Vilna to confer with the Polish commander of all forces on the Polish front. He granted the permits along with grave warnings about the terrible risks she would run. Heedless of the warnings, she headed victoriously back to Minsk.

Railway strikes and sabotage protracted her short trip over several days, but the delay gave Dr. Karlin time to arrange for a sleigh with the help of Jewish contrabanders who were running goods illegally across the border.

The little party crept out of Minsk in the predawn chill of midwinter, keeping watch lest they be intercepted by the Beresina troops. By nightfall they had reached a Jewish home on the outskirts of Berysov, about eighty miles from Minsk, having outfoxed the Minsk commander.

A plunge through the Polish front lines was their next hurdle. Marguerite's safe-conduct pass netted them a Polish soldier as a driver and they started on the morning of February 8, 1920, across a ravaged countryside. Roads were rutted by the passage of heavy guns, forests were slashed by abandoned trenches that had to be bridged with spruce boughs. At the last outpost an officer awaiting them in a camouflaged dugout, alerted to their arrival, was ready with a barrage of Bolshevik atrocity stories to discourage further travel. He little relished his order to conduct them to no man's land, assuring Marguerite she would be shot within twenty-four hours, and doubtless fearing for his own safety.

With Red army detachments stationed close by, the two women and their guide set out on foot, picking their way through barbed wire entanglements lacing the dense forest, the Polish officer in the lead lugging Marguerite's sleeping bag. In her heavy fur-lined coat, she stumbled behind him through the snow, carrying her suitcase, musette bag, and typewriter. Dr. Karlin, with little more than what she wore, puffed along in the rear.

At the edge of the woods, no man's land stretched before them, wide snowy fields with a peasant village lying peacefully in the distance. Not a Red soldier in sight. It was shockingly tranquil. They crossed the exposed fields swiftly. At a house in the village, a peasant, obeying the officer's order, reluctantly brought out his horse and rig. The outfit was so dilapidated the women piled in only their luggage and themselves walked the half-hour distance to the next stop, a schoolhouse where the Polish officer left them to their fate in the hands of the resident teacher.

Marguerite wrote later that she was "almost speechless with astonishment." She had expected an armed frontier, desolation, possibly immediate arrest. But here they were in an outpost of the Russian front, on soil under Russian command, invited out of the subzero cold to hot tea from a steaming samovar. Muslin curtains, potted geraniums, a peaceful landscape; they sat waiting for the appearance of the Red patrol. It had been their luck, they learned, to strike a moment of tacit armistice because of the bitter weather. The front was in a period of suspenseful waiting. So far so good. But they still had to face the Red patrol when he arrived. They could yet be court-martialed in the village and shot as Polish spies.

The Red patrol was a young peasant who could not read the strange passports handed him and after some indecision sent the two women in a sleigh to the command post some miles away. Buffeted by a heavy storm, they did not arrive until after dark, chilled and uncertain of their reception. They were now well inside Russia.

But they were actually welcomed in the remote, lonely post as fresh faces who broke the monotony. Well billeted, well fed, they were invited to inspect the local schools the next morning. As before, no one knew quite what to do with the strange birds who had alighted so unexpectedly, so they were sent on to a regimental headquarters sixteen miles farther.

They were now traveling in two sleighs with two drivers, one for themselves, another for their luggage. The storm howled unabated, but they had begun actually to enjoy the trip and the irony of the situation.

The bored officers staffing the regimental headquarters were so delighted at the arrival of interesting guests they turned the evening into a festive party, with Russian folk songs and dancing until five o'clock the next morning. One cannot help but wonder what would have happened if these had been two men making the same audacious break. Marguerite's good looks and lively personality must surely have worked some of the magic.

The next day the two women were again considered too "hot" or mysterious or baffling to handle, so they were dispatched from the regimental headquarters to brigade headquarters in Krupki. This was a railhead where they could catch a train for Moscow if permitted. But in Krupki they were at last up against a different breed of brass. Tough, upper-echelon officers listened suspiciously to Marguerite's tale that she was an American journalist sent to tell the Russian proletarian story to the outside world. They decided to hold her and Dr. Karlin a week for observation.

The women were questioned, but again their presence in Russia seemed so puzzling the authorities were confounded. The buck was passed once more. They were sent along to a yet higher command, the divisional headquarters in Vitebsk. For this trip they were deposited in a boxcar with eight other passengers. They slept on hay-covered shelves and cooked on a wood-burning stove, the only heat. During long frequent stops, the passengers got off and walked to stretch their legs. It took three days and two nights to cover the two hundred miles to Vitebsk.

In Vitebsk their luck still held. The commissar's wife was longing to go to Moscow. The visitors provided the commissar an excuse to assign her as an escort. They departed Vitebsk that very evening, again in a boxcar. The train was jammed to overflowing, but Marguerite as usual made light of the discomforts.

They arrived in Moscow, the Bolshevik stronghold, on the morning of the second day. Dr. Karlin telephoned the Soviet Foreign Office from the railway station and announced the arrival of an American foreign correspondent who awaited instructions on how to proceed. The women were instructed to wait. One can imagine the astonishment and consternation in the Foreign Office.

A representative of the Western Section of the Commissariat of Foreign Affairs arrived at the station within minutes. Marguerite said he was extremely annoyed. How had an American newspaperwoman gotten to Moscow without the authorities' knowledge? he demanded. His annoyance increased as Marguerite described how they had been admitted through the lines of the Russo-Polish front and passed along to the capital. "Do you know that you have done a dangerous and absolutely illegal thing in coming to Moscow without permission?" he stormed. "You have rendered yourself liable to immediate deportation — if not something worse." He took all their papers from them.

But they were conducted to an official guesthouse, a splendid home, formerly owned by some person of wealth, that had been preempted by the government, and luxuriously ensconced for the night after a courteous search of their luggage. They dined with other official guests in an oak-paneled dining room, and Marguerite sank into a comfortable bed that night in high spirits.

"I had penetrated the wall of bayonets that had shut the Soviet republic off from the rest of the world," she exulted. The thrill of seeing the Kremlin walls for the first time the next day dominated her thoughts. If there was any quiver of trepidation, she doesn't mention it in her memoirs.

Despite her illegal entrance and despite the Soviet government's refusals to let other bourgeois news correspondents into Russia, the commissar of foreign affairs decided she might remain in Moscow for two weeks. Marguerite rushed to radio home a message that she had arrived and immediately began arranging interviews. She also began the same wide-ranging opinion gathering she had conducted in Berlin, attending all kinds of meetings, talking with many types of individuals. Her Russian improved steadily. This was fortunate, for Dr. Karlin meanwhile had arranged to remain in Russia and had gone her own way.

Marguerite was instantly taken with the Russian people — all Russians, "Communists and reactionaries, alike," she declared. Russia became the first of her passionate attachments to the East.

She was elated therefore when she was informed rather casually that she might remain an additional month in Moscow. It was, she felt, typical Russian kindness.

She redoubled her attempt to absorb as much as she could of Russian artistic and intellectual life. She attended a speech by Lenin, interviewed Trotsky briefly, saw Koussevitzky conduct, heard the superb Chaliapin sing, and met Alexandra Kolontai, later Soviet ambassador to Mexico. Every conversation confirmed her conviction that the Bolsheviks were firmly in the saddle and would only be strengthened by foreign intervention.

Most nights, Marguerite could be found at the Foreign Office, usually until quite late. She would wait for the nightly midnight bulletin and incorporate it into articles she wrote on the spot. These had to be approved by the Foreign Office, and the only international telegraph service in Moscow was there. Sometimes she didn't finish until two or three o'clock in the morning. The streets were safe for a woman at any hour, so she made the half-hour walk back to her quarters alone.

One evening as she was walking home, a Russian soldier stopped her and asked for her name. "'Margherita Bernardovna Garrison,'" she responded, giving the Russian version, as she later recorded this episode. "'You are under arrest,'" he answered, handing her confirming papers.

Marguerite apparently was taken completely by surprise. She had sent no intelligence reports, having committed to memory any data she would carry home. She thought her cover was intact.

She protested vigorously but was nonetheless firmly escorted to the feared prison for political and espionage prisoners, the Lubianka No. 2. Once headquarters for the Russian Life Insurance Company, its doorway bore the cryptic advice, "It is prudent to insure your life."

Although shocked, Marguerite felt certain that the situation would be straightened out and all would end well. It therefore did not bother her greatly that she was searched, photographed, and finger printed, all politely, and that standard arrest procedures followed. She was then taken to a small bare room, where she threw herself down on the naked boards of her plank bed, covered herself with her heavy coat, and promptly fell into a sound sleep.

There's Always Tomorrow, the title of Marguerite's autobiography, aptly sums up her optimistic attitude toward life.

Several ranking members of the Soviet secret police, the Cheka, awaited her in a large well-furnished office warmed by a glowing fire to which she was ushered the next day. Formal greetings were exchanged. And then, to Marguerite's amazement, a dark, slender "black puma" of a man, whose name was Moghilievsky, declared, "'We know perfectly well that you are here as a representative of the American Secret Service. You acted in a similar capacity in Germany last year. We have reports from both America and Germany to prove this.'" The Cheka had been watching her for some time, he said.

Moghilievsky was a member of the presidium of the Cheka who handled espionage and counterrevolution. He first cited a long and accurate list of her activities. Then he delivered the crowning evidence by handing her a copy of one of her confidential messages from Germany to the MID, clear indication of the existence of a MID leak she had not suspected. (At this point, she says, she was also ignorant of another betrayal that had occurred just before her departure from the United States. A treacherous article had been published in *The Army & Navy Journal* referring to undercover work performed in Berlin immediately after the armistice by "an American woman agent." The Russians had somehow learned she had been a secret agent in Germany and, she later realized, thus had put two and two together and had been watching her movements in Russia. The mysterious stranger on shipboard could have been an agent of the Cheka.) Too late, she saw that the Cheka's "underground army of spies and informers" had been gradually "collecting bits of damning evidence . . . playing with me like a cat with a mouse," and she had been "blissfully unconscious of the fact."

No choice was left now as she stood before Moghilievsky but to admit she was an agent for the United States government. But she insisted she had acted merely as an observer, had stolen no information, and had transmitted nothing.

No matter, she was harshly told. She was a spy. She could even be shot as a Polish spy, Moghilievsky said, referring to her activities in Warsaw. (So they had probably watched her there as well!)

178

Then Moghilievsky's manner became flattering. Such an "exceedingly intelligent woman" was too useful for such drastic action, he said. He had a proposition for her to consider. "'We are prepared to give you your liberty, Citizeness Garrison, but under certain conditions.'" These were that she become a counterspy, providing information about the foreign visitors who would be staying in the official guesthouse with her.

Marguerite faced an excruciating decision. She had to choose between immediate imprisonment and a play for time. With time, she might get a message through to General Churchill by underground means. Meanwhile, for as long as possible, she could try to delude the Cheka with harmless reports, knowing, of course, they inevitably would discover her double-cross. She chose the role of counterspy.

"In that moment, I renounced everything that hitherto made up my existence," she later wrote. "It was finished — and I felt as if I had already died and been born into a new nightmare world. I looked Moghilievsky full in the eyes. 'I accept your proposition,' I answered calmly — so calmly that I wondered at myself."

Although outwardly unchanged, her days were now filled with anxious covert activity. She smuggled information to U.S. military attachés in several European capitals, including messages to relatives that she had been "caught like a rat in a trap." She warned friends in Moscow to stay clear of her, struggled through draining sessions with Moghilievsky, ducked men who tailed her, fought a sense of isolation, depression, and a morbid feeling of unreality. It was only a matter of time until the Cheka detected her trickery. Ultimate arrest was certain; she felt with resignation that every day free was borrowed time.

To add to her problems, Mrs. Harding, the British journalist, appeared on the scene as a correspondent for the *New York World*. Through extremely complex machinations, Moghilievsky maneuvered to make it appear that Mrs. Harding's prompt arrest was due to Marguerite's denouncement of her as a spy. No attempt at explanation or reconciliation ever assuaged Mrs. Harding's anger or obsessive belief that Marguerite had betrayed her. Marguerite's MID file even contains a letter from the Intelligence Division to her faithful stepfather-in-law, Dr. Ames, assuring him that no evidence existed to connect Marguerite with Mrs. Harding's arrest. Nevertheless, after her release from the Soviet prison, Mrs. Harding carried the matter to the British Parliament and even demanded redress from the United States government. She also attempted to interfere with distribution of Marguerite's autobiography in England when it was published there in 1936 under the title *Born for Trouble: The Story of a Chequered Life.* In it Marguerite had related her own side of the episode.

Initially, MID officials were optimistic about Marguerite's situation. She had cleverly managed to send coded messages through Estonia on Danish and German bank notes, as well as through trusted travelers, warning that she had been compelled to save herself by counterespionage and alerting them to the leak that led to her arrest.

"I think we can rely on her cleverness to deceive the Bolsheviks," Colonel A. B. Coxe, acting director of military intelligence, cheerfully wrote to a colleague. To Dr. Ames he wrote that the MID was "bringing pressure" on the Soviet economic representative in London to get Mrs. Harrison out, although they had "the greatest confidence" in her ability "to extricate herself," despite the fact that "she is practically held a prisoner."

H. N. Brailsford, an English journalist who had seen Marguerite in Moscow during this period, wrote Dr. Ames from London that she was not uncomfortable. "Nonetheless she is free only in the sense that within Moscow she can go about as she chooses. She is, formally or informally, kept as a hostage under surveillance. She is most anxious to return home, but has been refused permission repeatedly, finally told only in exchange for someone of real importance; e.g. in return for the release of Eugene V. Debs. She is physically well but painfully anxious and unhappy."

As the summer dragged on, Marguerite's one comfort was in helping British and American prisoners. Through Red Cross funds or her own remaining money, cached in her money belt, she bought food on the black market and delivered packages to them. One of the prisoners she managed to help was her friend from Warsaw, Colonel Merian C. Cooper, whose plane had been brought down near Kiev and captured by the Bolsheviks. She was able to communicate to his parents that he was still alive.

Moghilievsky, tiring of her bland reports, began threatening arrest, but Marguerite listened apathetically. "It was only a question of time anyway," she said. And one night when a knock came at her door she was so certain of its meaning she merely called "come in" without even rising. Two men and a woman from the Cheka searched her room, allowed her to pack a few things, and then conducted her in a car through the chilly autumn streets to the Lubianka prison. It was October 24, 1920.

She now entered that vast Soviet penal system that would be so vividly described decades later by the Russian writer Aleksandr I. Solzhenitsyn as the "Gulag Archipelago." Solzhenitsyn graphically likened the abominable conditions to a murderous sewage disposal system indiscriminately swallowing "enemies of the revolution" by the hundreds of thousands.

Marguerite spent ten nightmarish months in Lubianka, the first American woman ever to be held in a Bolshevik prison, and in these early days when conditions must have been at their worst. Afterward she wrote an account of her life as prisoner 2961. Her engrossing book, *Marooned in Moscow,* is one of the earliest memoirs in the literature of Soviet prison experience.

Marguerite accepted her imprisonment without bitterness as being a reasonable result of having transgressed Soviet law. During an initial period of solitary confinement in a dark, tiny cell, she began practicing a sort of self-hypnosis. "I began to work out a certain philosophy that sustained me through the many weary months to come and gradually made prison not only bearable but almost enjoyable," she wrote. "Little by little I learned to detach myself utterly from the world which seemed irretrievably lost and to find a new world of my own, bounded physically by four walls, but spiritually limitless. Under such conditions a person either goes under or lives for things of the mind and spirit. There is no middle course."

For six months she was held in a small room variously occupied by from seven to fourteen women, some sleeping on the floor when most crowded. They shared the common chore of cleaning the filthy toilet serving 125 persons, hunted daily for vermin, and created entertainment to stave off madness. Many succumbed and were carried away raving; three cases of typhus and several virulent syphilis cases had to be removed.

As the months passed, her own health began to fail, and the

onset of tuberculosis was evidenced. Her repeated petitions for a transfer to a prison where she could get fresh air and sunshine were at last heeded and she was told to pack her things for a move. With her luggage, she "half walked, half fell" down four flights of stairs, trembling from weakness. Then she was standing half-blinded by the sunshine on a street in front of the prison.

The teenage boy who guarded her had no conveyance, no funds, and did not even know where the Novinsky prison, her new destination, was located. Marguerite had to take charge. (Solzhenitsyn likewise describes having to direct ignorant guards to the prison when he was arrested.) Hailing cabs, Marguerite offered personal belongings in lieu of money, of which she had none, and at last found a driver who would deliver her at her own expense to her new penal address. She said she was "almost in despair of ever being able to get locked up again."

Novinsky was a "terrestrial paradise," Marguerite found, compared with Lubianka; it had a cheerful hospital, real beds, and flowers in the yard. She composed herself to accept Novinsky as her probable home until death.

But back in the United States, her name was very much in the news. Soviet imprisonment of a socially prominent Baltimore woman was a major international incident, exacerbating the U.S.-Soviet breach. The State Department professed itself helpless in the absence of diplomatic relations, however. Marguerite's personal friends, the *Baltimore Sun,* and the MID were thus left to spearhead efforts to save her. The *Sun* sent food, clothing, and money; none of it ever reached her. Cables were dispatched to ambassadors in several countries, to the League of Nations, and to various congressmen, appealing for aid. Maryland's Governor Ritchie, Dr. Ames, and a *Sun* spokesman conferred in New York with Ludwig C. V. Martens, head of the Soviet trade bureau, a quasi-ambassador for the Communist government.

Newspapers kept alive the suspenseful tale that the daughter of B. N. Baker of the U.S. Shipping Board was "in dire straits in a Moscow cell," was "in danger of execution," or was being held "to compel U.S. recognition." Speculation and exaggeration, in the absence of awareness of her double role as an American secret agent, built an aura of intrigue and high danger. One rumor had it that she was not in prison at all but living as the mistress of Trotsky.

Marguerite knew nothing of all this. She had received no letters from home even before her imprisonment, there being no postal communication between the United States and Russia. She was relieved, however, to get verbal assurance that Tommy had been returned to his grandmother in Baltimore.

She was therefore dumbfounded when she found the U.S. senator from Maryland, Joseph I. France, waiting in the prison superintendent's office one day in July. She was being released through the intervention of the American Relief Administration, whose offer of food to famine-starved Russia stipulated the release of all American prisoners. Senator France would take her home.

A battery of reporters and government officials met her in Riga, Latvia. A "pale and thin" figure wearing the old suit she had been arrested in and men's shoes many sizes too big, she was a "sorry sight" when she stepped from the train.

Merian Cooper met her train in Berlin. He had escaped the Soviet prison while working with a railway prison gang, slipped into Latvia disguised as a peasant, and returned to Warsaw to rejoin the Polish air force. He had been plotting to rescue Marguerite from Novinsky, he said. At the moment of her release, he was on the verge of landing a Polish army plane in a meadow near the prison to pick her up and fly her to Warsaw. He had arranged to bribe a prison guard to smuggle her out. Such was Cooper's gratitude for Marguerite's kindness while he was himself a prisoner.

Van-Lear Black, owner of the *Baltimore Sun,* was waiting for her in New York with his yacht loaded with friends, and she sailed to Baltimore in triumph. No reunion was more joyous than with her son. The Children's Hospital School of Baltimore, which Marguerite had been active in founding in 1905 on family property donated by her father, had erected a handsome plaque in her memory, never expecting her to return. It was now hastily removed. (It was reinstalled years later, after her death.) Frank Kent, managing editor of the *Sun,* offered her her old job.

Reporting to General Churchill in Washington, Marguerite learned that the leak in the MID that had led to her arrest had been spotted and excised. But the treacherous article published in *The*

Army & Navy Journal just as she departed from the United States, which had helped to betray her cover, was never explained. Despite her ten long months of suffering in prison, she terminated her connection with the MID feeling adequately rewarded by General Churchill's congratulations on the high caliber of her work.

She now devoted herself to writing *Marooned in Moscow* and magazine articles and to lecturing. She was forced to rely completely on memory since her notes had been confiscated when she was imprisoned, and paper and pencils had been forbidden. She used every opportunity to put forth her conviction that United States recognition of the Communist government was essential for the country's own economic and trade advantage. As was so often the case, she was years ahead of her time.

By the spring of 1922, the urban luxuries she had dreamed of in prison had become tedious to her, and she was anxious once more to investigate foreign cultures. The Far East now seized her imagination. Japanese and Chinese nationalism were on the rise, and she was eager to "probe the meaning of the new movements stirring among the yellow races."

In June 1922, only ten months after her release from prison, she set forth for Japan with a magazine assignment to write a series of articles about conditions in the Far East. Her route appears to have been only roughly thought out, but would cut across some of the most primitive regions of eastern Asia. Quite unexpectedly, her voyage took her around the world, though she could hardly have imagined such a thing as she steamed from Vancouver for Yokohama. On shipboard she completed her second book in ten months, first published as a series of vignettes in *Cosmopolitan* and later as *Unfinished Tales from a Russian Prison*.

National boundaries have altered in the years since her voyage and place names have changed, so it is not always easy to trace each step today on newer maps. But only by following her general path on a map of eastern Asia can one appreciate the immense swing of her travels. Her status and credentials as a journalist opened doors to the highest officials and finest homes in urban centers. In Tokyo, Peking, and larger cities, she was swept into the social whirl of the foreign community, interviewed the interesting political and military figures, and met the foremost personalities of the place. But in the remote villages and rural countryside, she was simply an American woman traveling on her own, wholly dependent upon her own resources. In the early 1920s, anything off the beaten track was likely to present conditions redolent of the Middle Ages.

She spent two months in Tokyo, taking only a short trip down to Kyoto, the old capital of Japan. Then she left for the northernmost point of the Japanese archipelago, the strategic outpost island of Sakhalin. Possession of the northern half of the island was then in dispute between the Japanese, who were occupying the area, and the Soviet government, which claimed it as part of Siberia. Only one American journalist had been there since its occupation and no other foreigners had been allowed in for over two years. The Japanese granted Marguerite a permit only on condition that she be accompanied by an official government guide, a Dr. Honda, who might have been a spy observing her, for all she knew. But he was so urbane and witty she found him a delightful companion.

She and Dr. Honda departed Tokyo late in July 1922 bound for the port of Otaru, from which they sailed on up through the sea of Japan to Alexandrovsk, the only large town in northern Sakhalin. They paused two days at Hakodate and were guests in a real Japanese hotel, where Marguerite slept on the floor on a quilt with a wooden head rest and had eel omelette, bean curd soup, and pickled plums for breakfast. The coastal steamer from Otaru to Alexandrovsk was infested with roaches which "swarmed over me by the thousands in my bunk at night," Marguerite remarked. But the food was excellent, she added, evidently not speculating upon the state of the kitchen.

She was billeted by the Japanese army in Sakhalin, and by good fortune in Alexandrovsk she became the only woman guest at an extremely elegant dinner with fifteen or twenty Japanese officers, all in full-dress uniform. She was the first woman guest the Japanese General Staff had ever entertained, she was told. She and Dr. Honda were driven to some of the few scattered interior villages along the lumber trails. The region was a primitive wilderness rich in resources, a "treasure house of coal, oil, and timber." The villages were populated by Russian criminals or descendents of criminals, for Sakhalin had been a Russian penal colony before the

Marguerite in 1922 at Nikolayevsk, with the officers of the Japanese General Staff, a U.S. military attaché next to her, and Dr. Matsujiro Honda, her Japanese guide, holding an umbrella

Soviet revolution. Sakhalin was Marguerite's last stop in Japan, and she left convinced that Japan was fired with the ambition of dominating the "yellow races" in the Far East.

From the port of Alexandrovsk, she and Dr. Honda crossed the Sea of Okhotsk, icebound for most of the year, to Nikolayevsk, on the Siberian mainland. As Marguerite's steamer approached Nikolayevsk, at the mouth of the golden, silt-heavy Amur River, her excitement mounted. Once again she would feel Russian soil beneath her feet, the Russia she loved despite her months of suffering there. "Ever since leaving Russia I had been homesick for the sound of Russian voices, for the broad sweep of the Russian wheat fields, for the homely little villages with their wooden *izbas,* for the childlike, lovable people with whom I had lived through so much," she wrote.

Her memoirs acknowledge the contradictory forces that pulled her back to Russia. She told herself, she said, that she was in Siberia to determine if the Japanese were carrying out their pledge

186

to evacuate the portion of the Siberian mainland they had occupied along with northern Sakhalin. But "deep down in my heart I knew that this was not the real reason I had wanted to go to Siberia," she admitted. Russia was her lodestar, her deeply loved land, and it still drew her irresistibly. Now this immense eastern portion of Russia beckoned "with its mystery and its illimitable spaces." While her imprisonment by the Communists precluded her return to Soviet Russia, she felt she could move with impunity in the area of Siberia not under Soviet domination.

She therefore undertook the picturesque but very rugged trip to Vladivostok overland, disdaining the easier seaborne route. Bidding farewell to Dr. Honda, who returned to Japan, she boarded an antiquated paddle-wheel riverboat — "a ramshackle old tub" — for the six-hundred-mile trip up the Amur River to Khabarovsk, where she would catch a train to Vladivostok. The river scene was as colorful as the second-class passengers with whom she chose to fraternize (the first-class crowd struck her as dull). She toured the villages at the many stops. Chinese, Russian, and Korean prospectors at every landing were selling sacks of gold dust to Chinese contrabanders, armed desperadoes who bootlegged the loot across the Manchurian border. She was told that that part of Siberia was "seamed with gold." The aboriginal inhabitants of the Amur region, a tribe of Mongol origin known as the Giliaks, were strikingly like American Indians of the Northwest: they lived in lodges, had totem poles, wrapped their babies like papooses, and grew and smoked tobacco.

In Khabarovsk Marguerite had to fight her way onto a train made up of boxcars and fourth-class Russian sleepers jammed with a hoard of marvelously costumed ethnic people from all over the region. The train was so crowded the only space remaining for her was a top tier of bunks in the car that carried the train crew and guards. Perched on high, she was watching the mass of Oriental faces below when she realized her typewriter had been stolen. The train commander was ready to order the entire train emptied and a wholesale search instituted, but she knew this would incur enmity. She refused the offer and shrugged off the loss as a welcome lightening of her luggage.

At Ussuri passengers transferred to open flatcars that were

pushed from behind by two men. Some cars were drawn by a horse, which had to be unhitched on downhill grades, then recoupled at the bottom. Where bridges had been blown up by the Japanese, passengers walked around the trestles, leaving the cars to thread their way precariously across makeshift repairs. Between a constant watch for bandits and the alert for missing bridges, the trip offered new excitements every minute. Oblivious to clouds of mosquitoes, flies, and gnats, to danger and discomfort, Marguerite's romantic spirit soared. "I could have gone on indefinitely thus," she exclaimed.

In Vladivostok the American consul gave her a secondhand typewriter and she boarded a coastal steamer for Korea. Her aims in her quick dash across Korea, Manchuria, and China were largely journalistic. She interviewed leaders and tasted the social life of the cities, particularly in Peking (Beijing, today). Her goals were more personal in the next and most exotic phase of her journey: a trip to Chita, the capital of a vast area in southeastern Siberia that had set up a Social Democratic republic known as the Far Eastern Republic, independent of the Soviet government in Moscow. After the Bolshevik revolution, the Far Eastern Republic had laid claim to a huge region embracing eastern Siberia westward to Lake Baykal.

Chita had been Marguerite's ultimate goal when she left New York, after which she planned to return home. In Peking, however, it occurred to her that she might be able to return by way of Russia itself. Amnesty might be granted her to allow such a journey. She applied at the Soviet mission in Peking for a visa to enter Russia, arranging for the notification to be delivered to her in Chita. She already held a visa to enter the Far Eastern Republic.

Chita could be reached from Peking by rail, but Marguerite chose the hazardous trip across the Mongolian plateau that would take her to the little-known city of Urga (today Ulan Bator), the capital of Outer Mongolia. The trip had to be made by automobile, an audacious trek as it was already nearly October and early winter snow and ice might sweep across the great barren stretches of the plateau. Due back in New York to start her lecture tour in November, Marguerite had only the thinnest margin for delay. "A foolhardy and senseless undertaking from many points of view," she acknowledged.

*During a trip across the steppes of Inner Mongolia in 1922,
in a battered, overloaded Ford, a team of bullocks hauls the party
out of a marshy ditch.*

But the "lure of Mongolia was irresistible," so she left Peking despite the efforts of friends to dissuade her. Kalgan (later changed to Changkiakow), located about one hundred twenty-five miles from Peking, was the last "civilized" outpost, and the jumping off place for Urga. Marguerite expected to travel in one of the Chinese commercial hacks that ran regularly from Kalgan to Urga, but officials at the American consulate in Peking said this would be madness. Reckless drivers and overcrowded jitneys would make the four- or five-day trip a horror. They put her in touch with an English fur trader who invited her to ride in his private car.

The host, the driver, Marguerite, and one other passenger were jammed into the five-passenger car with bales of goods to be traded for furs in Urga. They struck out along the old caravan route that had once carried tea, silks, and other treasures of the Orient to Moscow. Walled Chinese farmhouses dotted the landscape. Farther on, only herds of ponies and cattle with nomad herders could be seen. The car wheels sank in sand and gravel. Four bullocks hauled them up three thousand feet in the Hanibar Pass through the Great Khingan Mountains. Sharp narrow curves on the mountains often left the car hanging perilously over the edge. At the summit of the Khingans separating China from Mongolia, the steppes of Inner Mongolia stretched thrillingly ahead.

At every stop through the Gobi Desert, Marguerite picked up the wind-polished pebbles of lovely colors that covered the steplike plateaus. Hundreds of caravans passed, the camel bells and creaking wooden wheels of bullock carts the only interruption in the boundless silence.

Urga, cut off from the world by the immense Gobi Desert, was a bizarre, self-contained universe, half-Russian, half-Chinese, and semibarbaric. Towering above Urga's simple native houses were the gold-roofed temples of the Lama City, the sacred home of the priests. Seat of the Living Buddha, second in prestige only to the Dalai Lama of Lhasa, the Lama City housed in its narrow streets twenty thousand lamas and numerous temples. Marguerite attended services in the central temple, the Gon Don, where a bronze Buddha sixty feet high stood among gifts from the faithful. The ritual was strangely Catholic, she observed.

The huge open-air bazaar of Urga, where goods from all over the globe were sold, was the quintessence of Oriental pageantry. Marguerite vividly described the flamboyantly displayed merchandise and flamboyantly dressed crowd: "Mongol princes, dressed in magnificent fur-trimmed robes with superbly wrought silver knives in their belts, peacock feathers floating from their hats, shopped on horseback, jostling the humbler folk, dressed in costumes all the colors of the rainbow, who swarmed about the booths bargaining and bartering with the dark-robed Chinese."

Prospects for the next leg of her journey were extremely discouraging, she soon began to discover. Few travelers since the Bolshevik revolution had made the trip from Urga to Verkhne-Udinsk in Siberia, where she would be able to take a train to Chita. She was strongly advised against undertaking the trip. "Trade with Russia was dead, political conditions uncertain and traveling not altogether safe. Besides, it was the worst possible season for such a journey," she conceded. Rivers were just beginning to freeze so would be impassable until more solid ice formed. Bandits roamed; and try as she might she could find no one in Urga willing to go with her. She despaired that she would have to go alone.

At last an old prerevolutionary stagecoach driver named Kosakov announced he was prepared to convey her in his *tarantas* and *troike,* carriage and three horses. After his reassuring picture of the rig, she was shocked at what drove up. The ancient vehicle had no springs, one horse was lame, another decrepit, and the third was an unbroken colt. But Marguerite was determined, and they set out one morning in the bitter cold, Marguerite already shivering in her fur-lined coat and felt boots.

Verkhne-Udinsk was roughly four hundred miles as the crow flies, the countryside almost barren of villages and drafty log houses the only post stops, where guests slept around a mud stove on plank beds. The first two nights Marguerite stayed at guesthouses so crowded that people had to sleep on the floor. The third she spent with a family of Russian peasants so backward the children ate the foil on the candy she offered. On the fifth day in the town of Troitsk-Kosavsk, she learned that the rivers ahead had not frozen, making them impassable. She had to mark time for a week, housed by the driver Kosakov and his wife in their minuscule log home, until the rivers could be crossed.

A young Cossack courier carrying diplomatic mail from the Russian consulate to Chita accompanied them when they left. Armed, he was able to fire at bandits and wolves lurking in the dense forest through which they had to pass during the week it took them to reach Verkhne-Udinsk.

Marguerite reveled in these vicissitudes. "I did not mind the cold or the discomforts, I was not homesick, lonely, or afraid. This vagabond life had a curious fascination for me. I did not want to go home . . . When I saw the roofs of Verkhne-Udinsk in the distance, I heaved a sigh of regret at the thought my adventures were over," she wrote.

The first night in Verkhne-Udinsk she slept in a brothel, the only available shelter. The town had now fallen into Communist hands and strangers were suspect; the young Cossack guided her to the only door that would receive her. Business went on as usual all night but Marguerite slept well. The second night, however, a raid impended, and the Cossack helped her check out barely in time to escape the police. They slept in the cold railway station waiting room on hard benches until the train arrived next morning, when Marguerite boarded for Chita.

Marguerite was startled to read in the newspaper en route to Chita that the Far Eastern Republic had been taken over by the

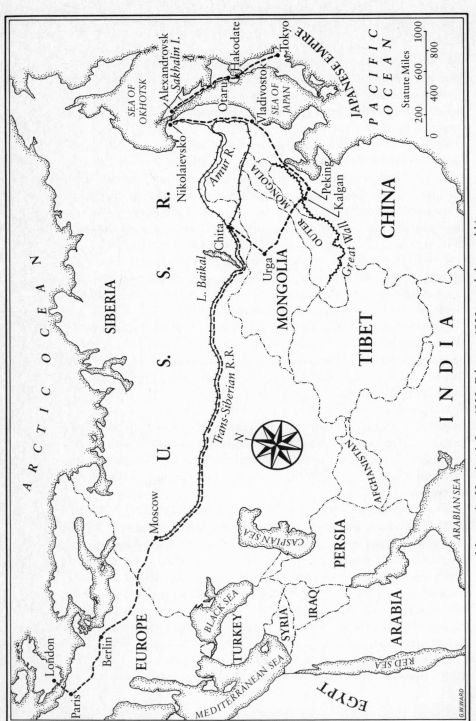

Marguerite Harrison's June 1922–February 1923 round-the-world journey

Soviets on the previous day. She had thus inadvertently been on Soviet soil for some twenty-four hours. However, she held a valid passport to the Far Eastern Republic. Although she was not particularly nervous, nevertheless, at a convenient train stop, she wired the United States' vice-consul in Chita, advising him of her arrival. He met her train on the morning of November 19.

Two days later, she was arrested while walking along a street in Chita. A Red soldier, revolver in hand, escorted her to the local version of the Cheka — by then known as the GPU (Government Political Department) — where the commandant informed her she had been arrested on orders from Moscow, charged with espionage for the United States government, and would be sent to Moscow on the next train.

Held four days in the Chita prison, she was conducted under armed guard to the railway station to commence the interminable eight-day trip on the Trans-Siberian Railway to Moscow. The U.S. vice-consul was at the station to assure her he would communicate her plight to Washington from Manchuria, where he was going immediately.

Marguerite's stamina faltered. "The iron self-control to which I had schooled myself almost gave way," she remembered later. "At the time of my former arrest, I had welcomed it as a deliverance from an intolerable strain and the inevitable consequences of my own actions. I had at least done something to deserve it. But this time I was innocent, and I could not understand why the old charges had been revived against me. I knew perfectly well that there was some motive behind it all which I could not fathom. It was baffling and disheartening."

She was even more alarmed when she was taken off the train four nights later in the middle of the night and placed in a provincial prison far from Moscow. Here, she knew, she could perish in oblivion, lost without a trace. The stench of putrid food and filthy bodies was overwhelming. "In all my experiences I had never seen anything so horrible as the small room to which I was conducted," she said; it was dark, heatless, crawling with vermin. The occupants had no pallets or covering, had had no baths. Marguerite gave her coat to a freezing woman and shared her soap.

To her relief, she was shipped on toward Moscow the next day.

193

As she had done before, she melted the hearts of the tough, unfriendly guards and soon was making coffee over her spirit lamp, sharing chocolates and cigarettes. One guard awakened in agony on the following morning with a serious illness. Marguerite helped nurse him for three days before a doctor could come aboard. The doctor diagnosed the highly contagious erysipelas. But since no authority existed to remove the patient, he remained with Marguerite and the other guard until their arrival in Moscow where he was carried from the train, raving with pain.

Marguerite was first placed in the Lubianka prison, then shifted to Boutierky, then back to Lubianka, finally being settled in a cell not far from her old quarters. Weeks passed as she waited for her cross-examination, her morale and energy declining steadily. Finally, after New Year's, she was taken to the offices of the presidium. Her old adversary, Moghilievsky, awaited her. He readily admitted he had ordered her arrest, had had his agents track her in Siberia, and had known she had applied in Peking for a visa to return to Russia.

What did he plan to do with her? she demanded. He answered flatteringly that when she had placed herself where he could retrieve her "'talents,'" the "'opportunity was too tempting'" to resist. He considered the whole affair a compliment to her abilities. He had journeyed especially from the Caucasus to make her "'a most liberal offer.'" If she accepted, she would be freed immediately.

The offer, which Marguerite later recorded, was this: "'You will remain in Russia. I shall not ask you to inform on British or Americans. Past experience has shown me that I could never depend on you to do that. Your work will be among the Russians. You speak the language almost perfectly. They will trust you as a foreigner and give you information which they would not give to any Russian. You will have a comfortable apartment, all your living expenses and a salary paid in gold, equivalent to two hundred and fifty dollars a month in American money.'" Her son would be brought to Russia at government expense to finish his education at the University of Moscow.

Marguerite declared she would rather die in prison. She would never become a defector.

In that case, she was told, she would have to stand trial for her old indictment: espionage and high treason. "'You will probably be sentenced to death,'" Moghilievsky said, "'and the best you can expect is ten years in Siberia.'

"I rose, forcing myself to look unconcerned though I was trembling in every limb," she recalled. She returned to her cell exhausted.

Thereafter she was grilled regularly. Her MID file reveals that her interrogators tried to trap her into admitting espionage work against other countries, but she made no such admissions. The Soviet officials also repeated a conversation she had held with two American army officers in Washington, D.C., on May 21, 1922, revealing further leaks in the American intelligence organization. Marguerite's son, Thomas Bullitt Harrison, declares that the ultimate hope of the Soviets was to secure her services as a Soviet spy operating in the United States. "They put tremendous pressures on Mother," he said when interviewed. "They grilled her over and over, day after day. They kept stressing, 'We've got you, nobody knows where you are,' making her feel helpless. They were ready to do anything to get her to sign up to work as a Soviet agent in the United States. But she wouldn't do it."

Nor did she reveal this in her autobiography. Her son says he does not precisely know the reason for this. But Marguerite was ever compassionate, and concealed many facets of her experiences for fear of damaging some person, institution, or cause.

Her feelings for Moghilievsky, the instigator of this stressful situation, are also puzzling. A mysterious passage in her autobiography suggests a strange tolerance for her jailer and a speculative possibility that the Soviet official might have had an eye for her that was not purely businesslike:

From the first we had been enemies — Moghilievsky had spied on me, I had double-crossed him, we had matched wits in many a verbal duel. Logically we would have hated each other and yet there had been a certain *camaraderie* between us. I had always felt an unwilling admiration for Moghilievsky — he even attracted me in a curious fashion, and during our long talks together I had seen something of the human side of his character. I sensed that I

195

had appealed to him in much the same way and I wondered as I lay staring into the darkness what was the motive that had impelled him to follow my movements after I had left Russia and to scheme and plot to get me back again to Moscow.

Marguerite had been in prison ten weeks when her trial was finally scheduled, but by then she was physically too weak to care. "I had no appetite whatever and I spent most of the time lying on my plank bed in a stupor. Once in a while the remnants of my old sense of humor came to my rescue and I smiled when I pictured my friends at home saying, 'Well! What do you think? Marguerite Harrison has got herself into prison again!' Because unless one knew the circumstances, it seemed too frightfully stupid to have walked into the trap a second time."

In this despairing state of mind and health, she was wholly unprepared for the sudden announcement that she was being discharged. Schooled to show no emotion before the Bolsheviks, she said it was now "only by a superhuman effort" that she refrained from bursting into tears. She packed tremblingly, and before she knew it she was standing in the snowy street in front of the prison, dazed at her abrupt dismissal from the dim nether world where she had languished so long. Given a week to clear out of the country, she used the days to rush about Moscow to observe the changes, crossing the frontier only fifteen minutes before her permit expired.

Coincidence alone accounted for her release. An American Relief Administration officer visiting the prison's foreign espionage section recognized her in the corridor, reported his discovery to his office, and the ARA immediately demanded her release. With American food pouring in to feed the starving population, the Bolsheviks dared not risk a furor over an American prisoner, so let her go.

Marguerite arrived home on the S.S. *President Monroe* in March 1923 with "a plea for recognition of the Soviet Government by the U.S." for our own economic and commercial advantage. Twice imprisoned by the Soviets, she nonetheless had not altered her opinions concerning practical politics. But for the remainder of her life, she was unable to remain in a room with the blinds closed.

Settled in the old Hotel Schuyler in midtown Manhattan with

Tommy, now twenty-one, she lectured on her adventures in Russia and the Far East and began a book on Russian and Japanese expansionist ambitions, which would be published in 1924 as *Red Bear or Yellow Dragon*. Her income was sufficient, life was amusing, and she had had enough excitement for most lifetimes.

But by the spring of 1925, only a few months since her release from prison, she was prey to the old wanderlust. "During the late spring nights I lay awake listening to the sirens of the ocean liners that were leaving for distant ports," she wrote in her memoirs of the magical throb of the ships at the Hudson River piers. "They were truly sirens to me, urging, enticing, irresistible. Finally, I could stand it no longer. I made up my mind that I would have to go somewhere before the summer was over."

It was in this mood that she ran into her old friend Colonel Merian C. Cooper, who credited her with saving his life with the medicines and food she smuggled to him in prison. They began to meet frequently. Cooper, now interested in filmmaking, had just returned from Abyssinia with cameraman Ernest Beaumont Schoedsack where they had filmed the pageantry of the Abyssinian court. Cooper was intrigued with the film industry, then in its infancy, and with the potentials for travel films. He found travel films of their day routinely awful, simplistic sightseeing tours of one tourist mecca or another. Marguerite agreed. "Why doesn't somebody do something different — something imaginative, something with a new attack," they asked one another.

Her lively imagination fired, Marguerite was soon agreeing with Cooper they could "do something different" themselves. They would make a new kind of travel film, one with a story that unfolded by virtue of the dynamics of a situation. They could film some ethnic group whose daily existence was in itself a drama. They decided an ideal subject would be a nomadic tribe struggling to survive in an authentic pastoral setting. These people would supply the only cast of characters, their real lives provide the storyline. No phony studio sets, no contrived Hollywood folderol! With no money, backing, or anything more than their marvelous idea and their restless spirits, Marguerite and Cooper formed an informal partnership pledged to execute this scheme.

They invited Schoedsack, the cameraman, to join them for one-third interest in the project. As footloose at the time as the other two, Schoedsack readily accepted. A breezy midwesterner from Council Bluffs, Iowa, nicknamed "Shorty" despite a six-foot-five-inch frame, Schoedsack had been a cameraman for Mack Sennett in Hollywood and filmed infantry action under heavy fire for the U.S. Army Signal Corps during the war.

Through the help of friends, Marguerite was able to assemble ten thousand dollars and thus became the financial backer as well as the first woman documentary film producer.

None of the three had any idea where to look for a suitably interesting tribe of nomads, one firmly rooted in their own traditions and unblemished by an alien civilization. Marguerite volunteered to go to Washington, D.C., to consult with a friend, Harry Dwight, who had lived in the Middle East and written short stories set in the region between the Persian Gulf and the Black Sea, where nomads abounded.

Because they were colorful and comparatively accessible, Dwight recommended the Kurds of Anatolia (Asiatic Turkey), but he said that by making a longer, more costly journey they would find far more exciting subjects among the lesser-known Bakhtiari of Persia. The Bakhtiari still followed the simple, pastoral ways of their ancestors, migrating seasonally with their flocks and possessions as in Biblical times. The tribes camped during winter months on the plains near the Persian Gulf, but with the onslaught of the hot, parching spring migrated to the higher valleys of central Persia, crossing six ranges of mountains and the flooding Karun River on the outward journey, only to repeat the hazardous trek on their return in the fall. Dwight considered the Bakhtiari an ideal example of humans adapting for survival in marginal conditions.

Back in Manhattan, Marguerite discovered that, except for Orientalists, importers of Oriental rugs, and some people who had lived in the Middle East, few individuals in this country seemed aware of the Bakhtiari. Cooper, searching for more information, turned up almost no contemporary references in the New York Public Library. The few accounts available dated from the previous century. The intrepid nineteenth-century English explorer Sir Austen Henry Layard, who excavated Nineveh and traveled extensively in the Middle East, had dwelled among the Bakhtiari between 1840 and 1842. He recorded that his experience had been one of lavish hospitality intermixed with inhuman brutality. The Bakhtiari, in his opinion, were "arrant robbers and free booters, living upon the plunder of their neighbors and of caravans, or of the pusillanimous populations of the plains, amongst which they were in the habit of carrying their forrays [*sic*] with impunity."

Shortage of cash rather than this fearsome description turned the film partners toward the Kurds, however. With their limited funds, they would have to "count every penny twice before spending it," Marguerite said. For travelers using water and land transportation in those days, the Kurds of Turkey were considerably closer to Manhattan than the Bakhtiari of Persia.

"We departed not knowing where we were going to find our great picture, but quite sure that we would find it, with nothing in the world but a camera, fifty thousand feet of precious film and our ten thousand dollars," Marguerite wrote afterward. At the pier their "ill assorted jumble of miscellaneous crates, bags, and boxes" would have struck a sharp contrast to the massive armaments assembled by a film expedition shooting on location today. Their personal luggage was geared to transportation by camel or horseback: a duffel bag, knapsack, and army blanket for each man, a duffel bag, two suitcases, a toilet case, bedroll, and rubber bathtub for Marguerite. The technical equipment consisted of the camera and sealed film and a collection of gifts for the nomads: cheap wrist watches, knives, beads, and scarves.

The party was also strangely assorted in personalities and appearance, Merian short and stubby, Schoedsack a towering giant, Marguerite smallish and chic in an outfit suitable for a European cruise rather than for a ride among the nomads. She was forty-four, albeit a glamorous forty-four, while the men were both thirty.

On shipboard Marguerite assiduously completed *Red Bear or Yellow Dragon* — her third book in four years. The men remained in Paris to purchase additional equipment and arrange for reception of the exposed footage they would send back. Marguerite went on to Constantinople (Istanbul), the Turkish capital, to apply for permits to film the Kurds in Kurdish Anatolia, known as Kurdistan.

But the Middle East was a cauldron of unrest at the time and the Turkish capital had been moved to Angora (Ankara today), where permission to film would have to be secured. So Marguerite first had to get a permit to go to Angora. She was still waiting for the

*Sharing a meal of wild goat in Turkey's Taurus Mountains during
the long 1924 overland trip from Istanbul to Persia, en route to
join the Bakhtiari*

Angora permit when the two men arrived, expecting to start immediately for the Kurds. At the end of a nervous week, Merian
decided to start the film in Constantinople, concocting a flimsy
theme of a world-weary American woman (Marguerite) on a mystic quest for a "Forgotten People" (possibly her own ancestors)
supposedly dwelling in the heart of Asia. The search would lead to
the nomads, of course.

In Angora at last, they were firmly refused entrance to Kurdistan
because the Kurds were on the brink of open uprising. (Marguerite
later reported the outbreak for the *New York Times*.) They decided
instead to go in search of nomads said to be living in southern
Anatolia. But before they set out, Merian fell ill and had to be
operated on in Angora's "dilapidated" Turkish military hospital,
poorly equipped and providing only stifling, fly-filled rooms for
recovery. "I have never seen any other man who so reveled in
personal discomfort or who got such a grim satisfaction from physical suffering," Marguerite wrote, still horrified that Cooper had
refused to return to the American hospital in Constantinople. She

Riding sidesaddle, Marguerite travels by mule in Turkey in 1924,
in search of nomads to film.

used the time, however, to interview the new Turkish leader, Mustapha Kemal Pasha.

By late November they were able to proceed in a horse-drawn *araba,* resembling an American covered wagon, painted bright green with floral decorations but lacking springs and with a seat only for the driver. They bounced across the barren Salt Desert along an ancient caravan trail, camping in the open at night, cooking on an oil stove, once falling in with a camel caravan of wild-looking, turbaned Turkomans with whom they shared an evening meal and a night in a massive old caravansary.

They were headed for the seaport of Adana on the Mediterranean Sea, but midway at Konia bogged down again awaiting new travel permits to continue. Marguerite had time to observe the famous whirling dervishes of Konia, the Mevlevi-Khané, whose dances of religious ecstasy she later described in an article for *Asia* magazine. The new permits specified a direct train trip from Konia to Adana, but wanting to see the scenic Taurus Mountains, they risked arrest by jumping off the train in the black of night at a stop

The trek continues on camel at Al Qä'im in Mesopotamia, near the Syrian frontier.

at a high pass. Unfortunately, they were snowbound three weeks in a nearby village. Barely escaping arrest by gendarmes sent to catch them, they rode on by mule over the ancient trail through the Cilician Gates where Roman legions once marched and three days later reached the "dreary" town of Adana.

Here new disappointments awaited them. The nomads in the outlying districts were impossible, "a squalid, moth-eaten lot," Marguerite said in disgust. "Most of the men had discarded their picturesque costumes for castoff army uniforms and their annual migration was a short trek over an easy road. There was nothing epic about their effort to keep themselves and their miserable herds of sheep and goats alive."

So after all, their subject would have to be the Bakhtiari of Persia — an additional fifteen hundred miles away across Syria and Iraq. Marguerite abandoned her study of Turkish and dug into the Persian grammar she had bought in Paris.

They reached Aleppo in Syria by train, then wedged themselves into a guttering old Ford to travel through central Syria toward

202

Baghdad, following the Euphrates River Road, a route so infested by bandits there were few guests at the inns where they passed the nights. French cavalry patrolled the Syrian end, and camel-mounted Iraqi desert corps patrolled the Iraqi side. After five rattling days in the car, they stopped at Abu Kemal near the Iraqi border, rested, then continued on to Baghdad. Marguerite could detect no vestige of the eighth-century splendors of Caliph Haroun al-Raschid in the "straggling town of unpaved streets and ugly semi-modern houses." But she found compensation for her disappointment in meeting and forming an "instant friendship" with Gertrude Bell, the noted British Orientalist, author, and scholar on the Middle East, whose peerless knowledge of Eastern languages, geography, and Arab leaders had been of invaluable help to the British government during World War I.

Gertrude Bell knew much about the Bakhtiari and now urged the Americans to hasten. The nomads' spring migration would begin in April and it was then nearly March. Once the nomads broke winter encampment and were on the move, it would be impossible to join them. Careful preliminary negotiations were necessary for foreigners to be accepted by a people so strongly independent they answered only to the rule of their chieftains. Bell counseled entering Persia at the port of Mohammerah (modern Khorramshahr), at the head of the Persian Gulf, and inquiring there how to contact the tribesmen.

Merian and Schoedsack elected to make the trip from Baghdad by a small steamer down the Tigris River to Basra near the gulf. But Marguerite characteristically chose the more risky route. She accepted an invitation to ride with an American vice-consul across the nearly trackless desert as far as a car could go. She would then catch a Tigris riverboat for Basra and join her partners there.

Not surprisingly, the car trip was slow and arduous. The road had been washed away, and Marguerite and the vice-consul had to walk along searching for the faint tracks. On their route lay deep, bridgeless canals, sometimes fifteen to twenty feet wide, over which they threw a makeshift suspension bridge so that the car could pass.

When the partners at last trod upon Persian soil in Mohammerah, they had been on the move for seven months, and they still had not gotten a single shot of a migration.

Anglo-Persian Oil Company officials in Mohammerah were hospitable in response to the film crew's letters of introduction, but they knew little more about the Bakhtiari than that the Americans would need a "mandate" from the tribesmen before they could travel in Bakhtiari country. "We could surely be robbed and murdered unless we had such a guarantee for our safety," Marguerite said. "We were told that while the ruling family were suave, polished Persians, the tribesmen were quite untouched by modern civilization, a wild unruly lot."

They learned that Captain E. G. Peel, a British consul, was the recognized authority on the tribesmen and could probably arrange an introduction to the chieftains. Peel was stationed at Ahwaz, the gateway to the Persian oil fields, a steamer voyage up the Karun River. When the Americans arrived, British oil field technicians at the isolated outpost eagerly greeted the newcomers with plans to entertain them for days. But Peel advised them to leave immediately before the tribesmen began to move. At that very moment the Bakhtiari princes, on their annual tour of the tribes, were camped near the town of Shushtar, fifty miles farther up the Karun River. Most of the year the princes were scattered, living in Teheran or in their mountain castles, so the Americans were lucky to catch them together now. Peel knew the princes personally and dispatched a message introducing the newcomers, whom he advised to wait in Shushtar for an answer. He also wrote a letter to Shushtar's governor general.

The trio dashed off under a burning sun to drive the fifty miles to Shushtar, aware now that every minute counted. Crops along the dusty road were already ripening in the summerlike spring heat. Arabistan, through which they were traveling, was "one of the hottest places in the world," Marguerite decided. As they approached Shushtar, the car was suddenly surrounded by mounted Persian gendarmes wearing cossack-style Russian blouses, fur-banded caps, baggy trousers, and high leather boots. Fears of capture subsided when they learned this was an honor guard dispatched by Shushtar's governor general to escort them. They entered Shushtar in grand style.

The governor general, a "melancholy looking" old gentleman, "wearing the traditional long black frock coat of the Persian official," entertained them with an excellent meal and warm, civilized hospitality. But Marguerite observed that he "smiled pityingly" when they said they planned to live with the Bakhtiari tribespeople during the migration. Life in Shushtar was wretched enough, he murmured, but among the tribes it was impossible. He personally would prefer to live in Teheran. Marguerite sensed again and again this schism between the city Persians and the tribespeople. The urban dweller despised the uncouth nomad; the nomad regarded the city slicker as weak, cowardly, and caddish.

The governor general arranged for the most comfortable home in the crumbling city to be put at their disposal while they awaited word from the Bakhtiari. It belonged to Mustafi Agha, a gracious host who spoke little English. Through Marguerite's slender command of Persian, they learned how the beautiful city that had flourished in the fourteenth century had become a pile of sunbaked brick and rubbish through invasions, floods, and finally, in 1885, the collapse of Valerians Bridge, a combination bridge-dam in the irrigation system that had helped make Shushtar an oasis.

One day at tea in Mustafi Agha's small garden, their answer arrived from the Bakhtiari in a most unusual fashion. Marguerite vividly described the scene later. As they idly conversed, a picturesque figure suddenly arrived "leaping lightly up the terrace steps." Young, graceful, slim, with clear skin and handsome features, he wore a European riding habit, a burnoose over his shoulders, and a small black cap on his head. He stood slashing sportily at his boots with his riding crop, white teeth flashing below a close-trimmed mustache. Behind him stood five dramatically clad attendants, wearing long coats over long full black trousers topped by white waistbands.

Speaking English with a decidedly American accent, the young man introduced himself as Rahim Khan. He had been sent by his uncle, the Il-Khani, chief of the Bakhtiari, to invite them to visit his camp. Startled though they were to behold this sophisticated, Westernized youth instead of the expected "wild" tribesman, the Americans accepted eagerly, promising to be ready very early the following morning.

But it was long past "very early" when Rahim Khan finally arrived next morning mounted on a splendid horse. Mounted cohorts led horses for the guests and two mules for their baggage. Rahim Khan dismounted and, in the most leisurely fashion, partook of a good breakfast on the terrace, while behind his chair his personal barber stood quoting long verses of Persian poetry.

The party at last got under way, thundering through the narrow streets of Shushtar, scattering townspeople and splattering mud on the multicolored coats of the pedestrians, an arrogance that did not escape Marguerite's notice.

During their forenoon ride, the partners learned that Rahim Khan had been educated at the American College at Beirut, that his ambition was to go to New York, and that he despised the savage life of the nomads but was proud of the ruling family of thirteen princes to which he belonged. They controlled fifty to one hundred thousand nomads (statistics were only a guess) living in the mountains between Isfahan, Shīrāz, and Shushtar. The princes' considerable yearly income consisted of rentals and payments in crops from villages and dependent tribes, and royalties from the Anglo-Persian Oil Company, which had drilled for oil on Bakhtiari land.

At midday the cavalcade reached a guesthouse. Marguerite now learned that when the Bakhtiari princes traveled through the country they and their entire retinue were supported by the local feudal subjects. Here a stupendous feast awaited them, "enough for twenty starving men," Marguerite said. The banquet was an unforgettable experience: "The bare walls and floor of the guest house had been covered with rugs, the divan on which we sat piled high with cushions and half a dozen barefoot villagers brought in a series of dishes on their heads, placing them on a white cloth which had been spread by Rahim's attendants. There were roast chickens and mutton, huge bowls of pilau, curds and sour milk, heavenly drinks made of lime or date juice, nuts, raisins, sweet cakes and bonbons stuffed with nuts, and many other dainties. We ate ravenously. Even the knowledge that the poor villagers had been compelled to feed us at their own expense did not mar our enjoyment of the feast."

During the long, sweltering meal three servants stood fanning the perspiring guests. His hunger satisfied at last, Rahim leaned back upon his cushions and proceeded to fall soundly asleep, first covering his head with his burnoose. The others, equally drowsy but lacking this "portable mosquito net," as Merian called it, stayed awake fighting off flies. It was late afternoon when their host, refreshed, sprang up and ordered the horses to be brought and the cortege continued on its way.

At sunset they caught their first sight of the royal encampment of the Bakhtiari princes. The riders gazed down into a valley tinted with gold from the sunset, where a river rushed from a deep gorge in craggy cliffs, "full five hundred feet high," Merian wrote. At the base of the cliffs was pitched a camp of fifty many-colored tents. "The amber glow lay like a shimmering veil on the black and orange and white and brown of them; it tinted and dyed with its warm hue the black cloaked figures, the steel of the rifle barrels of scores of horsemen, the flocks of grazing sheep. All were covered with this golden light."

Darkness fell as they rode down to the tent-dotted plain, but Marguerite made out the encampment's outlines by the "flickering points of light from many candles" and "the campfires that glowed against the darkness." The lounging, dark-cloaked figures around the fires eyed the newcomers silently as they rode through the camp.

Three comfortable tents facing the river awaited them. The reception tent, lit with candles in silver holders, was filled with carpets and cushions, the walls hung with flowered satin. Rahim had thoughtfully equipped Marguerite's tent with a camp bed; the men's tent, Merian reported, was spread only with rugs on which to lay their bedding, "since we were to sleep on the ground as did every man of the encampment from princes to the lowest drawer of water."

Rahim's servants attended them graciously. Marguerite welcomed the silver basin of hot water and a chance to wash after the long hot trip, and she slipped into a clean dress before joining the men in the guest tent to await the Il-Khani.

He arrived with superb panache. Two elderly major-domos "bearing huge silver-topped staffs of office" strode in first and stood at attention on either side of the entrance. The Il-Khani then entered in full Bakhtiari costume: a black coat, white sash, black skirtlike trousers, soft white shoes, and a round black hat. Marguerite later described him as "a powerful looking old man with fine rugged features," and Merian noted how "his big walrus mustache showed white against the brown of a face tanned and lined by a life spent in the open."

He was followed by another man, clearly of a different breed and generation, a city Persian, short, stout, middle-aged, wearing a frock coat, gold-rimmed eyeglasses, a huge diamond ring, and a gold wrist watch. This was Il-Begi, the second man in the Bakhtiari hierarchy, named Amir Jang.

"Peace be with you," "And to you peace" — the customary greetings were exchanged amid polite bowing. The princes sank into camp chairs placed by their servants. The guests returned to their cushions. Rahim joined them. Amir Jang, who spoke fair English, was a cousin of the Il-Khani who was khan of all the Bakhtiari, and would hear their petition, although he did not understand English.

With Rahim's assistance, they presented their request to live with one of the tribes during a migration so that they might tell the story on the screen. They would eat, sleep, and travel with the tribe, living as they did. The route they wished to follow was the northernmost of the five trails used by different tribal groups. It was the most dangerous and difficult but the most likely to be pictorially exciting. They had been told it had never been traversed by a foreigner.

Marguerite said that when Amir Jang comprehended their request, he laughed at their foolhardiness "until the tears came." He could hardly believe they were serious. He himself, he said, had the good judgment always to choose the Lynch Road, the easy, comfortable route built by the British before the war. But he quickly gained the Il-Khani's consent, and it looked as if the filmmakers' project would finally be realized.

Tea was served Marguerite next morning in her exotic tent as she lay in her camp bed. She was the only female in the camp; during their tours, the princes left their womenfolk in their mountain castles in the Chahar Mahal Valley region. The encampment comprised five members of the ruling family, each with a retinue of servants — cooks, barbers, and armed riders who were bodyguards — a total of some three hundred people who had been settled at this spot for a month, supplying themselves from local stores of food — something the villagers might not consider much of an honor, Marguerite speculated. The Il-Khani also received bags of silver, sacks of grain, or flocks of sheep as "taxes" from his subjects. The princes were as eager to receive these taxes, Rahim pointed out, as they were adamant against paying any to the central government.

As Marguerite strolled through the camp with Rahim, she was regaled with tales about the fierce independence of the tribespeople, who even then were resisting orders from the central government to give up arms. A governmental regiment sent into Bakhtiari country had been ambushed, stripped of their clothing, and sent back to their leader naked. Even worse violence had occurred among the tribal group to the north, the Lurs. The governor general of Luristan had invited twelve leading khans to a conference, then had hanged all twelve men in the public square. The Lurs retaliated by boiling alive all the officers of the federal troops they could catch.

Such disclosures appear not to have diminished Marguerite's growing enjoyment of the Middle East. And now her feeling of a fundamental affinity with the region was to be even more strengthened during the dreamlike trip arranged for the group by Amir Jang. They were to return the next day to Shushtar by way of the Karun River, there to await a guide who would lead them to the camp of the Baba Ahmedi, the tribal group with whom they would travel. They bade the old Il-Khani good-by.

For the twenty-mile trip downstream, Amir Jang had had constructed a barge made of goatskins strung on a wooden frame, a light, commodious craft of a type known in this part of the world as far back as memory could reach. The film crew gathered with the prince, Amir Jang, and his party on the riverbank, some twenty people all together. One of Jang's retainers tossed Marguerite on his back, waded out to the barge, and settled her among piles of silken cushions and rich rugs spread under a crimson satin canopy shielding the passengers from the sun. All the passengers, including Amir Jang, as well as the tall, gangling Shorty, were piggybacked aboard in this manner. Jang gave a signal and they cast off, the barge skimming like a leaf into the swift waters.

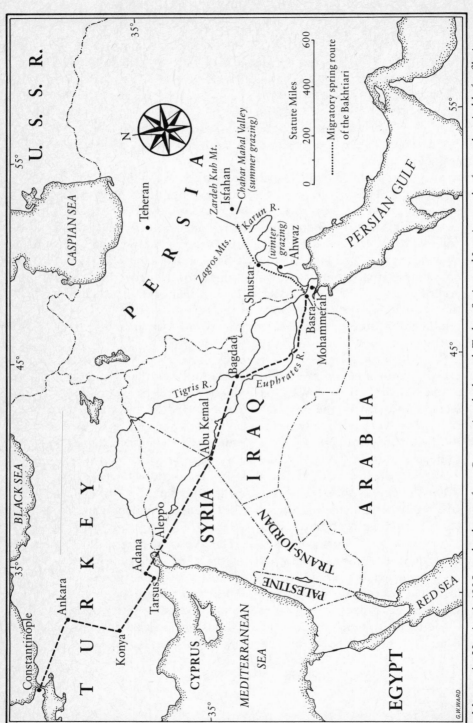

Marguerite Harrison's 1925 overland route from Constantinople through Turkey, Syria, and Iraq in search of nomads suitable for filming

A servant soon placed a brazier of hot coals before Jang, who genially prepared an opium pipe for each guest. Smoking her pipe and reclining upon her cushions, Marguerite watched the spectacular scenery sweep by. For her the experience was deeply spiritual, and it filled her with an overwhelming impression of déjà-vu:

> It seemed the most natural thing in the world that I should be riding on a barge of goatskins down a mountain river. Somewhere, sometime, I knew that I had done it before, and the opium was not entirely responsible for the feeling . . . In Persia as in Russia, I experienced the same sensation of complete and absolute familiarity with my surroundings. When I arrived in Moscow I knew that I had seen it before. When I talked with Russians I instinctively understood their point of view. Their language came to my tongue with uncanny facility.
>
> I had learned Turkish and Persian with the same ease. I could sit crossed-legged or on my heels for hours at a stretch without feeling fatigued. I adapted myself without effort to the customs, manners, and foods of the peoples of the Middle East. In the Far East I always felt myself an alien, but in Russia, Turkey, and Persia I was at home.

Once in Shushtar, haggling began for mounts to carry the foreigners and their equipment. They were advised to use mules rather than horses, which had to be unshod to cross the heights. For the movie equipment and baggage, an Arab named Hadji, owner of three donkeys, was hired. Hadji was terrified of the "wild" Bakhtiari but was unable to resist the good pay offered him. On the trail, however, Marguerite had to goad him constantly to get him started each morning. Captain Peel dispatched an interpreter named Mohammed, who would prove invaluable.

By the time the guide from the Baba Ahmedi arrived, preparations were completed. The entourage set out from Shushtar on a hot, dry morning. All day they rode through desolate, treeless country, and at nightfall reached the first shelter, a one-room mud hut. The miserable place was so dirty the men disdained to throw their blankets on the soiled floor and stretched out under the stars. Marguerite, however, was able to unfold her camp bed inside.

The next day they climbed steadily through bare, serrated ridges, mounting the foothills of the great mountain range to the east, which they would soon be crossing. Toward evening they were astonished suddenly to come upon the tents of the princes. The encampment had moved to a new location and here Rahim was in charge. With him was Haidar Khan, chief of the Baba Ahmedi, who was to be their new host and protector during the long days of migration through the Persian wilderness.

Haidar Khan's grim stare bespoke his displeasure. Summoned by Amir Jang to take charge of the visiting Americans, he communicated in every aspect of his muscular frame the impression that responsibility for them was being forced upon him. But Amir Jang's order was law, and when the visitors arose next morning Haidar Khan was waiting to conduct them to the camp of the Baba Ahmedi. The tents of the princes had vanished; only Rahim remained to bid them good-by. Then he galloped off. For better or worse, they were now in the hands of Haidar Khan.

Around noontime four black tents were spotted ahead in a vast valley, the camp of the Baba Ahmedi. To exclamations of dismay at the meagerness of the camp, Mohammed hastened to explain these were only a fraction of the three hundred "tents" (families) of five hundred "rifles" (men) commanded by Haidar Khan. The families were dispersed for better grazing of their flocks.

Though a grudging host, Haidar Khan upheld Bakhtiari honor by killing a sheep to welcome his guests. Presently Marguerite found herself sitting cross-legged on the floor of one of the tents with several tribesmen, dipping her hand into the shared dishes and drinking goat's milk from the communal earthenware bowl. They were now with real nomads, the authentic, unspoiled tribespeople for whom they had been searching since leaving New York the August before. (Decades later, the humanistic philosopher Jacob Bronowski would write of the Bakhtiari, "They are as near as any surviving, vanishing people can be to the nomad ways of ten thousand years ago.")

Marguerite began her study of these archaic people in the days while they were waiting for the migration to begin. The women were striking, "tall and straight, dressed in full skirts of dark blue or black cotton that came to their ankles, with flowered calico jackets and bright kerchiefs. Their long black hair was braided and the thick braids crossed under the chin." Vigorous, muscular, free moving, they appeared on the whole to enjoy a position of respect, "although in no way treated as equals of men." They were the busy keepers of the camp, milking the sheep and goats, souring the milk in goatskins hung over a low fire, cooking the one meal in the evening over dried dung burned in a shallow pit. The men meanwhile lounged around camp, traded horses, or visited other camps. Marguerite at first found them unbelievably lazy, smoking their water pipes, drinking tea, and gossiping the whole day through.

Haidar had two wives, both unveiled, as were all the tribeswomen. Wife Number 1, mother of four, was "a superb woman, dark, vivid and handsome," while Wife Number 2 was a young girl who because she had no children was "treated like a slave and did all the heavy work." Female prestige resided solely in childbearing. Yet in these lawless mountains, Marguerite was told, a woman could travel without fear.

The tribes had no written language of their own, no written history, even few legends, and a lineage that would be hard to prove, although known to be ancient. The Bakhtiari claimed to be descendents of the original prehistoric Aryan inhabitants of Persia. (And they are so regarded by students today, in the accepted ethnographic sense that denotes a linguistic stock who speak proto-Indo-European, not in the distorted Nazi usage of the term.) Purportedly Moslem, the Baba Ahmedi tribe struck Marguerite as being not at all devout. Indeed, they seemed to lack religious or even superstitious practices, the constant movement of nomadic life being scarcely conducive to sustaining traditions.

But while spiritual longing seemed nonexistent, they were avid for medical help for their physical problems. Before she had even reached the Baba Ahmedi, Marguerite had become known as the "Lady Doctor" or "Hakim Khan." All Western visitors were automatically assumed to be oracles of medical wisdom. During Marguerite's various trips out of Shushtar, when the party stopped at villages, the poor had flocked around her seeking treatment or medication. Marguerite's extraordinary linguistic facility, augmented by her supply of simple medicines, readily dispensed, confirmed the belief she was a medical expert with near-magical powers.

In Haidar Khan's camp she was soon swamped with requests from the sick and ailing, a situation that would continue throughout the migration. "Every morning when I opened the flap of my tent at least a dozen patients were waiting outside," she wrote later. "I was appalled by the responsibility, for I knew nothing whatever about medicine. My experience as an amateur physician during my three months with the tribes would fill volumes. Some were funny, others tragic." She was able to identify three "terrible scourges" that were creating havoc: malaria, venereal disease, and eye troubles, both ophthalmia and trachoma. "I treated all these ills as best I could," she wrote. "For malaria I had quinine. For those who had venereal disease I could do nothing except bathe the suppurating sores with permanganese solution, and I treated the eyes with boric acid." Stomachache called for castor oil and cathartic pills. She expelled a leech by making a child drink salt water. She even performed minor surgery, amputating a finger, "which was hanging by a thread." Luckily, she said, "none of my patients died, and my supply of medicines made our work easier, for the poor people were immensely grateful for what little help I could give them."

Cooper confirmed the significance of her medical efforts as well as her linguistic skill. Gratitude to Marguerite influenced the tribespeople to suffer the persistent filming for weeks on end, to ignore the cameras and tolerate the foreigners while going about their daily life. According to Cooper, Marguerite also won over Haidar, who was fascinated by all her accouterments, and particularly by the box of gold-tipped cigarettes she presented him.

The heat was now growing more intense each day. The grass was withering before their eyes. The spring dust storms would soon begin to rake the arid, baking land. The flocks must be taken to new grass.

Suddenly the tempo of camp life quickened. The lounging came to an end. Black-robed men from neighboring camps galloped in to huddle with Haidar and then departed. Three of Haidar's brothers — out of a family of nine brothers, all khans — rode in, according to Merian the biggest men with the hardest faces they had yet seen. More huddled conferences. More arrivals and departures.

Then one night Haidar Khan gave the word: the migration would start at dawn! The great drama was about to unfold. The date was April 16, 1924.

Cooper kept a diary intermittently during the migration, which later served as the basis of his book *Grass*. He also wrote a series of articles for *Asia* magazine. His descriptions augment those of Marguerite's autobiography, *There's Always Tomorrow,* which details the story of the *Grass* expedition from its inception in New York. Marguerite also wrote magazine and newspaper articles on her return. These sources plus the film *Grass* itself, which can still be viewed in the United States in a few libraries or through private rental, supply a vivid account of the incredible trek.

On the first morning of the migration, long before first light, the black tents were rolled and stored in stone cairns. (Only a few leaders carried tents on the journey.) Pots, kettles, rugs, and the scant furnishings were packed into saddlebags lashed to cows and donkeys. Children, puppies, and newborn lambs were also tied to the animals. The smallest babies were carried on their mothers' backs in shawls or wooden cradles. Number 1 wives were permitted to ride, but the rest of the people walked, either barefoot or in white canvas slippers.

People began to pour into the valley from every direction as Haidar's three hundred "tents" assembled. The movement got under way in the most haphazard fashion, people and animals straggling along without a sign of organization. More tribes kept joining the march throughout the day.

By the next day Marguerite estimated there were perhaps five thousand people with fifty thousand head of livestock on the move — sheep, goats, cattle, asses, horses, and dogs — all raising an impenetrable cloud of dust and a stupendous cacophony. Noisiest of all was the incessant barking of innumerable dogs. Each family had its own fierce guard dogs to protect its herd from thievery.

Merian exulted at "the gorgeous colorful torrent of humanity" that poured onto the trail. Marguerite, from the back of her recalcitrant white mule, viewed the shapeless tide, lacking both discipline and command, with a mixture of dismay and admiration. To her it seemed more a rout than a migration.

But she began to discover a pattern in the chaos. As days passed she decided that age-old routes and rituals were being followed, unwritten but ingrained in every individual. Rules of survival had been long ago established. Thus every night they managed to camp in a fertile valley where there was grass and water for the animals. Clans or groups of families had positions they knew well, dispersed so each could enjoy separate pasturage. Each slept inside a circle of saddlebags stacked to form a compound lighted by campfires. The animals milled in the middle, safe from thieves, even from the thievery of neighbors, a threat to be constantly reckoned with.

By day the hoard became a long river of people and flocks traveling in continuous file. By night they were scattered again. "When we crossed the successive mountain ranges the great stream of humanity came together. When the valleys were reached it spread out like a huge fan, each tribe occupying its allotted territory," Marguerite said.

The various discomforts of a nomadic style of travel emerged as the days settled into a routine. Merian remembered the incredible dust. "When the Bakhtiari hordes were on the march, the dust was unbelievable for thickness and dryness. We tied handkerchiefs over our mouths and noses, we even drank water through handkerchiefs, for the dust got into everything, even the goatskin water bags slung under the bellies of the horses or on the backs of donkeys. The latter animals, by the way, had had their nostrils slit in the common fashion of that country, to make it less difficult for them to breathe."

For Marguerite, flies were "the worst of the minor discomforts I had to endure during the trip." Swarms hovered around the herds when they were driven into camp at night (for protection against bears, as well as thieves). The flies remained inactive during the chilly night, but they assailed her at the sun's first rays. They got into her hair, eyes, clothing, and food and continued their assault throughout the day. The animal noises that went on outside her tent during the night did not bother her, however. She was too tired to care, and slept soundly.

In rain, wind, and, later, snow, her two American companions slept out in the open, their single blanket apiece for cover. In violent thunderstorms, of which there were several, the two men along with Hadji and Mohammed all piled into her tiny tent, extremely "close quarters indeed," she commented wryly.

The precious film cases and moneybags were all kept under Marguerite's camp bed. She took her guardianship, which amounted to a twenty-four-hour alert, very seriously. Their developed film was irreplaceable and new film was unattainable. The moneybags were heavy and bulky because the tribes would accept only silver coin. Enough tender had to be carried to pay the salaries of their personal retinue as well as to pay Haidar Khan for their food, an unfortunate arrangement, they soon discovered, since Haidar Khan cheated them steadily. They were afraid to protest, fearing his anger; but their slender budget did not allow for extra supplies.

By now they had been four or five days on the road. The Karun River, deep, swift, icy, two hundred yards to a quarter of a mile wide, presented their first formidable challenge. Boats could not be launched in the foaming, swirling torrent, and there was no bridge. Marguerite could not imagine how thousands of people and animals, newborn babies, the aged, and all the worldly belongings of the tribes could ever reach the other side. But tribes had been crossing this river from time immemorial. Already goatskin rafts, smaller versions of Amir Jang's barge, were being constructed, each raft designed to convey six or eight people with belongings.

Watching the first launchings, Marguerite saw that the rafts were bounced around like twigs in the dangerous rapids and whirlpools. It seemed certain they would overturn, but two steersmen aboard each raft kept them afloat. After the passengers had disembarked on the opposite shore, the current itself brought the rafts back to a bend on the launching bank a quarter-mile downstream. The rafts were then portaged back upstream to the starting point by the steersmen.

The languid Haidar Khan and his "lazy" tribesmen were galvanized into frenzied activity. Fearless and commanding, Haidar was in and out of the river, leading the bawling mass of animals, supervising the disorderly loadings. The men swam hour after hour in the icy water, once working straight through the night. Their courage and stamina were no longer in doubt. Goatskin water wings under their stomachs kept the swimmers from being swept away as they guided and prodded the animals into the water — all but the goats, which refused to swim and had to be flung onto the rafts. Dozens of animals drowned, sucked under by the currents.

Marguerite's turn came at last. "I piled onto the raft with half a dozen saddlebags, my own belongings, three women and five goats. We shot out into the current, whirled round and round dizzily until I had to shut my eyes to keep from falling off into the water, and at last reached the opposite bank — then a steep rocky ascent, several miles of scrambling over a rough trail, and we came out on a grassy plateau."

In the film *Grass,* the sequences of the Karun River crossing are among the most exciting and dramatic. The spectacle of so many humans battling against the mighty river inspires wonder and admiration.

A full week went by in this struggle before all the people and animals were brought across. Then several days had to be spent in sorting and resting the animals. But at last the migration pushed on.

Days of threading through narrow valleys and clinging to sheer ledges passed. They were climbing ever-higher ridges, mounting toward the towering ranges in the east.

The next major rest stop was at Shimbar, a high mountain valley, where the thousands of people and animals congregated once more. The scene of this massing of the tribes in the expansive valley, with the campfires, the colorful clothing, the restless animals — the exotic spectacle of it all, evocative of the Old Testament — moved Marguerite deeply.

After Shimbar they traveled in closer formation, as they were to pass through hostile lands. It was now mid-May and the frightful heat meant that camp had to be broken before dawn and a long rest stop taken at midday. "The trail was so difficult we seldom made more than ten miles a day," Marguerite recalled, "but at that, we were on the move for at least twelve hours out of the twenty-four."

One of Haidar's wives brought supper to Marguerite's tent each night, a monotonous menu of rice cooked in mutton fat, un-

Marguerite, Cooper, and Schoedsack with their equipment on the Bakhtiari migration

leavened bread, sour milk, and tea. "Cast iron pancakes," Merian called the Bakhtiari bread and recalled that Marguerite had cracked a tooth on her first bite. They lived off the tribes' "shockingly inadequate" diet, Marguerite admitted, only because their funds were too skimpy for extra supplies, which they might have purchased at an occasional farm or village. She learned to eat the pith in thistles' stems, wild onions, and a kind of wild berry to supplement the tribes' rations.

Dead tired after a day on the trail, Marguerite still faced various nightly chores before she could collapse on her camp bed. A fastidious woman, she had to attend to her toilette each night. "I had to bathe and wash my clothes at night with the small amount of water that could be heated over a fire of dried dung. Most of the time I wore riding suits of natural pongee. I could not have withstood anything else in the heat, and I was particular about washing them out and keeping them clean."

In photographs of the migration, Marguerite appears both stylish and decorous. Her smart riding outfits were trousered but had long tunic jackets, and her legs were modestly swathed with robes

219

as she rode. She was always chastely hatted. After *Grass* debuted in New York, film critics questioned whether she had actually been on such an arduous migration, "because I was much too well-groomed and spotless to have traveled over such country," she said indignantly. "They little knew how hard I had worked to look presentable."

On a day when she was to appear in the film, Marguerite applied her makeup before breaking camp. But scorching temperatures made it necessary to redo her cosmetics on the trail, balancing her kit on the mule's neck or on a rock. But Marguerite equated vanity with valor and even without a movie role would doubtless have contrived to remain attractive. "Even in prison in Russia I clung to my pocket mirror and my last grains of face powder, and I waved my hair on bits of rags or paper," she admitted. "These things have always helped me keep up my morale."

One wonders how she actually managed enough rest and privacy to function since her tent had become the place of rendezvous not only for her partners but for Haidar Khan and his cohorts as well. They stopped by nearly every evening with their water pipes and "sat solemnly for hours, talking little but smoking and drinking countless cups of tea," she said. Of the women only Haidar's venerable mother, "a hag with red-dyed hair and a cackling laugh," ever came, her exalted confidence deriving from having borne twenty-two children, ten of them sons. She still rode daily with the tribes.

Marguerite also missed out on the daily siesta during the afternoon rest stop. While the others were sleeping, she was holding her medical consultations. In his diary, Merian described a typical hot afternoon during which the "Lady Doctor" was busily engaged while others rested: "Schoedsack and I lay under the shade of Mrs. Harrison's tent-fly and dozed . . . but this was Mrs. Harrison's time of work. Soon the sick from all the camps around began to crowd about, and she dressed wounds, or gave out medicine for internal ills, Mohammed acting as her assistant. Though Mohammed acts as her interpreter, she already has learned sufficient Persian to carry on an ordinary conversation. She is a far better linguist than either Schoedsack or I."

Marguerite bore up under the strenuous schedule until around

May 19. She had been five or six weeks on the migration when she came down with malaria. Now in the grip of chills and high fever, she had to become her own physician. With a fever of 106 degrees, she called for water and sponged herself, although very weak and nearly blind from the forty grains of quinine she was taking daily. The fever dropped. On the fourth day she was able to be lifted, still limp, to the back of her mule, and to continue.

"Haidar redeemed himself during Mrs. Harrison's illness," Cooper recorded in his diary. "He stopped the movement of all the Baba Ahmedi for a day or so until she should be well enough to move, and has shown every possible consideration." (Marguerite, never trusting Haidar, remarked sourly in her memoirs that it was "the only time I ever saw him display any decent feeling.")

Merian perceived other evidences of humanity and kindness. "When news got about that Mrs. Harrison was ill and we had no medicine left, every single one of the Baba Ahmedi khans brought the few pills of quinine that he had saved out of those she had given; and not a khan failed to make a personal call each day . . . to inquire with grave and kindly courtesy after her health, and to offer her anything the tribes had in the way of food, though, indeed, there was little variety from which to choose."

The ascent became increasingly difficult each day, until at last the tribes faced their final, most terrible barrier. This was Zardeh Kuh, the "Yellow Mountain" that towers nearly fifteen thousand feet above sea level. Zardeh Kuh was the "personal enemy" of every member of the tribe, "grim and gigantic," a mass of "black and yellow rock and snow and more snow, rising straight up until the peaks are lost in the clouds," wrote Cooper.

As she stood gazing at the sheer icy peak, Marguerite later recalled, she wondered how the thousands of barefoot, lightly clad women, children, and men, and the thousands of animals, would ever scale this wall. But of course the tribesmen again had an answer: they would chop a path out of the ice and snow. The next morning before dawn a gang of men with flowing robes pulled up around their waists, barelegged and barefoot, began attacking the wall of ice with picks and shovels. Haidar Khan climbed ahead to mark the zigzag course, testing the ice and risking his neck at every step.

The migrating Bakhtiari attack the formidable Zardeh Kuh in the Zagros Mountains of Persia.

For four days Marguerite and the others watched them trench this impossible trail up the "frowning face" of Zardeh Kuh. Long after dark they returned to the camp, shivering and "blue with cold."

With the path finally finished, the tribespeople and their animals began to press forward impatiently, for their flocks were now running short of pasturage. Merian and Shorty dashed off to catch the oncoming horde. Marguerite was left to calm the hysterical Hadji and to goad him to start up the mountain by warning that he would probably be killed by bandits if he turned back alone now.

At last she and Hadji and his pack train fell into the single file of people and animals inching their way up the narrow, treacherous trail, a chiseled trench with snow mounded two or three feet high on the exposed side and the wall of the mountain on the other. To start up its length was an irrevocable move; there was no turning back.

The peril and audacity of the ascent come through even in Marguerite's matter-of-fact, unsensational chronicle of this climb:

On one side of us was an almost perpendicular slope that stretched up and up till it seemed to touch the blue sky, on the other an equally dizzy drop which increased from a few feet to hundreds, then to thousands, as we worked our way up the mountain in horizontal zigzags.

A sharp wind cut our faces and tore at the flimsy cotton garments of the tribespeople but they shouted cheerily as they drove their animals along the narrow path. I walked along leading my white mule. In front of me was an old man crawling painfully on two sticks, a child of two or three perched on his shoulders. Behind me was a little girl carrying a baby calf.

Above me was a long line of moving figures that grew smaller and smaller, until they looked like flies crawling up the sides of a gigantic sugar loaf. In the rear were thousands of men and beasts moving slowly and laboriously. Once on the trail it was impossible to turn back or even to stop for long to get one's breath. The stream of people moved ceaselessly and remorselessly . . . up and up until late at night.

A donkey lost its footing just ahead and catapulted out of sight over the side, followed by the frantic owner, who miraculously was caught on the twisting path below and saved.

Marguerite gained the summit in late afternoon, to find that her partners had encountered some frightening moments. Shorty had stepped outside the trail, trying to catch a shot, slipped, and slid helplessly until his tripod caught in the ice and held.

Merian was almost beside himself with excitement. He was thrilled by the spectacle of the migration — a cast of thousands set against the mountain of ice — and responded with typically dramatic fervor. He wrote later of the "crawling cable of men and animals" toiling upward, of the "stupendous, primitive scene" seeming to be a "fierce drama of the Old Testament. Man, nearly naked man, pitted against naked nature."

The crossing of the Karun River, the pageantry of the procession, the scaling of Zardeh Kuh — for Merian the sheer drama provided sufficient visual material for his film. But Marguerite, more searching, wanted the human story. She wished to portray on film the diverse aspects of the tribes' lives: the way they ate, slept, cooked, raised children. The divergent points of view of the two partners must have been evident during the journey; certainly they became clear after the film was finished.

On Zardeh Kuh's windswept summit that night, Marguerite nearly froze in her sleeping bag inside her little tent. The migrants slept out in the open without a shred of protection. "It made me shudder when I thought of the thousands of women and children outside in their cotton garments, with bleeding chilblained feet, lying under the stars rolled in a few miserable rags beside feeble smouldering campfires of dried dung," she remembered.

The next morning Marguerite stood in the floodlight of the mountain sun and gazed back down the sheer slope the tribes had ascended, some throughout the night. As she looked to the east, she saw an amazing sight: gleeful tribespeople were sliding down a long, snow-filled ravine as if it were a gigantic toboggan, shouting with delight. With the dangers behind them, the weary marchers were now romping "like children at recess."

The remainder of the journey entailed only a short march. The "Promised Land," their final destination, lay in the region of Chahar Mahal, or the Four Districts, among the seven- to eight-thousand-foot valleys of the upper Karun River and its tributaries. The nomads settled in an immense valley covered with "huge carpets of wild narcissi, beds of tulips that might have graced any garden, and clumps of mammoth black irises." Families set up their tents in groups around campfires, the women resumed their daily chores, and the men "relapsed into the lazy creatures they had been." The abundant grass would support their flock for the entire summer.

To her credit, Marguerite did not view the Bakhtiari migration as quaint, romantic, or heroic. Nature had dictated the terms, and the tribes had adapted in order to survive. Somewhat of a stoic herself, she saw their accommodation to their environment as that of other stoics resigned to their destiny. "They all seemed unconscious of the fact that they had done anything remarkable or endured any particular hardships," she said. "Their ancestors had done the same thing for countless generations, and the migration to them was quite a commonplace affair. Thus, every year, all unconsciously, they staged a drama which was all the more thrilling [to an outsider] because of its supreme naturalness."

224

Marguerite ended her sojourn with little affection for the nomads, although acknowledging their hardihood and perseverance.
She had lost interest in the Baba Ahmedi women early on, finding
them to be merely workhorses and childbearers. "Our leave-taking
was unaccompanied by any regrets on my part or Shorty's," she
said. "Merian was the only one of our party who developed a
liking for the Bakhtiari. They were not a lovable or an interesting
people — hard, treacherous, thieves and robbers, without cultural
background, living under a remorseless feudal system, crassly material and devoid of sentiment or spirituality. Their two outstanding qualities were an arrogant pride of race and a contempt for
physical weakness." "They have no poetry and no gardens," one of
the city Persians later said; and with their grinding, wandering life,
how could they?

But even as the migration ended, Marguerite was to enjoy another sample of the hospitality of the upper-echelon rulers of the
tribes. From the summer encampment, the trio rode on to the castle
of one of the princes, a cousin of Rahim's. It was a feudal palace
with battlemented walls of dried mud, containing vast quarters for
servants, others for the women and the slaves, still others for
guests. Marguerite estimated that her room measured at least fifty
feet square. Magnificent rugs adorned the walls and floors, but
there was no furniture other than a low divan.

As soon as Marguerite arrived, servants brought her a large
copper tub steaming with hot water scented with roses and left her
to revel in her first real bath since Baghdad, nearly four months
ago. (They had left Baghdad in early March; it was now mid-June.)
That evening a sumptuous fifteen-course meal was served on a
velvet tablecloth heavily embroidered in gold. Back in her room the
divan had been made into a bed with a crimson counterpane and
white silk sheets. Memories of her hard little camp bed and the
dusty trail subsided instantly in this delicious comfort.

The following night they were invited to Rahim's father's castle,
"twice as large and twice as splendid." Here the entertainment was
of such "sumptuous Oriental luxury" Marguerite felt she was "re-
living a page of Arabian Nights."

The filmmakers proceeded to Teheran by car, "well satisfied"
that they had obtained a "fairly complete picture" that was
"unique of its kind," although Marguerite regretted that because

225

of lack of equipment they had been unable to film certain scenes, such as the campfires at night and the candle-lit tents glowing along the glistening river. Robert W. Imbrie, the American consul in Teheran (later slain by fanatics) attested in a letter that they were the first foreigners to make the entire forty-eight-day migration with the Bakhtiari over the Zardeh Kuh trail from the Jungari district in Arabistan to the Chahar Mahal valley in Ehleck. Before leaving Teheran, Marguerite interviewed the man who would become dictator a year later, Reza Shah Pahlavi, father of the Mohammed Reza Pahlavi who was deposed in 1979 by Islamic revolution led by the Ayatollah Ruholla Khomeini.

Grass was given a private showing at the Plaza Hotel in Manhattan in March 1925 and a public debut a few weeks later at the Criterion Theater. "Our Bakhtiari picture has so far been most favorably reviewed," Marguerite wrote a friend. But in fact the critics didn't know what to make of the movie. The concept of the "documentary" was unknown, and critics lacked the vocabulary for judging such a film. One critic thought it would have been improved with a love plot. Another that it could have been a "big movie" with a leading man like Rudolph Valentino. A few reviewers praised the "honest approach" and the "sincere unposed method." But even when they sensed the appearance of a new genre or an innovative departure, it was with bafflement.

Professional geographers, however, immediately discerned that a new form had emerged, and statements from geographic leaders were enthusiastic. Dr. Isaiah Bowman, director of the American Geographical Society, thought it the finest film he had ever seen, and Louis D. Froelick, the editor of *Asia* magazine, praised the co-producers as "dramatists of reality."

The only person supremely disappointed in the final film, and sharply critical of it, was Marguerite Harrison. Some ten years after the film's premiere, in her autobiography, she described how her purpose had been distorted in the production process:

> I suppose I should have been thrilled over its production and over the fact that it ran for four whole months at The Criterion. But I was not. I went to see it just once, and after that I could not

set foot in the theater again. I could not bear to see it on the screen because I loathed the manner in which it was presented.

We had made an authentic record of a stupendous, natural drama, and I felt that it should be treated in an absolutely natural manner. Those were the days of the silent pictures, so that our film had to have titles and subtitles explaining the various episodes. I wanted to tell the story of the migration simply and straightforwardly without overstatement or exaggeration, but I was over-ruled by Merian and Shorty, and the scenario writer from the editorial staff of Famous Players who collaborated with them. Their titles were melodramatic, artificial, and of the theater. They put impossible speeches into the mouths of the Bakhtiari tribesmen, whose language was as primitive as their lives.

Viewers of the film today wholly agree. The subtitles are jarring, frivolous, frequently so alien in tone they are ludicrous.

"Br-r-r. This water's cold" is scarcely the utterance of a hardy Bakhtiari stepping into frigid glacial waters. A small tribal girl carrying a lamb is captioned, "Everywhere that Mary went . . ." and so on, entirely without relation to the culture portrayed or to the native language. And descriptive subtitles at moments of dramatic tension are presented in the breathless style that today might be used to report a boxing match on television.

But for all the crudity of early black-and-white filming and the movie's awful subtitles, *Grass* remains an epic film. It was one of those turning points that open a new door, a pioneering, exploratory, inventive assault that changed history. *Grass*'s stature in documentary film history would grow as the cinema itself evolved, and also as ethnographic perspective changed. In those days, for instance, racism and primitivism were attitudes accepted by ethnographers. *Grass* opened a door not only to the geographic and ethnographic documentary in particular but to the whole method of documentary treatment of life, leading toward that staple of instruction and entertainment that we know today as the documentary film.

Grass was not a financial bonanza. The capital invested in the film was repaid, plus several thousand dollars in royalties for each partner. Thereafter, the threesome went their separate ways.

Shorty joined the famed William Beebe expedition that sailed to film and study the Galápagos Islands, while Merian wrote his book about the Bakhtiari expedition, also entitled *Grass*. He later became a leading Hollywood director-producer, heading his own company and working with the celebrated John Ford. He and Schoedsack created other benchmark documentaries, such as *Chang*, and entertainment films that included the immortal science fiction gem *King Kong*.

When she arrived back in New York, Marguerite was once again, as on previous occasions, irritated by her reception by the press. On her return from earlier excursions, reporters had greeted her with such frivolous and sexist questions as did she use lipstick in the Gobi Desert, or had she "had a love affair with a Bolshevik commissar"; now they asked "if she had become enamoured of a shiek." "They were not interested in what I had actually seen and learned," she complained.

Her annoyance with this attitude inspired her to join with several other women to form a society that would provide intellectual companionship for female writers, explorers, journalists, and serious travelers like herself, and that would dignify their professional image so they were not treated as eccentrics or mere globe-trotting dilettantes. On a snowy winter day in early 1925, Marguerite Harrison and three other women explorers — Blair Niles, Gertrude Mathews Selby, and Gertrude Emerson — formed the Society of Woman Geographers, for women who had "blazed new trails in geography, ethnology, natural history, and kindred sciences." It was destined to become an international body with headquarters in Washington, D.C., and has included some of the most distinguished women of the twentieth century, maintaining even today its strictly professional qualifications for active membership. Until the end of her life, Marguerite counted her role in founding this society and her part in establishing the Children's Hospital School in Baltimore her most prized accomplishments.

In 1926, at age forty-seven, Marguerite remarried. Her new husband was Arthur Middleton Blake, an attractive English actor. "The prospect of wandering over the world alone did not appeal to me anymore," she said. She had been described as a "man's woman," as having left a "trail of broken hearts." But she did not see herself in such a light. While men had always "played a large part in her life," she said, friendships with them after her husband's death had been merely "interludes." Men had been attracted to her, even in love with her, according to her MID file, but she maintained that "during all my wander years I had never met any man for whose sake I would have given up even a small part of my personal freedom." But now she was ready for marriage. "Although I was thoroughly unconventional in most respects, I still held rather old-fashioned views with regard to marriage. I believed people who marry assume certain mutual obligations that cannot be shirked."

Following her marriage, Marguerite continued to work as hard as she had since her first husband's death, lecturing and writing articles and books. She published her most solid work, *Asia Reborn,* in 1928, a political and economic analysis of the new movements in the Far East which, according to her son, was standard reading in political science classes at Harvard University for years. Her exuberant autobiography, *There's Always Tomorrow,* was published in 1935, the same year as her translation from the German of Edward Stucken's *The Dissolute Years: A Pageant of Stuart England*. At some point she and her husband moved to Hollywood to allow Blake to act in films.

After Blake's death in 1949, Marguerite, now seventy-one, moved back to Baltimore and settled near her son and his second wife and their daughter. (His first marriage had ended in divorce; the couple had had five children.) Despite her early absences, the bond between mother and son was still strong.

Marguerite continued to travel, though less than she had during her most prodigious years from 1918 to 1924. At seventy-eight she journeyed by freight boat to South America. Another trip to South America by air included a visit to some soaring Andean spot where the tour director begged her to inhale oxygen, which she haughtily refused — without dire consequences. She managed to cover large areas of Africa, touched Australia, and was in her eighties when she flew to post–World War II Berlin, somehow, alone and without trouble, passing through forbidden Communist East Berlin, probably by grace of her still-brazen nerve and her skill with both German and Russian.

Her health remained remarkably intact until the last three years of her life when it began to decline. Long a chain smoker — resorting to a ladies' pipe in her later years — she ceased smoking entirely after her first small stroke. She died, after other strokes, at age eighty-eight, on July 16, 1967.

When her son Tommy, then seventy-two, was interviewed in his Baltimore home, he reflected on his lifelong awe of his mother's talents. "She could do anything she attempted," he said. "She was a fine pianist, she spoke five languages fluently, could pick up the rudiments of a new one swiftly. She made the most beautiful clothes, embroidered, did wood carving, was a gourmet cook and a great gardener. She was a marvelous bridge player, always in demand. And when she lectured there was a rare quality of naturalness that carried the audience along with her every word."

Tommy and his wife hired a boat in Ocean City, Maryland, to take her ashes out into the Atlantic to be scattered as she had requested. But such an irrepressible spirit would not leave the stage blandly. A strong nor'easter blew up and held the couple waiting for several days. At last they carried her ashes to the bridge between Assateague Island and Maryland, where Tommy, uttering a prayer, flung them into a powerful ebb tide which carried them out to sea.

"Mother loved the ocean," he said, "and I thought there was an appropriate symbolism that her last remains should have gone out on the ebb tide to be swept restlessly on and on across the face of the earth by the tides of the ocean."

LOUISE ARNER BOYD

1887–1972

ALMOST FROM THE MOMENT her ship weighed anchor, Louise Boyd's 1937 summer expedition to Greenland met with hostile weather. The *Veslekari,* a husky little Norwegian sealing vessel, was beset by a ferocious southwest gale immediately after leaving Bear Island in the Spitsbergen archipelago far above the Arctic Circle. The ship was on a course set for Jan Mayen Island in the Greenland Sea, bound for the majestic fiords of East Greenland.

Louise Boyd, the expedition's leader, gazed apprehensively out over the turbulent waters: "Heavy seas sweeping over our decks put so much water on them that the iron door of the galley had to be closed to keep the water from splashing on the stove and scalding the cook. Hip rubber boots were an absolute necessity not only on deck but even in our mess room where, despite the closing of the iron door, the sea surged in around our legs, often knee-deep. The ship had to be navigated at from half to slow speed much of the time."

Now guiding her fifth expedition into the Arctic, Louise Boyd was hardly a stranger to the gales of northern seas or to the bitter chill of fog, snow, sleet, pelting rain, and Arctic ice in its many forms — pack ice, inland ice, ice floes, icebergs, and glaciers. After five Arctic expeditions, she well knew that the quixotic behavior of ice and weather could spell success or failure.

Greenland has itself been compared to a gigantic bowl of ice. The world's largest island, rimmed by coastal ranges, its inland ice cap covering most of the island, is more than two miles thick in places, forming a permanent sheet whose weight depresses the ground surface over eleven feet below sea level.

The Louise Arner Boyd East Greenland Expedition of 1937 was not bound for the desolation of the inland ice cap but for the wondrous east coast of Greenland, that dramatic littoral "traversed by some of the profoundest fiords in the world." To those who imagined Greenland as a monotonous white wilderness, Louise would snap back an impatient denial. The fiords, with mile-high rock walls, brilliant color, and infinite forms, rivaled the spectacle of the Grand Canyon, she declared. Add to this landscape of vivid cliffs and shimmering snow-covered mountains "a sea dotted with icebergs or fringed with pack ice and great floes," and you have "a picture of such majesty and on so vast a scale that no explanation need be given by any explorer for wishing to revisit such a scene."

And revisit it time and again was what she had done since her initial trip to Spitsbergen on a small tourist ship in 1924, when she caught her first dazzling glimpse of pack ice. She wrote ecstatically of her discovery: "Far north, hidden behind grim barriers of pack ice, are lands that hold one spellbound. Gigantic imaginary gates . . . seem to guard these lands. The gates swing open, and one enters another world where men are insignificant amid the awesome immensity of lovely mountains, fiords, and glaciers."

These fanciful "imaginary gates" opened nearly half a century of association with the Arctic for her, during which she organized, financed, and led seven expeditions. At age sixty-seven, she climaxed her career by flying over the North Pole. Toward the end of her life, she was described as "the only woman to achieve an outstanding position in Arctic exploration."

A figure of mystifying paradoxes, Louise is not easy to place in focus. She seemed to have two distinct personalities. One sees her, a rugged, tomboyish figure, striding about the deck in her oil skins, hip boots, and sou'wester, bracing against the bulkheads on a ship "rail under in sea water," in a struggle to keep from being swept overboard; or being a good sport as she gamely grabs for the door of the head flung open by the cavorting vessel. Or again, one watches her stoically wading ashore through icy slush, trudging across miles of rocky moraines for a long day of photographic work.

Yet time and again she would declare to interviewers, "I may have worn breeches and boots and even slept in them at times, but I have no use for masculine women. At sea, I didn't bother with my hands, except to keep them from being frozen. But I powdered my nose before going on deck no matter how rough the sea was. There is no reason why a woman can't rough it and still remain feminine."

Back in her native San Francisco Bay Area, one sees her as the *grande dame* of San Francisco society, the elegant socialite who graced every important social event, the wealthy, sybaritic lady coddled by a staff of nine on her suburban estate, Maple Lawn. Society reporters described her as "tall, blue-eyed, graceful, slender, erect, and elegant." Never pretty, her features were craggy but "strikingly handsome." Gracious, gregarious, stylish, she was an imposing presence. Her fame was such that she was always adequately identified as merely "Miss Boyd." On her shoulder she wore a camellia, usually king-size, from the prized collection in her greenhouses. "I don't feel dressed unless I'm wearing flowers. Even in Greenland, I'd find something and wear it with a safety pin," she said. And like the queen of England, she was invariably hatted. "I've never thought of going without one unless it was to the dentist's."

Yet friends would watch her step into her waiting car, regal in a Paris gown and toque, only to see the chauffeur gun the motor and roar off like a shot, to her obvious approval.

At Maple Lawn she was fully, formally, impeccably dressed, whatever the hour. House guests would find her in the morning, gardening in a smart herringbone wool suit (with matching hat, of course), no matter how early. Yet this dainty person, who brought her own personal maid on her expeditions, would wear to shreds two pairs of heavy hobnailed boots during a two-and-a-half-month Greenland summer. And if outraged, she could curse like a stevedore.

To men who encountered her solely in her role of explorer, photographer, and expedition commander, she was "a hell of a gal," a boon pal, a gung ho type who knew what she wanted. But perhaps not the girl of their dreams.

She never mentioned money, it was said, was generous without limit on her expeditions, and made life a "party" for guests wherever they might be. But she could be canny and suspicious. When showing visitors through her superb greenhouses, she could coldly turn at the end of the tour and request that they please return the prized camellia cuttings surreptitiously snitched during the visit. She had the sensitivity of the very rich to being used.

Her emergence from a wealthy society background to become a significant explorer with serious credentials required that she buck up against even more derision than most women explorers of the day. Not only was she female and a wealthy socialite, but she was not a scientist. And as she would learn, even in the field of polar exploration she would not always be accepted by the snobbish little band of specialists.

Born on September 16, 1887, to a moneyed family, the social cream of San Francisco, she moved among families of immense fortunes from earliest childhood. Her great-grandfather, Ira Cook, had purchased Maple Lawn in San Rafael, now a San Francisco suburb, in 1870, twenty years after crossing the plains from New York. He planted trees still standing through Louise's lifetime. Her father was John Franklin Boyd, a successful mining magnate.

A *New York Times* society writer described the San Francisco "blue bloods" as "vigorous, acquisitive, outspoken, educated, well traveled, fashionably dressed and extravagantly housed." Miss Louise A. Boyd was listed among the top of this opulent ruling class, along with the elite of the sugar, railroad, newspaper, and banking industries, such names as Spreckles, Crocker, and Cameron, who had built the city at the Golden Gate.

Louise was taught by governesses, then attended Miss Stewart's School in San Rafael, and later Miss Murison's School in San Francisco. She did not go to college. She made her debut a year after the 1906 San Francisco earthquake and fire, it being obvious that life, even social life, must go on.

But while favored by birth, the young Louise spent her childhood tiptoeing about the huge San Rafael house amid a perpetual hospital hush. There was almost never a time in her early decades when the house was without day and night nurses. Illness and invalidism hung as a pall over the place. Louise's two brothers, John Franklin Boyd, Jr., and Seth Cook Boyd, both afflicted with rheumatic fever and frail from birth, died when they were sixteen and seventeen, respectively. Neither parent enjoyed good health. Her father, having lost his sons, brought his daughter into his business affairs; after his death she became head of the Boyd Investment Company. Her mother died in 1919, her father one year later.

Her parents' deaths left her at thirty-two quite alone, without near relatives. Unmarried, an heiress, suddenly freed from years of responsibility to her invalid family, she faced unlimited options, anything from a morbid retreat to an unbridled plunge into the reckless self-indulgence and profligacy of the 1920s.

She chose neither extreme. Maple Lawn emerged from its years of somberness to new vitality, with parties and house guests and a stream of visitors enjoying the estate's luxurious private swimming pool, still a novelty in those days. And Louise began to travel.

In 1920, Louise toured post–World War I France and Belgium with the socialite widow of General Conger Pratt. As she was chauffeured through battlefields in a Hotchkiss Motorcar, she scribbled in her diary, describing the ruined cities, bombed cathedrals, and devastated landscapes "bare of every tree." The next year, she and Sadie Pratt toured other European countries.

An intelligent sightseer and serious tourist comes through in the diaries, but there is no hint of the future Arctic explorer nor much of the personal opinions of the writer. One does learn that on shipboard the two ladies removed themselves from the captain's table in distaste for the other guests ("Common awful people!") and managed to meet some of the more interesting passengers, including a Rockefeller ("So simple and unassuming and thoroughbred").

It was in surprising contrast to this conventional Grand Tour background that Louise chose an extraordinary destination for her next trip. For reasons not now on record, she decided to go to Spitsbergen, a small archipelago lying in the Arctic Sea between the coasts of Norway and East Greenland. In the summer of 1924 it was so unorthodox a place to visit that a nascent pioneering spirit must have been guiding her choice. Afterward, she would explain rather lamely that she had been "fond of geography from earliest childhood," favoring books that took the armchair traveler "into high northern latitudes." Her trip in the small tourist boat to Spitsbergen and to the pack ice was a turning point, for, she said, "on that trip were laid the foundations of my subsequent seven expeditions to the Arctic." She had found the love of her life.

By summer 1926 she had chartered the M.S. *Hobby*, a Norwegian sealer (once the flagship of the noted Norwegian explorer Roald Amundsen) and gathered a small group of friends to hunt polar bears in Franz Josef Land. Franz Josef Land was an even more exotic choice than Spitsbergen: it is the northernmost land in the Eastern Hemisphere. Seventy tiny frozen islands, little visited except by seal- and walrus-hunting expeditions, they are so close to the North Pole they have several times been utilized as a base for polar dashes. After 1926 the USSR claimed the archipelago and it more or less "disappeared" behind the iron curtain. (In 1929, the Russians established there one of the most northerly meteorological stations in the world.)

En route to this far-flung and unlikely outpost, Louise stopped off in London to be presented at the Court of St. James, a measure of the lighthearted mood of the jaunt. Indeed, although afterward it was claimed that Louise was the first woman to set foot in Franz Josef Land (a claim she did not herself make), this expensive cruise was far more recreational than exploratory. Louise made the most of the time, however, by beginning the photography of Arctic topography and of sea and land ice that would become her lifework. Photographing lavishly, she began to build the invaluable record she ultimately left as her legacy, a pictorial documentation of every aspect of landscape from distant perspectives to close-up studies of cliffs, glaciers, inlets, ice in every form, animals, plants — an archive that would become of immense usefulness to her country during World War II.

The hunting party returned to San Francisco with a debatable number of polar bears. Some reports claimed the entire party had shot twenty-nine; other reports attributed all twenty-nine bears to Louise Boyd's gun. (It was known she was able to shoot a polar bear from a moving ship.) Years later, in 1963, when safaris both to jungle and Arctic were less admired, Louise said in an interview, "People are always exaggerating . . . for instance, it's not true I shot

*Louise Boyd with one of the polar bears that
fell to her gun*

19 polar bears in one day. That's a crazy story. I think it was only five or six and that was for food." In any case, she caught some fine photographs of the beautiful animals.

Gratified by her experience as an expedition leader, Louise chartered the *Hobby* for another summer expedition into Arctic waters in 1928. The ship was equipped and ready to sail from Norway when the world was startled by the sensational news that Roald Amundsen, Norway's cherished hero of Arctic and Antarctic ex-

AIDS SEARCH
FOR
AMUNDSEN.
Miss Louise Boyd,
of San Rafael,
Calif., who loan-
ed her chartered
yacht to aid
search for missing
explorer.

Louise Boyd in 1928

ploration, was missing. Amundsen had commanded the *Gjoa* on the first and only negotiation of the Northwest Passage, from 1903 to 1906, definitely establishing the North Magnetic Pole, though he was trapped by ice through three winters. In 1911 he discovered the South Pole. In 1918 he became the second in history to travel the Northeast Passage north of Europe and Siberia. After failing to fly planes across the North Pole, he flew on the dirigible *Norge* piloted by General Umberto Nobile on a seventy-two-hour flight from Spitsbergen to Alaska over hitherto unexplored areas of the central Arctic, finding no land. In 1928 Nobile attempted to fly to the North Pole in his dirigible, the *Italia*, and crashed. Although Amundsen and Nobile had quarreled over the *Norge* expedition, now Amundsen gallantly set forth with a party by plane to rescue the Italian explorers. And then Amundsen himself was declared missing.

Louise was in Tromsø, the popular starting point for polar ex-peditions, far up the Norwegian coast, when the rescue party and the press arrived there. Louise had never met Amundsen but he was as much a hero to her as he was to the rest of the world. She immediately abandoned her plans and placed her ship, equipment, and crew at the disposal of Norwegian search parties, declaring she would herself join in the hunt.

Later, after she had been elected to the Society of Woman Geographers, Louise reported on her three-month, ten-thousand-mile search for Amundsen's lost hydroplane, *Latham*. She sailed from Tromsø on July 1st under orders of the Norwegian government, she said, and at Kings Bay, Spitsbergen, took on board two hydroplanes, three mechanics, and three officers of the Royal Norwegian Navy. Her voyage encompassed an immense swing from Tromsø to the west coast of Spitsbergen and westward into the Greenland Sea, and then eastward to Franz Josef Land as far as 81°13' north latitude. She returned to Tromsø on September 22.

Louise photographed zealously the entire time, making both still and cinema records of the details of the search, the various ships involved — Norwegian, French, Italian, and Russian — the airplane flights, the areas visited, the pack ice in the Greenland Sea, Barents Sea, and Arctic Ocean — twenty thousand feet of motion-picture film and several thousand still photographs. "To the best of my knowledge, I am the only one who made such a detailed and complete photographic record of this Arctic tragedy," she wrote. "All negatives and one complete set of prints are in my possession. One complete set, also maps, I have donated to The American Geographical Society."

Elsewhere Louise described the exasperations of hunting for objects in the unstable atmosphere of the Arctic, which produces fantastic mirages that have tricked explorers from earliest reports. "Four of us stood watch around the clock. We would just stand there and look. Ice does such eerie things. There are illusions like mirages, and there were times we clearly could see tents. Then we'd lower boats and go off to investigate. But it always turned out the same — strange formations of the ice, nothing more."

Louise encountered another new experience during the search: fire at sea. In the Barents Sea, hundreds of miles from land, fire broke out on the *Hobby*. Louise was so terrified that afterward she made it her "personal responsibility" to see that "an ample supply of freshly filled fire extinguishers" was on board any of her expeditionary ships. Already, with characteristic thoroughness, she was building the information file that would make her future expeditions as foolproof as possible.

The search for Amundsen proved fruitless, although Nobile and those of his party still alive were rescued. The massive hunt for the ill-fated explorers made world headlines, and Louise's role was prominently featured. For her contribution to the arduous Amundsen search, which included generously paying all the expenses of her vessel and crew, she was decorated by Norway's King Haakon VII with the order of St. Olaf, First Class, the first non-Norwegian woman to receive this honor.

Louise's career was greatly spurred by the unprecedented contact with established polar explorers involved in the hunt. During trips to Norway and Denmark in connection with the search, she was thrown into repeated contact with the Scandinavian experts of the day, such prominent men as Dr. Lauge Koch, Ejnar Mikkelsen, Docent (Prof.) Adolf Hoel, Bernt Balchen, and Hjalmar Riiser-Larsen (who later founded the Scandinavian Air Service). These modern Vikings, seasoned explorers actively studying the Arctic region, inspired her with their tales of the fabled coast of East Greenland and descriptions of the "lonely magnificence" of the "dramatic alpine complex of waterways, mountains, and glaciers" to which her interrupted 1928 expedition had been directed. The Amundsen hunt had further familiarized her with "conditions of navigation in polar seas, and with the appearance and behavior of the different forms of marine ice," so now she felt ready to tackle "more hazardous waters, where the approach to land is rendered difficult by an exceptionally wide belt of ice." She now knew that "the reward of crossing this belt is access to a land of extraordinary grandeur and beauty."

She began organizing a serious scientific assault on these formidable shores for the summer of 1931, chartering the Norwegian sealer the *Veslekari,* already a veteran of Norwegian scientific expeditions into the fiord region. In the intervening summer of 1930, she squeezed in a two-month photographic trip to scenic points north of the Arctic Circle, returning to Franz Josef Land, where she collected botanical specimens and photographed Swedish and Finnish Lapps in the extreme northern regions of Scandinavia.

242

At last in the summer of 1931, she was ready to confront East Greenland, a region unknown to most of the world, though by no means unexplored. The fiord region especially had been surveyed, mapped, and studied by both Danish and Norwegian expeditions, as well as by others. But many scientific questions remained unanswered and Louise's contribution would be in making detailed surveys of typical small areas.

The fiord region lying between the 70th and 74th parallels is a coast fractured into the "largest ramification of fiords in the world." It comprises the intricate Franz Josef Fiord and King Oscar Fiord group, one of the most complicated fiord patterns anywhere, and the Scoresby Sound network. The most notable fiords of the globe are found in high coastal lands and in high latitudes: Labrador, Norway, British Columbia, Alaska, Patagonia, and New Zealand. But the great fiords of East Greenland are an extraordinary labyrinth of bays, connecting channels, and minor systems, and they have remarkable vertical dimensions, both in height of walls and in depth of water. The relatively narrow, steep-walled valleys flooded with seawater in the major fiord, called Franz Josef, are like an arm of the sea half a mile in maximum depth lying at the bottom of the Grand Canyon.

Louise would find the greatest menace in reaching the fiords to be the ice pack along the coast, although in good years the fiord region is more likely to be free of ice than the coast on either side of its limits. Above Cape Bismarck, the fiords' northern limit, the coast is nearly always blockaded by impenetrable ice, while the same is true below the southern limit, Scoresby Sound. From Scoresby Sound south nearly as far as Angmagssalik, a permanent barrier of compact ice guards the shores. Navigation through the pack into the fiords is usually possible during July and August, with a possible extension at one or the other end of this period in good years. In bad years, even in midsummer ships cannot get through at all to Franz Josef Fiord or into any part of the coast north of it. And of course in winter the entire east coast is frozen solid.

The striking contrast between Greenland's east coast and the coast of Norway in the same latitudes, one frigid, the other only moderately cold, is due to the different currents flowing along their coastlines. The East Greenland coast is affected throughout the year by the East Greenland Current, sweeping fiercely out of the Polar Basin at the top of the globe down along the entire length of the east coast. This current brings immense masses of pack ice, which influence navigation, exploration, even habitation, capriciously opening or closing off access to the coast during the brief summer and prohibiting it through the rest of the year. The Norwegian coast, however, is blessed with the warming North Cape Current sweeping from the south northward along Norway up as far north as the Russian port of Murmansk, which it keeps ice free throughout the year.

The veteran French explorer Jean Baptiste Charcot described this harsh difference in his North Atlantic and Greenland Sea studies of pack ice:

> Voyages along the west coast of Spitsbergen as far north as 80° and often beyond are hardly more risky than those along the shores and in the fiords of Norway; on the east coast of Greenland, as far south as latitude 61°N. (the latitude of Bergen and Oslo) they constitute veritable polar enterprises with the difficulties and dangers of ice navigation. Between Tromsø and King's Bay (Spitsbergen) from spring to September there is an uninterrupted procession of vessels of all tonnages . . . Farther west in the same sea and extending well to the south lies the sinister, implacable, and often murderous cortege of the ice floes, with its scattering of icebergs.

Louise's 1931 voyage to this "sinister" coast, in the company of six friends, was planned as a study and photographic reconnaissance, preparatory to more intensive work on later expeditions, which indeed it became in the sequence of her 1933, 1937, and 1938 expeditions. The *Veslekari* was a 125-foot, oak-ribbed sealer, built in 1918 in Aalesund, Norway, perhaps a mere cockle shell as maritime craft go, but it had bravely withstood years of battering by the northern seas.

The luck of the beginner, as well as a season of unusually favorable weather, smiled upon Louise on this trip, so that despite the lack of scientists in her party (she would assemble these for her

A camp set up during an overland trek in a stark landscape of avalanche boulders

next and all subsequent trips), she achieved astonishing results. Systematically following the coastline of every fiord and sound in the Franz Josef–King Oscar fiord region, making numerous shore stops, she photographed at a furious rate. By the season's end she had taken several thousand photographs of "typical topographic forms, glaciers, sea ice, fine scenery, animal life, and flora."

In the course of this methodical cruising, the *Veslekari* pushed into the very end of Ice Fiord, an arm of Franz Josef, an indentation deep inland and difficult to reach. Study of the area revealed errors in previous mapping. "After two attempts we reached the inner end of Ice Fiord," Louise recorded, "which, to the best of my knowledge, had never been visited by a ship and on all available maps was inaccurately drawn from observations made by previous expeditions from distant peaks."

A single glacier, the Jaette, had been shown on earlier maps to enter the terminus of Ice Fiord. Louise's survey showed that the Jaette discharged into the fiord from the southwest and that the head of the fiord terminated at another larger, entirely independent glacier, coming from the north. This was the De Geer Glacier, considered one of the three principal sources of icebergs in the entire fiord region. The Boyd survey sketch map recorded the considerable divergence from a map made in 1900, the best previous authority.

Further surprises came after a landing far inland at the head of Kjerulf Fiord. Here Louise and her party crossed by foot an unexplored valley sloping down to the fiord from the north. After five or six miles a large glacier spilled across the valley, subsequently shown to be Hisinger Glacier, which discharges into Dickson Fiord. The connection between Kjerulf and Dickson fiords was previously unsuspected. Entirely on the basis of more than two hundred photographs Louise took during this excursion, and without actual measurements in the field, Dr. Walter A. Wood, surveyor of the American Geographical Society, was later able to draw to scale and publish a map showing this connection between the two fiords — a feat of photographic skill as well as of mapmaking.

Louise started on this 1931 expedition with superbly modern camera equipment. She had fallen under the seminal influence of Dr. Isaiah Bowman, then director of the American Geographical Society, the New York research institution fostering original geographic investigations. (Later, Dr. Bowman became head of The Johns Hopkins University.) Dr. Bowman had explained to her new photogrammetric mapping techniques being used at the society that facilitated mapping of high relief at reconnaissance scales. These new methods made possible mapping from elevations and hard-to-reach terrain where details of landscape features were to be studied. Louise utilized these reconnaissance techniques on her 1931 voyage, with camera equipment selected for landscape photography with fine-grain film. This included a tripod-mounted aerial camera of calibrated focal length. Her photographic success in Kjerulf Fiord was doubtless due in part to her excellent equipment.

Louise was surprised a year later to find on a map published by the Geodaetizk Institute of Copenhagen that the inner reaches of Ice Fiord that she had charted had been named "Miss Boyd Land,"

*Highland ice fields of Miss Boyd Land are
the feeding grounds for this stream of ice,
the Louise Glacier at the head of Ice Fiord,
East Greenland.*

or in Danish "Weisboydlund." Quite unlike scores of explorers
whose stake in their profession was often the coveted honor of
bestowing a name upon some newly discovered spot, Louise was
modest about the designation of Miss Boyd Land in her honor. "I
am not guilty of giving the name 'Miss Boyd Land' to the land that
lies between the De Geer Glacier, which I had the good fortune
to discover in 1931, and the Jaette Glacier," she said. "My first
intimations that this land had been so designated came in a letter
from Dr. Lauge Koch and on seeing the name on his published
map." Koch was a leading Danish scientist and explorer of East
Greenland.

In 1943 the United States Board of Geographic Names under-

The 1931 Boyd expedition to the northeast coast of Greenland visited Scoresby Sound, the northernmost colony on this coast, settled by a few Eskimo families.

took a worldwide housecleaning of geographic nomenclature, eliminating many fragile claims or other marginal names. However, the region once uncharted at the head of Ice Fiord, whose center point is 73°31′N, 27°50′W, was officially recognized as "Miss Boyd Land" as the Danes had named it.

Before turning northward, the *Veslekari* anchored in Scoresby Sound near the only Eskimo settlement in the fiords, and the northernmost Eskimo settlement on the East Greenland coast. At this tiny habitation, unique and remote, the Danes also had a seismological and radio station. The visit was distinctly picturesque. At sight of the vessel, the entire population rushed out to the ship, the Danes in a dignified launch, the Eskimos in kayaks, paddling swiftly and rolling their craft over and over in the cold water like seals at play, exuberantly displaying their skill.

The curious little colony was only six years old. Eskimos had disappeared from the inhospitable East Greenland coast probably before the mid-nineteenth century, except for the much more southern, isolated community of some 750 souls discovered by Gustav Holm and named Angmagssalik, later renamed Tasiilaq by the Danes. In the 1920s when Denmark and Norway were disputing sovereignty of East Greenland, the Danes argued for colonization of the fiord region with its more open waters and longer summer growing season, to establish Danish jurisdiction. Accordingly, ninety pureblood Eskimos were transported by Ejnar Mikkelsen, the Danish explorer, from Angmagssalik for settlement in Scoresby Sound, a "land of untold wealth," according to Eskimo legend. Mikkelsen reported the joyous newcomers "lost no time in getting their umiaks (women's boats) into the water and to shore where they ran about, shouting, laughing, rolling themselves in luxuriant grass, taking possession of the land."

Six years later, Louise found the colony contentedly settled in houses of wood and turf, quite unlike any igloo, even boasting glass windows. The "charming" inhabitants smiled at the visitors, their faces "radiating kindness," and welcomed them with dancing, chanting, and singing "with much emotion and many gyrations" while beating noisily on tin pans (in lieu of drums). The men and women dressed very much alike, in soft, knee-high sealskin boots, dark cloth trousers, and cotton parkas, the women's boots trimmed in fur and embroidery. Both wore colorful blouses with beaded or embroidered collars, and jewelry. They dried their staple food, seal meat, on high wooden racks away from dogs and wild animals. Hunting in kayaks, their way of life, the men arranged a piece of cloth across the bow, hiding themselves as they stole quietly upon their prey. Paddles and harpoons were often embellished with narwhal and walrus tusk ivory.

On Sunday, August 16, the *Veslekari* cruised about picking up scattered families, and that evening eleven members of the Boyd party and twenty-seven Eskimos attended services in the small red and white Lutheran church where the sermon was in Greenlandic, a language so difficult it often defies the efforts of the most skilled linguist.

Louise was highly amused later as the *Veslekari* was returning the Eskimos to their homes. A bitter wind sweeping eastward off the inland ice cap suddenly emptied the decks of the native Greenlanders. These hardy sons and daughters of the North had scurried off, just like anyone else, to the engine room to keep warm.

Louise departed with affectionate feelings. "It was past three o'clock in the morning when these splendid, kindly people left our ship. We sent the women and children ashore in the launch, and the men in their kayaks raced each other to land, black silhouettes against the first rays of dawn. As we left, I saw seven flashes in a row and heard as many rifle shots. We blew the *Veslekari*'s whistle to acknowledge the salute. Then seven more flashes and shots rang out, bidding us farewell from the little group lined up on the shore.

Leaving the *Veslekari* in her home port, Aalesund, Louise returned to the United States by transatlantic steamer. Dr. Isaiah Bowman and certain members of the American Geographical Society's staff were on shipboard. Long conversations with them opened Louise's eyes to the advantages of study through integrating various sciences into a single program. Her quick grasp of this interdisciplinary approach to geographic study changed the course of her career. This concept guided the structure and purposes of her next three expeditions to East Greenland and began a long and mutually profitable association with the American Geographical Society (AGS). The AGS would sponsor and help staff and program her next three expeditions and also would publish her three books, extensively illustrated by maps, charts, and her own photographs. For their part, the AGS acquired a powerful friend and ally who possessed the financial and organizational means to investigate an environment she loved. The relationship would be useful to all parties, for now her expeditions could be directed toward purposeful ends with a trained, scientific staff.

Louise eagerly embraced the advantages of professionalism. For her next expedition, she sought out the best equipment available. A "firm believer" that explorers and scientists should be supplied "the most precise and practical instruments that modern times have developed," she later declared, "I spared no effort or expense in order to equip every branch of our work to obtain detailed knowledge in difficult areas where time was a factor" — not only her own cameras but "all other instruments."

A tide gauge loaned by the U.S. Coast and Geodetic Survey was included on her 1933 expedition as well as a Wild phototheodolite for surveying. But her proudest addition was the very latest ultra-sonic depth-measuring instrument, a new development at this time. "I have arranged with Henry Hughes & Sons, Ltd. to install on my ship, S.S. *Veslekari*, for the duration of our expedition the new Hughes Silent Magneto-Striction Echo Sounder with Recorder for obtaining Echo Soundings along the continental shelf . . . Then I went to Switzerland and made arrangements at the Institute for Technology at Zurich for the plotting of my phototheodolite plates on their autograph on our return from Greenland . . . I went to the Wild factory at Heerbrugg where my phototheodolite was made and had a most interesting time."

She even had alterations made in this new echo-sounding instru-ment. No instrument suitable for a *Veslekari*-type vessel had ever recorded depths greater than 1370 meters (750 fathoms), but her specifications for alterations guaranteed 1800 meters. Trials showed the soundings could actually reach at least 2200 meters (1200 fathoms) and probably more. This depth, Louise said, was "greater than that of any previous apparatus of this same size and type."

So it was a superbly equipped scientific expedition that sailed at last on June 28, 1933, on the *Veslekari* from its home port Aale-sund, Norway, with Louise as leader and photographer. Under the aegis of the AGS, Louise had assembled a team of brilliant scien-tists, including two from the society, as her guests and staff: from the AGS, O. M. Miller, surveyor, and Walter A. Wood, assistant surveyor; Professor J. Harlen Bretz, Department of Geology, University of Chicago, physiographer; William B. Drew, Gray Herbarium, Harvard University, botanist; and N. E. Odell of Cambridge, England, geologist. Odell's wife was also invited, at his urging. The scientists' expenses were paid to and from the port of departure, and some were placed on salary.

Appendicitis early in the voyage removed Drew, the botanist, from the scene. Louise, a devoted plant lover, already a collector on previous trips, took over the botanical functions and by the end of the expedition had collected eighty vascular plants at thirteen different stations.

Posh would be too strong a term to describe an expedition aboard any vessel as practical as a small sealer, but from many standpoints the expedition of 1933 was unusually luxurious. Not only was the vessel technically well equipped, but as far as possible Louise saw that her guests wanted for nothing. The scientists and Mrs. Odell were installed in six double cabins aft below deck where the library (salon) was housed. Aft on deck were the dining salon, radio room (which the radio operator also used as his cabin), the captain's cabin, chart room, and bridge, and a very small room for developing photographs. Amidship were two galleys, and one very small mess room for the crew.

Louise had added three single cabins on deck, one for herself, another for her maid, brought from Maple Lawn, and a third for the mess girl. Still another special cabin had been built for cameras, film, and scientific equipment. Below deck were quarters for the crew. A full crew, all Norwegian, included the captain, Johan Olsen, a first mate, second mate, chief engineer, assistant engineer, wireless operator, four sailors, two stokers, two porters to carry Louise's cameras, a steward, and a cook for the crew.

The vessel carried one large motor dory, one motor launch, two large rowboats, and two American canoes. The hold was filled with coal, barrels of fuel oil for the dories, launch and lights, and tanks of drinking water. An enclosed space provided access to the echo-sounding instrument which had been installed while the ship was at dry dock.

Meals served the scientists in formal style in the dining salon could have graced a first-class steamship. Delicacies from distant lands appeared as a matter of course (on July 4 the six scientists and their hostess polished off five pounds of caviar in a rousingly patriotic celebration).

The largess affected some of her guests in an unexpected manner. In choosing her cast of characters, Louise had taken for granted that a good scientist would naturally make a good expedition member. She pigeonholed the scientists according to their expertise, without asking whether their personalities were suitable for a two-and-a-half-month voyage in close quarters and under conditions often entailing physical hardship or danger. Perhaps she ought to have applied something of the selectivity today given to submarine crews and astronauts. Some of her guests, unaccustomed to such munificence, were not only uncomfortable but derisive. Jealousy and strains on loyalties developed. Louise was not only a woman in a man's realm, a nonscientist among scientists, but a capitalist who inadvertently riled the chip-on-the-shoulder have-nots. She chose to ignore these tensions and sailed along in serene indifference; but she did not later issue second invitations.

The glacial marginal features in the Franz Josef—King Oscar fiord region were the object of study. As noted, the Danes and Norwegians had already mapped the main contours of the outer coastline of East Greenland and the principal fiords, studies had been made of the geology, plant, and animal life, and some archeological studies had been made as well. But there remained uncharted areas in the inner reaches of some fiords, and incomplete mapping or hasty study left much work for scientific investigation.

The voyage began with a trial run to test the newly installed echo-sounder off the northwest coast of the Lofoten-Vesteraalen Islands, lying off the coast of Norway. The instrument began to indicate surprisingly shallow depths, while the record markings were not those usually produced by either a hard or a soft bottom. The engineer who had installed the instrument was still aboard and in puzzlement ordered the ship turned and the area retested. The strange recordings were at last attributed to dense schools of fish that frequented the waters at that time of year. The discovery resulted in a new use of the echo-sounder. "The manufacturer designated this particular type of echo-sounder as the *Veslekari* Model and it has since been extensively used on trawlers off the Norwegian coast for locating cod and herring," Louise wrote later.

Four days of stormy weather followed by fog brought them to the wild thirty-five-mile-long strip of rocky land midway between Norway and East Greenland known as Jan Mayen Island, belonging to Norway. Almost always covered by heavy clouds or drenched with rain through the summer, the coast is pounded by a heavy sea, making landings hazardous. The only permanent dwellers were the handful of Norwegians manning the vital weather station whose storm warnings saved the lives of thousands of fishermen along the Norwegian coast. When the weather allowed, a motor dory landing was made on the west side of Jameson Bay at the foot of Egg Bluff, and Louise delivered mail and provisions to the men, the first they had received in more than eleven months, so even old newspapers were welcomed.

During a cruise in the motor dory east of Jameson Bay, Louise one day observed one of the largest bird rookeries in the Arctic, where thousands of nesting birds exotic to all but the colder latitudes were found. "Here breed the gray gull (known as the sea horse), the auk, black and white in color, and the puffin or sea parrot, whose red razor bill contrasts with his black and white body." At the foot of a cliff, nourished by the bird droppings, flowers grew in profusion, including the old standby of field and roadside, the dandelion. At the summit of Egg Bluff, Louise found a plume of steam rising from a fissure, "so hot one can hardly hold a hand in it," a thermal phenomenon on an island totally barricaded by ice in winter.

Greenland's east coast was obligingly free of ice fields, and by July 13 the *Veslekari* had anchored at Myggbukta on the Hold-with-Hope Peninsula, one of only three wireless stations the length of the lonely coast. Two unpainted wooden sheds and a small cabin comprised this oasis of civilization. Appropriately, atop the cabin rode a giant mosquito-shaped weather vane: Myggbukta literally means "mosquito." The boggy land and low hills of this ice-free strip of land between the interior ice cap and the belt of sea ice, combined with moderate summer temperatures, made it a breeding ground for the insects. Swarms of them were so thick they clouded Louise's camera lens, making it impossible for her to take a shot without beating them away.

As an early landfall for any entry from the east, Myggbukta, with its good harbor, was a rendezvous site for explorers. While the *Veslekari* was at anchor, Dr. Lauge Koch, the distinguished Danish explorer and leader of a large scientific Danish government expedition at work in the fiord region, arrived in his seaplane. Then on July 22, the *Polarbjørn* sailed into the harbor with Docent Hoel of Oslo, leader of a Norwegian expedition. Hoel and his companions remained long enough to join the Boyd party for a jovial dinner on the *Veslekari*.

Koch reported that the fiords were solidly closed by heavy ice, so in the interval before they could weigh anchor, Louise explored the

The Veslekari *moored a mile off Bontekoe Island in heavy polar ice on July 16, 1933, before pressing into the mouth of Franz Josef Fiord.*

solitary strand of the Hold-with-Hope Peninsula, one of the earliest points discovered and named on the East Greenland coast by Henry Hudson in 1607. As she walked along in this wilderness, she was startled to stumble across a grave marked by a pile of stones and encircled by a low stone wall. On a hand-hewn cross fallen from its shaft and rotting on the ground was inscribed, "John Tutein, 1921 — Farvel Kaere Ven" (Farewell dear friend). Louise later wrote that "we nailed up the cross and replaced the stones on the grave — little enough to do for one who had walked these silent Arctic shores and passed to other shores beyond. Later in the summer I learned that the grave was that of an artist who, while painting, had been killed by a polar bear."

Ice conditions having improved, the *Veslekari* sailed into the wide, imposing mouth of Franz Josef Fiord on July 23, and on up to the western end of Ymer Island where the tide gauge was set up. Herds of musk ox were roaming the hills, and many Greenland hare bounded about. Pure white, large, and plentiful throughout the fiords, the Arctic hare were "too quick to be photographed,"

The Veslekari *at anchor in ice-free waters at the inner end of Franz Josef Fiord*

Louise complained, although she managed to get some excellent shots of the handsome creatures.

The *Veslekari* anchored in a small bay in Andrée Land, farther up the fiord, near the east face of a great rock mass called Teufelsschloss. One day the air was shattered by repeated blasts from the ship. These signals of alarm evoked an immediate fear of fire. The scientists, who had scattered to do their research, hastily rushed to the shore to meet the launch sent to fetch them. They learned the trouble was not that fire had broken out but that Docent Hoel, their recent dinner guest, had run aground in Alp Fiord, about eighty miles to the south, and the *Polarbjørn* had developed a "dangerous list." Help was urgently needed. Radio reception in the fiords being uncertain, his message had come by wireless by way of Myggbukta. The *Veslekari* responded it was starting immediately to help.

"All night, torn with anxiety, we steamed at full speed (8½ knots) southward through Antarctic Sound and King Oscar Fiord.

As there was fortunately very little ice in these waterways we were able to reach the entrance to Segelsallskapet Fiord in ten and a half hours. Here, much to our relief, we received another message — that the *Polarbjørn* had been safely floated at high tide and our services were not required."

The valiant effort was costly in time, which was a precious commodity on these short summer expeditions. Never knowing whether or when a particular site might be visited again for years to come, the scientists labored under intense pressure to make every minute and every opportunity for observation count. Now the overnight dash at forced speed had created engine trouble, which took another couple of hours to repair.

It all meant they had to drop further investigation of King Oscar Fiord and move toward their next site for study, the inner reaches of Franz Josef Fiord, which Louise had visited in 1931. The sheer walls of these narrowing waterways, along whose sides rise some of East Greenland's highest mountains, once more moved Louise to rhapsody. Here "the work of ice is displayed on a titanic scale," she said of the ring of diamond-white glaciers.

> Glaciers of many different types seem to pour over the summits and to cut through the rock walls of the canyon from heights of more than 5,000 feet. Some come all the way, others only part way, down to water level . . . One senses the approaches to inland ice and the great mountain ranges that border it. Below, far below the surface of the water, soundings show another 2,400 feet before the ground level of the canyon is reached. A tremendous cliff, "Attestupan," in Fraenkel Land, towers above the north side of the fiord. Its granite face forms an almost sheer precipice 6,000 feet high. Our ship seems like a mere speck against this monstrous wall.

Since the head of Franz Josef Fiord was to be the primary focus of study for the entire expedition, preliminary reconnaissance was necessary. The party split into two groups, Louise and Captain Olsen to go by motor dory and foot to the Kjerulf Fiord and Hisinger Glacier, areas of her 1931 discoveries, while the other scientists headed north into the area known as Fraenkel Land.

Louise again was awed by the massive Hisinger Glacier dominating the landscape. "The third or fourth largest river of ice in this part of Greenland," it was a veritable fountain of water and ice. Rising from the inland ice cap and fed by tributary glaciers coming from the ice-capped uplands, Hisinger like many glaciers was a source of numerous streams issuing from the icy edges. At a point the streams joined to empty into the fiord. Near the glacier grew dwarf willows, "the largest and tallest massed growth of [them]" Louise had seen anywhere in Greenland. These were two or three feet in height with "a spread of limb many times greater than this." Usually much smaller, Arctic willows are found wherever the narrow ice-free littoral allows growth of any kind.

Her excursion was memorable for a strange discovery. One day the sun had set behind the fiord wall, leaving the valley in deep shadow, with grounded icebergs standing in the water in stark contrast. Wanting to capture the beautiful scene, Louise dispatched one of the crew to bring her camera from the motor dory. As he approached the water's edge, he spied a floating bottle, an astonishing object in this unsullied landscape. Retrieving it, he found a note inside in both Swedish and English left by the chief surgeon of A. G. Nathorst's Swedish expedition of the summer of 1899. They had come to East Greenland in unsuccessful search of the lost balloonists Andrée, Strindberg, and Fraenkel. The note read: "This point, the inmost of Franz Josef Inlet, I have reached at the 12 August 1899, alone with a canoe: Dr. Josef Hammar, The Swedish Greenland Expedition 1899. Surgeon on Antarctic."

The message revived the grim story of still more lives sacrificed in exploration of this harsh land. Salomen August Andrée, a Swedish aeronautical engineer who had already made one failed attempt to be the first to cross the North Pole by balloon, had set forth from Spitsbergen with two other men in 1897 in the *Eagle*. Ill-supplied with clothing, they came down in the frozen wastes 298 miles away, where they managed to fit out three sledges, one with a boat, and to reach White Island (Kvitøya) in the Spitsbergen archipelago, where they died, possibly from exposure. For years expeditions searched for clues of the Andrée party. Not until 1930 did the *Bratvaag* expedition discover their remains and equipment, including Andrée's diaries and Strindberg's exposed film.

Discovery of this haunting message left three decades earlier in the icy fiord was, as Louise said, a startlingly "queer turn of events," involving her in a series of coincidences:

It marked the third time in as many years that these valiant balloonists, whom I had never known in life, had crossed my path. During our search for Amundsen in 1928 we had met Captain Eliassen on the Norwegian sealer, *Bratvaag*. While at White Island in 1930, Eliassen had found Andrée, chopped the ice from his body, recovered his diary and photographs; and had also found Fraenkel. Strindberg's body was recovered later; and thus was solved a mystery of thirty years' standing. By chance that same autumn I was in Stockholm and with Captain Eliassen and Docent Hoel I attended the funeral services of the three balloonists. In the spring of 1932 the Swedish Anthropological and Geographical Society conferred on me their Andrée Plaque.

With the return of the reconnoitering parties to the *Veslekari*, the scholars so pampered aboard the vessel now were to face a more rugged test of mettle. A land-based sojourn of three or four weeks was planned. The party would proceed across Fraenkel Land, periodically moving campsites forward as work progressed toward Jaette Glacier.

This would be no minor excursion. Elaborate preparations were required for the extended journey on foot across trackless stretches of rock-ribbed mountains, boulder-filled terraces, slippery glaciers, and icy streams. To transport all their gear and scientific equipment from the ship to the base camps and from one camp to the next, the party would have to carry everything on their backs. No native porters, pack animals, or vehicles were available in this uninhabited world, no trails to follow, no friendly villagers, no sources of food along the way, not even sledges and dogs. "The problem would not be so difficult in regions like Africa or Asia where labor is cheap and plentiful or in other regions where base camps can be reached by automobile or pack animal," wrote one of the scientists in the Boyd party, "but in our case we were dependent on the goodwill of the Norwegian crew of the *Veslekari*. We were indeed fortunate in that they were amiably disposed and worked their hearts out for the success of the expedition." Louise heartily agreed with this appraisal of the faithful crew.

Staggering under heavy loads, the party set forth on August 10, 1933, along the western side of Gregory Valley. Scrambling over rocky footing, they ascended along the banks of a large stream and established Camp One overlooking the stream's deep gorge. At 1991 feet and with plenty of good firewood from convenient dead willows, the camp was comfortable enough.

But the next camp, four and a half miles west of Camp One, and several hundred feet higher, was chilly by day and cold at night. A high mountain wall shut off the sun most of the day and there was no firewood. Cooking was done with petrol on Primus stoves. In Louise's photograph of this camp, one sees five frail tents, tiny dots on a barren terrace strewn with immense avalanche boulders, standing against a looming rock wall — a lifeless moonscape. The nearby stream froze at night but rose several feet each afternoon from sun melt at the valley head.

The third camp, set up on August 14 in an arid valley at 2476 feet, overlooked dry stream beds where autumn colors blazed: "bilberry, which resembles our blueberry and is delicious to eat, and the crowberry with its dark green foliage. Particularly brilliant were the fiery reds of the bearberry and the reds and yellow of the dwarf birch." Quantities of old, bleached reindeer horns lay on the valley floor. Nathorst was the last explorer to find live reindeer in this part of Greenland, and he attributed their disappearance in part to their having been killed by wolves.

Long, exhausting days in not always kindly weather brought the tired workers back to their tents late and ready to drop on their cots. Work often continued far into the evening because of the long daylight hours. Louise's photographs include many taken by the midnight light. On the day she climbed to Mystery Lakes with the surveyors to photograph, everything went wrong. A strong sand-filled wind battered her valuable cameras. "Regardless of all possible care, lenses and the innermost parts of the cameras fell victim." She was horrified when "even though the tripod was well braced with stones" her large camera was suddenly hurled by the wind down a bank and was damaged enough to require repairs back at camp. Her presence was essential until the surveyors' task was completed, however. "Not until late in the evening did I leave Mystery Lakes," she wrote. "A strong wind was blowing, drizzling rain with sleet was falling, and camp was eight or ten miles away."

In this vast emptiness, Louise was particularly impressed not by the silence but by the sounds. What appeared at first glance to be a lifeless landscape was in fact something very different to a person living in its midst. "Inanimate nature seemed almost alive in these valleys," Louise wrote.

Changes were continually taking place in the topography; rocks, large and small, single and in groups, constantly ripped down the steep mountain sides, forming deep troughs and rolling out on the valley floor. On the south wall, ice calved off from hanging glaciers thousands of feet above us and spilled fresh white substance over the varicolored rocks. . . .

Icebergs provide the chief source of noise in what Stefansson [leader of the famous Canadian Arctic Expedition of 1913–1918] calls the "misnamed Silent North!" You hear the trickle of small rivulets on the larger bergs, and the drip-drip of water splashing from their sides. The smaller ice formed from the calving of bergs makes a crackling sound in warm weather. Occasionally there is a swish against the shore of waves produced by the overturning and breaking up of some ponderous mass. Loudest of all, like the sound of cannonading, is the boom of a berg as it splits off from the parent glacier or the crash of bursting ice as a mighty berg collapses. These extraordinary sounds echo and reecho through the fiords.

To witness the moment of calving is a rare and coveted privilege for a scientist. One of the earliest such reports came from explorers encamped near the huge Storstrømmen Glacier, inland from Danmark Harbor, on September 20, 1912. A mammoth portion of the front unexpectedly split off, "producing a dozen icebergs and nearly carrying away the explorers and their stores."

Louise had the luck to view a calving on July 30, 1933, when the nearby Jaette Glacier suddenly split while she was working on a rocky cliff in Miss Boyd Land. The spectacle was unforgettable: "The resulting waves tossed our rowboat so high and so violently that only expert seamanship on the part of our second mate saved it from being dashed to pieces against the rocks. Waves and broken ice came up fully five or six feet on the cliff where we stood. There was no warning. Ice from the face of the glacier broke and with a booming sound disappeared under the surface of the water, to come up again many feet from where it had gone under. A succession of big waves was produced, with which were intermingled quantities of debris ice." Members of the crew left a wooden barrel safely above high water level elsewhere, only later to find the barrel in the fiord, its contents spoiled, the "victim of waves from a calving berg, or possibly from the capsizing of a large berg nearby."

Seeing a large berg capsize could be equally thrilling. Professor Bretz, the expedition's physical geographer, described one such episode: "The capsizing of a large berg near at hand is a spectacle, and an auditory experience, difficult to equal. Sharp reports of the preliminary riving are like greatly amplified rifle shots or the tearing crash of nearby thunder. The roar when the berg yields is a combination of more rivings, or crashings from ice falling on ice, and of the smiting of water by the falling ice. Splashing and fountaining are immediately added to the action and then comes cascading as submerged portions come up and tons of sea water flow off and fall back into the fiord. This is repeated in diminuendo as the berg rocks back and forth for some minutes."

One huge berg "turned turtle" while they were at the head of Franz Josef Fiord, presenting at rest an "almost half-egg shape, the water-melted bottom to the air." For twenty-four hours, Bretz said, the new top reflected "dazzlingly, like polished metal; after which it took on a matte surface." Waves from the capsizing berg were so long from trough to trough the *Veslekari* standing broadside rode with little swaying. Ricocheting about in the fiords, this turbulence whips up its own aftermath. "Spreading of these waves through the fiord induces other berg capsizings and collapses; and the water, previously only dotted with well-spaced bergs, may in half an hour be full of small floating ice. Impinging on shores, these waves are as effective as oceanic swells. We saw ice that had been tossed six meters back of the high-tide line. For hours after the tumult has died down, the fiord crackles like a fire in heavy, dry grass as the millions of compressed air bubbles continue to burst in the newly fractured surface of the comminuted ice."

The sheer fragility of the fiords' mammoth bergs astonished Louise. "So majestic in height and size," giving an impression of "permanence and everlasting durability," they could vanish like a wraith. "A booming sound — and an instant later what had seemed so indestructible is an unrecognizable mass of broken ice. The still waters and the reflections are gone, effaced by waves from the overturning and shattering of an icy giant. The power and movement of the ice are indescribable!"

Deeply involved in these extravaganzas of nature and in their investigations, the scientists and Louise were hardly ready for the unequivocal prophecies of oncoming winter that spelled an end to their stay. Finishing their work in Gregory Valley on August 23, they were aware the wintry face of the weather ordered an "imperative departure." Weeks of moderate to fine weather were swept aside by thick fog and heavy clouds that blanketed the mountaintops. "Shadows cast by the mountains on the fog layers were so inky blue, they looked almost artificial," Louise wrote.

The *Veslekari* retreated along the high-walled passage with occasional stops for observations and by September 3 had reached Geologist Fiord, headed by the large Nunatak Glacier. Here, edging toward shore at only a few knots to allow the scientists a brief landing before heading seaward, the ship ran aground. Good echo soundings had been taken the afternoon before, showing one hundred fathoms of water, so the sonic depth-measuring sounder, which would have warned of shallow water, was apparently not operating.

Captain Olsen quickly reversed the engines and threw all the ship's power into an attempt to back off. But the vessel could not be dislodged. All other standard procedures for helping a foundering vessel were attempted. But the *Veslekari* had run aground at high tide and the fiord bottom was composed of a sticky sediment that allowed the vessel to settle.

Always ready to dash to the rescue of other stranded ships, the *Veslekari* was now herself in grave need of help. The grim thought that stalked the decks, from crew to leader, was knowledge that this expedition was entirely alone on the empty, soon-to-be-frigid

East Greenland coast. The expedition had lingered later in the fiords than any other that season. If not released soon, the party could face the ordeal of ice entrapment through the Arctic winter.

While certain members of the expedition are reported to have been extremely nervous, Louise herself remained calm. But she was soberly aware of the implications of their situation. "To our best information all other ships had now left the East Coast of Greenland," she wrote, "or at least all those that had been north of Scoresby Sound." (Scoresby Sound itself was miles to the south, not within rescue range at this late date.) "Hence we were obliged to rely solely on our own resources to get afloat. Nor was this a simple matter. The tide went out and the ship settled a little more, although fortunately she maintained an upright position." Listing would be especially dangerous, adding to the difficulty of dragging the ship off the bottom. Herculean measures had to be taken to buoy the ship. "By the removal of 30 tons of sea-water ballast, 2 motor boats, 1 rowboat, 3½ tons of fuel oil, and 17 barrels of petrol she was lightened, and we hoped that the incoming tide would free her."

But the tide "came and went" and the *Veslekari* held fast. "Coal was next taken out. As we had no way of saving it, 15 tons were thrown overboard to waste. The ship had now been lightened 54½ tons." This was still not sufficient. Next, the ingenious Captain Olsen devised a means of utilizing an iceberg of modest size floating conveniently nearby. "About 720 feet away there happened to be an iceberg, some 20 feet long, 19 feet wide, and 6 feet high," Louise recorded. A cable was thrown around this berg and connected to the ship's winch. "The motor dory shoved the berg as the winch pulled on the cable, and the iceberg was grounded in a desired position aft of us. Fortunately for us, the next tide was the spring tide, and at high water (11:30 A.M.) on September 4, with the engines full speed astern and the winch pulling on the cable connected with the iceberg, the ship was floated undamaged. Here was a case when an iceberg was a friend."

Amid rejoicing, the petrol barrels and boats were retrieved and they got under way immediately, grateful that sufficient coal remained for the homeward journey. Characteristically, the scientists, missing no opportunity to note every interesting phenomenon, observed with interest that mud stirred up by the propeller in reverse created a putrid odor that permeated the entire ship. This indicated the presence of abundant marine organisms that closely follow the retreat of fiord glaciers. Glacial retreat was a focus of much study throughout the voyage.

Gales twice forced them back from Myggbukta as they attempted to set out from the coast, one gale bringing blinding snow and fifty-five-mile-an-hour winds. They had indeed overstayed their visit. "Nature was closing her doors on us! We had arrived in early July when the last winter's ice was still blocking the entrance to the fiords and on shore spring flowers were in full bloom! Now the snow of the coming winter had appeared. Extending from summit to sea level, as far as one could see, Greenland was white. Overhead were foehn clouds and northern lights, not in their real glory, but sufficiently to show that we had passed from one season into another — from a season of perpetual sunshine into one of darkness. Nature's warning to us was: 'Go Home!'"

In spite of the general eagerness to obey this "warning," the second departure from Myggbukta had to be delayed a day because the superstitious Norwegian sailors would not sail on a Friday. Despite good weather, the party waited over, calling this lost time "Superstition Day." On September 9 they departed Greenland from Mackenzie Bay, leaving Greenland decked in its "wintry mantle," and docked in Aalesund on September 16, ending a voyage of eighty days, of which sixty were spent in East Greenland.

Scientific results were encapsulated in the handsome book *The Fiord Region of East Greenland*, published by the American Geographical Society, co-authored by Louise with the five scientists and illustrated with 350 of her excellent black-and-white photographs selected from thousands taken on both the 1931 and 1933 trips. Several useful maps were also developed: three large-scale maps of photogrammetrical surveys of Louise Glacier in Miss Boyd Land, Arch Glacier, and Moraineless Glacier in Gregory Valley; a map of the hitherto unexplored Gregory Valley itself; echo-sounding maps reflecting the profile of the floor of Franz Josef Fiord; and a bathymetric map of the floor of the Greenland Sea as traversed by the *Veslekari* from Norway to East Greenland.

Dr. Isaiah Bowman was now instrumental in having Louise appointed a delegate to the International Geographical Congress in Warsaw in August 1934, representing both the U.S. government and the American Geographical Society. Ever ready to organize a tour, Louise put together a series of small groups to accompany her on a drive, before the congress opened, through the Polish corridor, the Danzig Free State, and East Prussia. She invited Dr. Bowman as her mentor and companion, and various Polish geographers as guests on different phases of the trip according to their regional expertise. In the deep hinterlands they passed very old towns and ancient farms. On one deeply rutted dirt "highway," Louise counted in less than an hour five hundred horse-drawn wagons, twenty-five pedestrians, and a bicycle; the horses were frightened by her car. This trip resulted in Louise's writing another book published by the American Geographical Society, *Polish Countrysides*, luxuriously illustrated with nearly five hundred of her black-and-white photographs of every aspect of Polish rural life.

But for Louise Poland was merely a pleasant morsel, consumed but soon forgotten in her voracious appetite for the northern latitudes. She now aspired to progress northward from King Oscar and Franz Josef fiords as far up the East Greenland coast as weather and ice would allow.

For her 1937 expedition, Louise once more boarded the *Veslekari*, with Captain Olsen in command and Captain Eliassen as assistant, and an all-Norwegian crew. The scientific staff included two paleogeologists, Dr. Richard Foster Flint and Dr. A. Lincoln Washburn; a surveyor, F. W. Buhler, who would focus on planetable techniques; and for the first time a hydrographer, James M. LeRoy, who would conduct the echo-sounding program, make studies of currents, monitor the tide gauge recordings, and carry on magnetic observations. The depth sounding of the 1933 expedition had been of such value Louise had decided to stress this work on any subsequent expeditions. A botanist, Dr. Henry J. Oosting, was included to examine plant communities that might reflect the effects of shrinking glaciers — an extension of the earlier study of glacial recession. An expert radio operator, Severre S. Remoy, was also along.

Before they even got under way, trouble with the sonic depth-

Women Here Are Preparing For Voyages of Exploration

Miss Louise Boyd   Times Wide World Photo.

*Miss Louise Boyd Will Head Expedition to
Arctic—Mrs. James L. Clark Packing
for Hunting Trip to the Congo*

*Louise Boyd on the eve of her 1937
East Greenland expedition, as pictured in a* New York Times *article
about women explorers*

finder made Louise decide to buy a new one. Again the trial run off
the Lofoten and Vesteraalen islands brought a dramatic surprise.
This time readings suddenly rose from normal depths for the ocean
floor at this point to a sharply more shallow depth, a significant
change in the profile of the sea bottom, revealing the existence of
an unknown and unrecorded ocean bank. This exciting discovery
would be further studied on Louise's 1938 expedition when it was
established that the 1937 point was a westernmost peak of the
bank, while soundings in 1938 disclosed a northwestern peak.
Lying between Bear Island and Jan Mayen Island, the bank came to
be named Louise A. Boyd Bank, a name that is retained today.

The violent gale that swept the decks and flooded the galley before they had reached Jan Mayen was prophetic. They left Jan Mayen Island threatened by new storms, facing Greenland with two questions in mind: When and where would they encounter ice? Would it be a good season or a bad? — questions haunting all mariners in these waters.

The amount and location of ice controlled every voyage along the East Greenland shores: new winter ice formed along the coast the previous season, icebergs drifting out of the fiords from the calving glaciers, and pack ice moving down from the Arctic ice cap. History abounds in tales of ships destroyed by ice in attempts to reach this coast. Most crushing are the immense floes of heavy pack ice from the far north, tabular slabs breaking from the frozen Arctic Ocean, which may be 165 feet thick and up to 435 square miles in area, larger than some Caribbean islands. Polar ice may be many years old, floating intact in these huge blocks for as long as thirty years before disintegrating. Drifting icebergs in the north Atlantic Ocean sank the S.S. *Titanic* south of Newfoundland on her maiden voyage of April 15, 1912, with a loss of over fifteen hundred lives, and in January 1959 the Danish *Hans Hedtoft* off south Greenland on her maiden trip with a loss of everyone aboard.

The *Veslekari* encountered ice at 73°53′ north latitude, 12°42′ west longitude on July 12, 1937, opposite Clavering Island in Gael Hamke Bay, considerably north of the Franz Josef–King Oscar fiord area. The presence of such a large and compact ice pack at such an early date so far south was an ominous sign to the veterans of the *Veslekari* crew.

The ice pack extended so far out into open waters that they traveled three days from the outer edge before they sighted land, and they didn't actually reach the Clavering coast until fourteen days later, a tortuous two weeks of inching through heavy ice fields, most of the time in fog and rain. "A tantalizing game of ice-pack tag," Louise called it, "a sort of hide-and-seek with the coast. Some days we were much nearer land than others, since we moved the ship whenever possible to what seemed to be a better position, even though it might for a time take us away from the coast instead of toward it. In one 30-hour period we drifted 15 miles southwestward." The engines worked at half speed, often less; and there were days "when we spent a good part of the time anchored to large ice fields."

The crew worked as hard as the engines, using heavy anchors to help push and pull. Imbedded in the ice, the flukes widened impossibly narrow lanes through which *Veslekari* forged, bumping and thrusting the ice aside — punishing work for the hull. But by brute force, threading their way through the leads opened, they at last arrived at Cape Mary on Clavering Island. Coming ashore in the motor dories, they found along the coast twenty-five-foot ice floes, tall as a two-story house.

Louise rather enjoyed the whole experience. It gave her a sense of what it might be like at the North Pole. "The ice, on our long struggle through it, was at all times fascinating and often beautiful," she wrote. "It gave one a good impression of what the true Far North is like and dispelled any idea that northeast Greenland is in all years easy of access. Hummocks on some of the floes were 12 to 15 feet high and occasionally were almost level with our motor dories on the davits. Some days rain made surface slush on the ice fields. We saw only one tabular iceberg [huge flat bergs like floating islands] on July 24 three miles off Cape Borlase Warren. Captain Olsen estimated it to be some 60 feet high and submerged to a depth of approximately 27 fathoms (162 feet). During our battle with the ice we had the company of polar bears, seals, and Fulmer petrels and as we neared the land a lone walrus was seen on one of the floes."

The *Veslekari* was the first ship of the year to get through to this coast, so it was joyfully welcomed by members of a French expedition hunkered ashore in a large, solitary, unpainted cabin, otherwise used in winter by Danish fox hunters. Led by Count Gaston Micard, the party had wintered aboard their ship, the *Quest*, anchored in Loch Fyne thirty-five miles to the west, and now in shore quarters, "were anxiously waiting for the ice to open and let them be on their way home."

After so much delay and confinement aboard ship, the scientists quickly set to work when they anchored at the head of Tyroler Fiord inland from Clavering Island. Louise was now working closely with the surveyor, he with his plane table and she with cameras, spending hour after hour developing data for mapping.

The work was tedious and tiring because of meticulous care needed to photograph the minute detail required for data to be used in developing large-scale maps. But getting to the sites was harder yet — a foot trip over a veritable obstacle course. Louise realized belatedly she should not have used the ship as a base but should have set up camp ashore.

Our days were long and more often than not we worked far from the ship. I regretted, when it was too late, that we had not set up camp for the party at the upper end of the valley; as it was, we had to spend a good deal of precious time getting to and from the ship.

Each morning the trip to the field involved wading ashore from the rowboats, tramping across the gravel delta, fording the numerous streams, often over the boot tops, and, finally, the time-consuming task of getting up into the high terminal moraines over loose rocks and stones. The going was made still more difficult in many places by slippery ice close beneath the surface. The return was a repetition of all this in reverse.

The men portaging the photographic and surveying equipment got the worst of it, trudging an hour and a half to two hours both ways with the heavy loads. And the final nuisance for everyone was changing boots each time they forded the knee-deep streams, from hip boots to hobnails, and later back to hip boots again. When photographing, Louise maintained a constant guard against a possible attack by a rogue musk ox. These Arctic ruminants grazed along the verdant edges of the coast. "It is perhaps worth warning prospective photographers in East Greenland of the menace of lone musk ox bulls in certain localities," Louise later advised. "When in herds or even in small groups, musk oxen usually avoid human beings, but a lone bull is apt to react differently." Several times she was ready to photograph when "over a hill would appear one of these wanderers. Seeing me and my crew he would charge upon us in a series of full-speed rushes, punctuated by halts during which he tore into the ground with horns and hoofs." Once they had to shoot the charging animal. (His stuffed head was later mounted for her Maple Lawn studio. "We got it before he got me,"

*Louise examines a curious hut of lumber and turf insulated inside
and out with musk-ox skins, used by hunters on winter rounds
of fox traps.*

Louise would tell visitors.) Usually, however, a gunshot in the air
drove the animal away, although "one day we had some unpleasant moments when our only rifle jammed." All ended well, but
thereafter she arranged for two rifles always to be brought along.

Her observant and practical eye noted that wherever musk ox
herds were found, as in Tyroler Fiord, their wool had "rubbed off
on banks, boulders, and low stands of birch and willow." On one
of her early expeditions, she had begun gathering the soft stuff shed
during the summer months and when she had enough had had two
mufflers handwoven by the Norwegian Home Industries in Aalesund. Subsequently she added more mufflers, a sweater, and a dress
and jacket. She was surprised to find "no evidence that the Danish
and Norwegian hunters or other visitors to Greenland gathered
[musk ox] wool; even when I told the hunters of its merits they
seemed to feel it was not worth bothering with."

Returning to the vessel one day, the party was astonished to
behold a strange motorboat in the fiord, like an apparition in such

a vacant landscape. It had been dispatched from the *Polarbjørn*. The Norwegian expedition was in trouble again: it had been stuck "fast aground" for three days on the north side of Young Sound, seaward toward Clavering Island, and all efforts to dislodge it had failed. Unable to contact the *Veslekari* by radio, the *Polarbjørn* dispatched one of the crew to get help.

Abandoning plans for further work in the area, Louise's party prepared for immediate departure and once more were speeding to the rescue of the *Polarbjørn*. Eight hours' effort went into pulling the ship free. Anchoring afterward off Sandodden on Young Sound, the *Veslekari* was engulfed by fog, and by the next day other portents indicated that any hope of an extended northward thrust along the coast must be forgone. Now they would be satisfied if they could manage some scientific investigations in Franz Josef Fiord.

As the party snaked their way southward along the outer coast, heavy, compacted ice held them three miles from shore. But they entered Franz Josef Fiord at last, to be greeted by at least thirty large icebergs in the mouth, and surrounding mountains covered with far heavier snow than in 1933. Excited as ever to return to the spectacular beauty of the 120-mile waterway, Louise yet had to acknowledge that adverse weather was threatening to rob them of working time.

Landing at the base of the 410-foot Nordenskiøld Glacier, they could see it had been actively calving, filling the fiord with icy debris. In 1931 at this same spot, the thermometer stood at over eighty degrees, a brilliant sun shone, grass was a foot and a half high, flowers blossomed, and gulls and ravens flew overhead. And the party had gone swimming. "Though surrounded by icebergs, glaciers, and the distant fringe of the ice cap, and though the water was bitterly cold, we had a most enjoyable dip in the fiord," Louise had recorded then. Now they sensed they could count on only a few more days for productive research.

Camping four days at Kjerulf Fiord's head, Louise photographed the entire Agassiz Valley with her Fairchild Aero K 6 camera. But snow was falling as they broke camp, and the next two days they sat at anchor in the storm. Then they made for the Danish wireless station at Solitaer Bay on Ella Island, at the time the only wireless

Louise Boyd's expedition staff always included a team of men to portage her various pieces of photographic equipment, including this Fairchild Aero K 6 camera. It was the first time this camera had ever been used for ground work.

station in the Franz Josef–King Oscar fiord region (and one of only three on the entire coast north of Scoresby Sound). Radishes and rhubarb still flourished in the station's small garden of hardy vegetables, an essential at these outposts "with supplies coming to the station but once a year and with even this annual visit sometimes prevented by the offshore ice."

Other landings were hampered by low-hanging clouds and fog which prevented the scientists from doing "anything constructive," while the relentlessly hostile weather cut visibility for photographing.

Meanwhile, Captain Olsen was daily becoming "more apprehensive." Continued bad weather and the drifting of pack ice so far into the fiords indicated that winter was setting in extremely early. But even the experienced Olsen had no idea the season was closing in as fast as was actually the case.

At last, however, he called it quits. "On August 23 he ordered us

273

to finish our work in King Oscar Fiord that day, as he was anxious to get out to the coast and see for himself what was happening. Nor was this last day, a fine one with the weather suddenly clearing, calculated to give us any inkling of the long, hard battle ahead of us."

By 6:30 P.M. all were on board and ready to leave. The captain chose the inland route to the sea, which meant circling to the north end of King Oscar Fiord and from there by way of the Antarctic Sound and Franz Josef Fiord to Foster Bay and the open waters. But when they entered Franz Josef Fiord, far inland from its mouth, they beheld a seeming infinity of ice. "Drifting ice over the whole of Franz Josef Fiord as far west as North Fiord and the size of the floes" heralded "difficulties ahead," probably with solid ice floes down to the sea, Louise recorded.

They had no choice but to push forward. "Although by 2:00 the next morning we had reached the outer end of the fiord at Foster Bay, we had had to make our way through thick, tight ice near Cape Franklin. Ten hours later we were no more than three miles southeast of the cape. As far as Captain Olsen could see from the crow's nest, north to Hold-with-Hope and south as far as Traill Island, heavy polar ice fields and floes blocked the coast."

Down the fiord at the Myggbukta coastal wireless station, the friendly men climbed to higher ground and made a visual survey of ice conditions out at sea for the *Veslekari* but reported back by wireless that no open water could be sighted anywhere. "Heavy polar ice had come south and moving in to the coast, had closed it to navigation for miles."

The *Veslekari* continued to force its way wherever it could. "The ship moved whenever there was the slightest opening, but all such moves were in vain, and finally at 10:00 P.M., our worst fears were realized. The ship was 'pinched' and tipped several degrees on her side."

The crew now resorted to dynamite to repel the entrapping ice. They attached about two kilograms of dynamite to a pole and poked the charge into small crevasses under the ice near the ship — but not too near; care had to be taken not to blow a hole in the side of the ship. The resulting series of explosions allowed the vessel at last to right itself undamaged.

By morning the ice had slackened enough so they could push northward toward Cape Bennett, but two hours later they were again blocked by large ice floes that reached to the coast. Now they were truly stymied. They could not reach open water by going forward, nor could they reenter Franz Josef Fiord. The passage they had come through so few hours before was now completely closed, and they faced the crucial question: Would the ice change and could they afford to wait on the chance that it might do so?

Waiting was too risky, they decided. They had only one option: to enter Sona Sound if possible and from there King Oscar Fiord, and then go south to the sea. The route was backward and required some retracing but, lying farther inland, might be freer of pack ice. "It would be well over a hundred miles out of our way," Louise said bravely, "but we had ample coal and there was no fear that the anticipated battle with the ice would cut our supply dangerously short."

At 10:00 A.M. on August 26 they started their hundred-mile detour through the west end of Foster Bay, for twelve hours plowing relentlessly through heavy floes. By nine that evening they struck open water off Cape Humbolt and could enter Sona Sound, which was relatively free of dangerous ice. But approaching King Oscar Fiord was "quite a different matter." Ice blocked the way once more. "From Ella Island southward heavy ice had come into the fiord and there were no open leads through which we could move. But we had to keep moving. Ours had come to be a struggle against time. Not only was there a possibility that ice might close in so tightly that we would be unable to get out that season, but there was even greater danger that the ship might be beset in the heavy ice and crushed."

The whole party pitched in to keep the vessel in motion and worked frenziedly throughout the night. "All hands, including the special assistants, willingly and cheerfully manned the ice anchors, leaping from floe to floe with the heavy equipment and hammering into the ice the anchors by which the ship got leverage for pulling and shoving. Many of the floes were as high as the *Veslekari*'s bow, 15 feet above the sea." Captain Olsen commanded the hazardous operations from his crow's nest, directing the men on the floating ice. The crew's galley stayed open all night, serving hot coffee and food. Men grabbed a bite when they could with no thought of regular meals.

The drama of that night was etched forever in Louise's memory. "No bunks were occupied that night, and some of the members of the expedition staff, including myself, were on deck all night. We had one brief respite when we found a small lead between the ice and the shore at Antarctic Harbor, but we were soon in heavy ice again, and our progress next day, August 28, was no less difficult than it had been the day before. That we were able to fill our drinking water tank, a three-hour task, from one large floe, indicates how slowly we moved in spite of our best efforts."

Snow and fog rolled in to make things even worse next day, but late in the afternoon as they inched forward they could detect that floes were diminishing in size. By midnight they emerged from the icebound nightmare of the past days into the open waters of the Greenland Sea. Their detour from start to open water, found at 71° 40′ north latitude, 20°21′ west longitude, between Cape Biot and Cape Simpson, was 120 miles. Not that all the ice had disappeared; as they emerged from King Oscar Fiord, heavy pack ice "blocked up against the shore" and extended for some thirty-five miles out to sea. But friendly open water gleamed between the floes, and the *Veslekari* could move normally once more. From midnight until two the next morning, the ship ran southeast simply to distance itself from the frozen pack, then set a course for Spitsbergen.

Relief surges through Louise's restrained comment on this moment of salvation: "The coast with its gripping polar ice was behind us . . . We got out although there were certainly long hours when it was doubtful if we should; but others at Clavering Island that summer did not get out, and no ship was able to get through to them until the following mid-summer." The *Veslekari* escaped such a harrowing ordeal, or worse, because of the "great skill of Captain Olsen" and his crew, and because of the *Veslekari*'s sturdy construction, she said.

"Records show that the ice fields of the Greenland coast have taken their toll," she wrote. And indeed considerably south of where the *Veslekari* finally wrested itself free lies the "ill-famed Liverpool coast," scene of many disasters. One of the most terrible occurred in 1777, when nearly fifty English and Dutch ships were sunk by ice, killing more than four hundred men — the greatest catastrophe in the history of the Arctic.

Moored safely in the home port of Aalesund, Captains Olsen and Eliassen assured Louise the 1937 voyage had been their "most difficult ice job" ever. Yet despite a short season and rapid or aborted reconnaissance work, science had been served and much accomplished. Dr. R. F. Flint's study of glacial geology and geomorphology was reviewed as an "eminent contribution to Arctic glaciology." Discovery of the Louise Boyd Bank was significant, and thousands of photographs were added to the Greenland archive Louise was building.

Not only was Louise ready to return to East Greenland after her 1937 escapade, but she was still determined to make a thrust through the ice belt as far north as she could land — the plan that bad weather had forced her to give up in 1937. By the next year she was all set to start out again. Same captain, same ship, same crew, but a smaller staff of scientists.

Louise had by now developed an authoritative catalogue of what a well-equipped Arctic expedition should carry along. Her diary for each expedition had listed "suggested additions to the equipment" that included not only major pieces such as the echo-sounding equipment or new radio outfit but small, practical, home-spun items of a particularly feminine cast. She always had with her inch-wide adhesive tape, "important not only for mending clothes, but for anchoring small objects, such as ink bottles, against rough weather." Safety pins, strong thread and needles, and an assortment of buttons were scarcely less important, while "a supply of unbleached cotton goods also has many uses," she said. Her medicine chest was equally homey, well stocked with standard remedies and first-aid items, of course ("including liniment for stiff muscles"), but with her own version of homeopathic aids. "I carry a supply of cayenne pepper. Taken in a glass of very hot water, it is an old remedy against chills or colds, recommended to me years ago by my family doctor, which has proved efficacious many times when members of the crew or staff came in soaked and shivering." (And, one can imagine, woe to the member of her party who resisted her administration of this fiery potion!)

There is ample testimony that Louise was clearly the boss on her expeditions. Not only did she hold the purse strings, but her systematic attention to detail, and her passion for converting her expeditions into serious instruments for contributing to knowledge of the polar regions, elevated her from the initial role of wealthy socialite indulging in an expensive hobby. She became a true leader, a presiding patron of scientifically trained personnel, a sponsor of science. While not pretending to be a scientist herself, and no more than an amateur writer, she was completely professional about her photography and her botanical efforts and about her responsibilities as an expedition leader.

While her lack of scientific background may have been denigrated by some of her staff, no one thought they could fool her; or they were "doomed to fail" if they did, one of the staff remarked. A glimpse of their respect is gained from a tale concerning the time she sent two of her scientists inland to examine a specific area. Competent men from reputable institutions, they nonetheless found this particular trek quite tiresome and turned back before reaching their goal, nevertheless reporting mission accomplished on their return. Imagine their dismay when Louise elected to make the same trip! There in the snow were their tracks to betray them. When they saw her returning to the ship, they reportedly said, "This is where we had better duck." For whatever reason, they were not along on her next expedition.

Once Louise recognized the potentials of photography for recording the unrecorded Arctic, she apprenticed herself to a good teacher. She also grasped that the job of photographer gave her a genuinely useful role as one of the working team. She designed her own light-proof bag of shutter cloth covered with black satinet, to which was attached short elastic-trimmed sleeves for changing film away from the ship — "a useful and practical darkroom in the field," she called it. She grew savvy about infrared film for shooting clouds, glaciers, and long-distance views over pack ice, yet decided that on the ground, infrared does not "give the results in the polar regions that it does farther south." Panchromatic film used with a red filter gave her "consistently better results," she said. Fiercely protective of her cameras and film, she worried about wind and dust and faithfully cleaned with a camel's-hair brush after every use of her precious tools. "At the end of each day on shore, no matter how tired I might be, I never called it a day until I had thoroughly cleaned all photographic equipment used that day and packed all exposed film, even though the task might take me well into the early hours of the next morning."

Equally earnest about her botanical efforts she matured into a collector of no mean stature. On her first expedition to Franz Josef Land, she plucked every growing thing she "could lay her hands on," and later discovered that almost anything from this remote part of the globe might be of interest to a trained botanist. A competent gardener and plant lover, she "knew enough to take each specimen from its roots to its tip and to record briefly the ecological conditions under which the plant grew." She was less sophisticated about methods of getting the specimen back home. For pressing and preserving, she had nothing better aboard on her first expeditions than the leaves of a book. But these "amateur efforts" paid off when a California botanist found that "one or more varieties had not been previously reported."

With future expeditions in mind, Louise sought out a botanist with the California Academy of Sciences, Alice Eastwood, for instruction in proper collecting and preserving methods, in correct equipment, and in handling in the field and on shipboard. She began also experimenting with collection devices and discarded as "inadequate" for polar work the standard metal plant container in general use in the U.S. It was not large enough to hold a full day's collection of specimen in the field, and "where time was so limited it was difficult to pack specimens in the vasculum [collecting case] with sufficient care to protect them until our return to the ship at the end of a long day ashore."

Standard wooden presses in which plants are stored between corrugated and blotting paper did not hold enough and were too heavy for portaging, so she also discarded these and developed her own system. "As with all branches of field work in the Arctic, methods must be adapted to meet peculiar requirements," she declared in explaining her practical adjustments.

For quantity collecting under the conditions in which we worked on these expeditions, the equipment that proved by far

279

the most practical and efficient was the standard frame rucksack. These bags were roomy, light in weight, and easily carried. Ordinary silk bandanas or squares of unbleached cotton cloth replaced the usual collecting papers in our equipment. Specimens were carefully packed in the squares, together with a sheet of tablet paper on which was noted the location, conditions of growth, data and hour of collecting — a record which corresponded to that in the key collecting book carried in my pocket. The bandanas were then tied by their four corners and placed in the rucksack; when the rucksacks were full, we tied bandanas to our belts. This method of collecting was entirely successful, and the specimens remained in perfect condition throughout the longest days on shore.

She also abandoned the old-fashioned preserving by pressing. Instead, "for drying plants, the pressing cases were suspended in the dry air of the engine room," spaces for the cases having been "planned for and arranged prior to sailing from Norway" — as might be expected from one so methodical.

Just as the radiant hues of the fiords dispelled the popular notion of a colorless wasteland, so did the flora of vivid palette in East Greenland, at least along the coastal areas. Here, Louise said, "nature has created . . . rock gardens that have a beauty almost beyond description — masses of brilliantly colored blooms in exquisite arrangement." She was intrigued by the degree to which growth rates varied from one summer to the next, affected by variations in snowfall, as well as by how different familiar flowers of the United States look in the Arctic. "In the higher latitudes they grow in miniature stands, display more intense color, and often have unusually large individual blossoms." For her, the "most characteristic flower of Greenland" because of its wide distribution along the eastern coast was the "vivid Epilobium," a willow-herb of the evening primrose family.

By the time of the 1938 expedition, Louise had collected botanical specimens "by force of habit" on so many previous voyages, she decided to dispense with a botanist and to continue the work herself.

The 1938 expedition put in as usual at Jan Mayen Island, the last landfall in the Greenland Sea from Tromsø, Norway, before the Greenland coast. Its weather is almost always hostile. This time the *Veslekari* had to ride a hard gale at anchor for two days in the island's lee while wind blew "at full storm force off the island, bringing with it so much silt that the ship was covered with fine, dark mud. The portholes were so coated that we could not see through them, and the silt penetrated everywhere, not sparing the camera room or even the well-cased cameras." After a cleanup from this strange mud bath, they ran up to Spitsbergen to observe pack ice, and then on July 21 started for the Greenland coast.

A landing was made at Bass Rock, just off Little Pendulum Island along the Greenland coast, where the party found two wooden cabins built in 1901 and stocked by the *Belgica* with food, clothing, ammunition, and other necessities for the United States Baldwin-Ziegler Expedition then attempting to reach the North Pole from Franz Josef Land. The expedition did not return by this route but the depot helped save the lives of two Danish explorers, Mylius-Erichsen and a companion, who passed two long winters there before being rescued in the summer of 1912. Returning from a reconnoitering excursion, they found that their ship, the *Alabama,* had been crushed by ice and foundered, and the rest of their party had been rescued.

Finishing scientific observations in the area on July 31, the *Veslekari* began its experimental northward journey up the Greenland coast aiming for the northernmost landing that weather and ice would permit. Favored by good weather and a minimum of drifting ice, the ship traveled at full speed along the coast, passing in turn Shannon Island, Great Koldewey Island (where they landed for photographs), and then Germania Land. By this point they had already entered the outer reaches of the limited extent of Arctic traffic along this coast. "From the southern tip of Germania Land northward we were in waters only rarely open for ships," Louise recorded with satisfaction.

Gone, however, was the majestic scenery of the fiords. Here was monotonous Greenland, a flat and regular shoreline without bays or indentations, and beyond, according to Louise's photographs, a cold, steely sky over endless plains of ice. But the expedition was surely nearing the realm of eternal winter, moving ever nearer to

The 1938 expedition landed at the northeast end of Île de France.
Towering shore ice almost conceals the Veslekari's *masts.*

the Arctic ice cap. Skaer Fiord's 120-mile-wide entrance was "completely blocked" by ice, and between Cape Amelie and the west side of Île de France "heavy polar ice was packed solid and unbroken as far as we could see."

The small Île de France far up the Greenland coast was the jumping-off place, beyond which ships never traveled. The *Veslekari* ran along the island's south coast, then along the east coast, until at midnight heavy polar ice halted further movement at 77°48′ north latitude, just south of Cape Montpensier, the northernmost tip of Île de France. Now they were only about eight hundred miles from the North Pole, whose latitude is 90°, far, far up at the top of the map, and, indeed, nearly on top of the globe. But they aspired for even more.

"There we lay drifting in the ice through the night and early morning of August 3," Louise wrote of this delicious moment, "hoping that the ice would change so that we would be able to continue northward, but it was obvious next morning that we had gone as far north as we could go."

Relinquishing a more extreme push, they now considered landing, not easy since an ice rampart guarded the coast. The *Veslekari* anchored to a field of grounded ice that was frozen solidly to the shore and towered high as the ship's bow, fifteen feet above the water. A ladder had to be used to climb from the ship to the ice, then came a scramble to reach the shore by foot over the "rough surface" broken by more towering hummocks. Altogether a wet, cold, dangerous hike, where one could turn an ankle, break a leg, suffer a bruising fall, or disappear into a tidal crack. Ahead the shore itself loomed menacingly.

"Where the ice field butted against the shore we had to cross heaps of rock debris which had been pushed up by the ice. There was much melt water flowing from the ice cap that occupied practically the full length of the center of the island, with the result that we had also to flounder knee-deep through a wide strip of mud to get from the ice to dry land."

The party remained ashore for only a brief stay: Captain Olsen called them to the ship by four in the afternoon, fearing the southbound ice packs. During their few hours of observations in extremely clear weather, Louise photographed without stint, catching the dim outline of Franske Island far to the northwest and of the masts of the *Veslekari* barely surmounting the mountains of shore ice.

Good timing, at the very height of the Arctic summer, and good weather were the fortuitous combination that granted the expedition a notable breakthrough. The Île de France landing was a triumph.

The northerly penetration was of such moment that Louise sent a wireless dispatch to the *New York Times,* dated September 7, 1938, carrying the dateline: "Louise A. Boyd Arctic Expedition on the Steamship *Veslekari.*" The story ran on September 9, with a map of the expedition's route and a photograph of Louise swathed in a fur-lined parka. In a separate but accompanying comment, Dr. John K. Wright of the American Geographical Society, writing from New York, declared, "Miss Boyd may claim the credit of having gone farther north in a ship along the East Greenland shore than any other American and of having attained what is probably the second highest latitude ever reached by a vessel in these waters."

In her book *The Coast of Northeast Greenland,* Louise herself stressed the landing. "To the best of my knowledge, ours was at

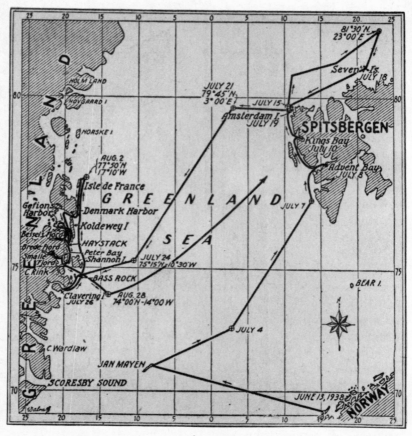

Louise Boyd's report of her Île de France landing on August 3, 1938, appeared in the New York Times *with this route map.*

that time the farthest north landing ever made from a ship on the east coast of Greenland. On July 30, 1905, the expedition led by the Duke of Orleans in the ship *Belgica*, which discovered Île de France, got as far north as latitude 78°16′ N, longitude 16°48′ W, or nearly 30 miles northeastward from Cape Montpensier, but was able to land only on the south coast of the island."

But Louise well knew that her success was partly a matter of luck. A day or two earlier, and "we might have had a good chance of getting still farther north than we did." A day or so later, and

284

they might not have made it at all. A Norwegian-French expedition in the *En Avant* attempted to go north from Danmark Harbor a few days after the returning *Veslekari* arrived there and was checked by ice off Germania Land, miles south of Louise's northernmost point.

Louise turned southward with no regrets. "All we could do this far north had been accomplished. I had spent profitable hours ashore with my camera at our one stop and had continued my photography from the deck of the ship going and returning, in order to get as full a record as possible of this seldom-visited coast."

The notion that any ship might travel farther north than this supposed end of the shipping trail was probably not entertained by any member of the Boyd expedition. But within Louise's lifetime, on August 3, 1958, a ship would cross the North Pole beneath the Arctic ice. This was the first atomic-powered submarine, the U.S.S. *Nautilus*, under Commander William R. Anderson. Then on August 16, 1977, the Soviet nuclear icebreaker *Arktika* reached the North Pole and became the first surface ship to break through the Arctic ice pack to the very top of the world.

Louise looked forward on her return to the United States to publication by the American Geographical Society of the scientific data and photographs amassed during the 1937 and 1938 expeditions. On her way home at the end of the 1938 expedition, she stored much of her equipment, as usual, in Aalesund, in anticipation of a future expedition.

But her plans were to be profoundly affected by the specter of World War II, which was already hanging over Europe even as she was starting the 1938 voyage. Hitler had annexed Austria in March of that year, and by May the United States had warily passed the Naval Expansion Act. In the swiftly succeeding events after the German attack on Poland in 1939, German forces by April 1940 were staging blitzkrieg attacks that conquered neutral Denmark, Norway, and the Low Countries, and defeated France. Areas visited by Louise in 1937 and 1938 and earlier became part of the war zone from the moment of the invasion of Denmark and Norway: Greenland was Danish territory and Jan Mayen Island and Spitsbergen, Norwegian. The United States grew nervously aware that German intruders were in Greenland monitoring the weather patterns shaped by this crucial landmass. By 1941 we had occupied Iceland.

Almost overnight, Louise Boyd's corner of the globe, the Greenland Sea and its various shores, had become a "hot spot" and her expertise was in urgent demand by her government. All her years of travel and photographing and growing intimacy with the region now began to acquire a new meaning and destiny.

"Information regarding Northeast Greenland prior to our entering the war was extremely scanty," wrote Rear Admiral Edward H. Smith of the U.S. Coast Guard — an understatement notable for its discretion. American ignorance was not surprising. For years the Danes and Norwegians had been the active explorers and scientists in the region. They had set up weather and wireless stations, and their fishermen, sealers, and hunters had roamed the waters. U.S. involvement in these essentially foreign waters had been limited. We did not even have a consul in the Greenland capital of Godthaab (known as Nuuk today), on the populated west coast, until 1941. Yet Greenland backs up very closely to the North American continent, lying cheek by jowl with Arctic Canada. It is a very near neighbor indeed.

After Louise's return in 1938, the AGS conferred its highest honor upon her, the Cullum Geographical Medal, making her only the second woman the society had honored in its eighty-six years. The "dauntless leader of scientific expeditions into the Arctic, she has captured the spirit of the polar world in photographs of rare beauty," the medal was inscribed. In announcing the award, newspapers called her "the only woman to achieve an outstanding position in Arctic exploration." The flurry of attention brought her work under a more intense spotlight.

Louise was officially requested to postpone publication of the findings of her last two expeditions, clearly indicating the strategic and navigational significance of this material. "The well advanced plans of the American Geographical Society and myself to publish this book in the fall of 1940 were brought to a sudden halt when officials of our government advised me of the possible value of our reports and photographic material to the invader and requested that publication be deferred and the reports made available to the interested departments of the government," Louise wrote in a foreword to the book that was finally published after the war, in 1948, as *The Coast of Northeast Greenland.* "Immediately I put into 'security' not only the material contained in this book," her account continues, "but also my extensive library of photographs taken on these and my previous Arctic expeditions and the hundreds of maps and miscellaneous publications, dealing with the northern countries of Europe as well as with the Arctic, that I had collected over the years. All of this material was turned over to departments of our government upon request and restricted to their use for the duration of the war."

She also made a spirited dash from New York to German-held Oslo to recover her canoes, cameras, radios, sounding equipment, and Arctic clothing, which the Nazis had impounded when they took over Norway. She was just in the nick of time, for a year later, with the United States in the war, transatlantic travel became impossible.

Louise's useful knowledge was drawn to the attention of the War Department by the above-mentioned Rear Admiral "Iceberg" Smith, so nicknamed because of his expertise in ice navigation. While Iceberg Smith was preparing for a mission to Northeast Greenland in the summer of 1940, he was advised to consult Miss Boyd. He was overwhelmed with the "exceedingly helpful" data she and her staff piled upon him: "voluminous photographs, including splendid panoramic views of important headlands," and assistance in identifying topographic features — information of "great assistance in the navigation of these little known ice-infested waters," he said.

By 1941 Louise had been appointed a consulting expert by the National Bureau of Standards and was heading a unique scientific expedition into Arctic waters. The purpose of the expedition, which left Washington, D.C., on June 11, was to obtain data affecting long-distance radio transmission, particularly conditions of the ionosphere in the Arctic, of special military significance for radio transmission to and through the Arctic. Portable ionosphere equipment developed by the bureau had been used in Texas and in Brazil during solar eclipses, but data from points in the Arctic region was lacking. The United States Coast Guard and the Department of Terrestrial Magnetism of the Carnegie Institution were to cooperate and benefit from the findings. Reporting this project to the Society of Woman Geographers, Louise noted, "The route of the expedition and other details will not be made public," reflecting the mission's secrecy.

The legendary schooner *Effie M. Morrissey* was chartered by Louise for the expedition, with its equally legendary captain, Robert Abram Bartlett, in command, now a stalwart sixty-six. A more picturesque combination of personalities and conveyance could hardly be contrived. Louise, now on her seventh expedition to the Arctic, familiar with every nook and cranny of the East Greenland fiord region, was an old hand in Arctic waters and was without question the one woman most conversant with the region, a unique figure among polar explorers. At age fifty-five, vigorous, enthusiastic, eager, her purse strings still open for an appealing cause, she was not one to be taken for granted. Long ago she had made it clear that she could establish her authority as an expedition leader.

Captain Bartlett was one of the great polar heroes of the era, a man of almost countless expeditions into the northern waters. Beginning in 1897 he had accompanied Robert E. Peary on various expeditions; on the final Peary trip he was leader of the last of the supporting parties that Peary sent back before making his final dash for the North Pole. In an adventure-filled career, Bartlett had commanded expeditions to North Greenland, northwest Alaska, Ellesmere Island, to the west shores of Baffin Island, to Siberia, and to Labrador, and he was regarded as one of the great ice navigators of all time. Neither could he be taken for granted.

Equally a "personality" was the small, coal-black, two-masted schooner, *Effie M. Morrissey*, which Bartlett had already commanded on fifteen previous expeditions. Launched in 1894, built of oak planking and greenheart sheathing, she was ninety-seven feet long with a beam of twenty-three feet (the *Veslekari* was a leviathan by comparison) and had been used by many prestigious American museums and scientific organizations.

This seemed a setup for a spectacular epic of the Arctic: a couple of explorers with years of polar experience behind them, a man

*Louise as leader of the U.S. Bureau of Standards' 1941 Greenland
expedition, with scientists on the deck of the schooner*
Effie M. Morrissey

and a woman, co-leaders on a mission of extreme secrecy and possible danger. German raiders might be on the prowl; the Arctic was always uncertain. Were they to be heroes together? Would romance blossom? Or at least a lifelong attachment?

Nothing of the kind. They scarcely spoke during the four-month cruise, according to Louise's friend, Dr. Walter A. Wood. Bartlett, a grizzled, tough old polar bear of a seaman, could not accept being teamed with a woman, a "society dame" at that, and in his opinion an upstart in the select little band of seasoned polar explorers. Afterward, according to intimates, Louise never mentioned this unpleasant situation.

The *Morrissey* team included two radio men from the Bureau of Standards, a radio operator from the U.S. Coast Guard, a physician, and a crew of eleven. The schooner sailed up the west coast of Greenland far into Smith Sound off Ellesmere Island, returning down the coast of Baffin Island and Labrador, landing in Washington on November 3, 1941. Louise published no later report because of the confidentiality of the work. The Department of Commerce news release reported: "Many thrilling experiences were related by Miss Boyd. At one time the *Morrissey*, a small but stout

289

vessel, was battered by a 100-mile gale, with waves 60 feet high. Everything movable on board was thrown about, including members of the party. Nobody knew whether the vessel would survive, but there was no sign of panic among either members of the crew or technical personnel."

The success of the expedition was commended in the *Technical News Bulletin* of the Bureau of Standards: "The Government is indebted to Miss Boyd for her effective leadership of the expedition and is gratified with the results achieved." The government indeed had reason to be indebted, for Louise had chartered the ship and crew, paid all expenses, and was herself serving on the so-called dollar a year basis by which many experts volunteered their services during World War II.

On this same basis she served in Washington from March 1942 to July 1943 as special consultant to the Military Intelligence Division on matters relating to the Greenland-Spitsbergen arena, lands she had surveyed and photographed in detail. Her utter seriousness about the confidentiality and importance of her task in the shrouded atmosphere of war is shown in notes she wrote the Washington group of the Society of Woman Geographers during her stay in the capital. To her 1942 report, in which she lists herself "Expert Consultant for U.S. Government," she attached a message on small, exquisite blue notepaper (bearing only the name "Miss Boyd"): "For good reasons please do not add anything to this . . . Am sure you will understand." Regretting that she could not attend one of the Saturday meetings, she wrote, "We in the Government work all day Saturday."

This work for her country gained her a Certificate of Appreciation after the war, "For outstanding patriotic service to the Army as a contributor to geographic knowledge and consultant during the critical period prior to and after the start of World War II."

Louise had never set out to "conquer" or "discover"; she more or less stumbled upon what became Miss Boyd Land and the Louise Boyd Bank. So when she at last decided to go to the North Pole, her motive was curiosity and a need for emotional satisfaction rather than ambition. She had never really thirsted for that glory that drives people to the high stakes of original discovery; and besides, the North Pole had long since been "discovered." She had simply dreamed as a little girl, she said, "of going to one very special place," the North Pole.

"So it was that on June 16, 1955, I chartered a special plane, gathered an American crew and took off from Bodø, Norway." She was sixty-seven at the time. Later, she wrote an appealing tale of this whimsical saga for *Parade* magazine:

North, north, north we flew. Soon we left all land behind us. From the cabin window I saw great stretches of ocean flecked with patches of white floating ice. Now the ice became denser, its jagged edges surrounding open pools of sea. And as I saw the ocean change to massive fields of solid white, my heart leaped up. I knew we were approaching my goal.

Then — in a moment of happiness which I shall never forget — our instruments told me we were there. For directly below us, 9,000 feet down, lay the North Pole. No cloud in the brilliant blue sky hid our view of this glorious field of shining ice. Suddenly I felt we had an invisible passenger — the Almighty.

In a moment of silent and reverent awe the crew and I gave thanks for this priceless sight. We crossed the Pole, then circled it, flying "around the world" in a matter of minutes. Then we departed. My Arctic dream had come true.

This adventure in wish fulfillment established several firsts. It was the first flight over the North Pole in a nonmilitary or commercial plane, the first to be privately financed, and the first to make the trip from mainland Norway.

From Oslo on her return Louise cabled the Society of Woman Geographers in more scientific detail.

Flew over North Pole yesterday morning at nine fifteen and circled the Pole. Did so in brilliant sunshine and cloudless blue sky and perfect visibility. Flew at nine thousand feet. Mostly very cloudy over rest of Polar Basin and rest of flight. Flew as Louise A. Boyd North Pole Expedition using specially chartered American DC4 airplane. Accompanied in flight by Lieutenant General

Finn Lambrechts, Commander in Chief of Royal Norwegian Air Force, and Lieutenant Colonel Steffan Olsen, also of Norwegian Air Force. American Ambassador to Norway and Admiral John Carson of American Embassy, Oslo, saw us off at start of flight. We refueled at Bodø, Northern Norway, and from there to North Pole and return to Bodø took sixteen hours non-stop. Flying from Oslo to North Pole and return to Oslo took twenty-five hours flying. Will be Grant Hotel, Oslo, for another ten days. Greetings to all woman geographers.

The North Pole foray was her final expedition, but she continued to spend four or five months out of each year traveling. Her spring 1958 itinerary in the Far and Near East included Japan, Hong Kong, and the Portuguese colony of Macao off the China coast, Saigon, Bangkok, Cambodia and Angkor, Kashmir, Pakistan, through the Khyber Pass into Afghanistan and thus to Turkey, and then home — once more around the world! In 1964 she arrived in Fairbanks, Alaska, on the heels of the catastrophic Alaskan earthquake of 8.5 magnitude. She had been invited by the University of Alaska and in connection with plans for the two-million-dollar Naval Arctic Research Laboratory at Point Barrow. In the aftermath of the quake, starving huskies were attacking people; the university was a vast refugee camp.

Louise was eighty when, in 1967, *The New Yorker* reported her arrival at the annual Explorers Club Dinner in Manhattan, in a pink dress "festooned with white orchids," where she was introduced as "one of the world's greatest woman explorers." Throughout all these frenetic years she had maintained her highly visible civic role in the San Francisco Bay Area. For twenty years she was on the director's board of the San Francisco Symphony, had been president of the Marin Music Chest, a charter member of the Marin County Historical Society, and an officer in the San Francisco Garden Club, the California Botanical Society, and others.

But by 1962 she had concluded she could no longer keep up Maple Lawn. Three-quarters of the grounds had already been deeded to San Rafael and is still today known as Boyd Park. The estate, with its fifty-seven-foot library, countless rooms, and winding driveway entrance, was sold to the San Rafael Elks Club and became Lodge No. 1108; Louise was promptly made an honorary member. Today the large, scantily furnished rooms echo hollowly with the shuffling of card games and the rustle of newspapers. The elegant furnishings that made Maple Lawn a showplace of Marin County had been sold at auction, but before that Ansel Adams, the noted photographer, had recorded in detail the rooms as they were in their heyday, when Louise entertained kings, diplomats, and the famous who visited San Francisco. Efficient as ever, she donated her valuable library of Arctic and Scandinavian books to the Universities of Alaska and California, and her books on California wildflowers and natural science to the Louise Boyd Natural Science Museum of San Rafael. Among the saddest to lose the great estate were the local firemen and policemen for whose families Louise had annually staged a marvelous Christmas party. Louise moved with her Coromandel screens, Irish chandeliers, and priceless collection of Queen Anne chairs to an apartment on Nob Hill in San Francisco.

Honors had accumulated. After receiving the Knight Cross of the Order of St. Olaf from the King of Norway, the Andrée Plaque of the Swedish Anthropological and Geological Society, and the American Geographical Society's Cullum Geographical Medal, she was elected a chevalier of the French Legion of Honor, and was awarded King Christian X's Medal of Liberation in appreciation of her contribution to Denmark's liberation. ("This was because I had saved my records from the Germans in World War II," she would say with a smile.) The American Polar Society honored her with a scroll crediting her efforts with contributing more to the knowledge of Greenland, Spitsbergen, Franz Josef Land, and the Greenland Sea "than has the work of any other explorer." She became the first woman in the 108-year history of the American Geographical Society to be elected to the Council of Fellows. She was a member of the Royal Geographical and the Royal Horticultural societies.

In 1969, when she was eighty-one, she returned to Fairbanks to receive her third honorary degree, a doctorate of science from the University of Alaska. She had been awarded honorary doctorate of law degrees from the University of California and Mills College earlier. While in Alaska she attended the dedication of the now completed Naval Arctic Research Laboratory at Point Barrow.

Louise realized that polar work had changed after World War II. "Land as well as air operations are now on such a vast scale of personnel and equipment, that I am fully cognizant that small expeditions such as mine . . . would be but a dot among the others and of very questionable good. We pioneered where others now carry on. I am happy to record that considerable of my Arctic equipment continues to function in the Arctic in my behalf through the Arctic Institute of North America," she wrote in a 1950 article in *Photogrammetric Engineering*.

Not only polar study but Greenland itself has altered radically since Louise's voyages. Changes in the Danish Constitution in 1953 brought Greenland out of its colonial status to become a county of Denmark, where Greenlanders enjoy the same rights and duties as other Danish subjects. The Ice Age stillness broken by the construction of American airfields during World War II has been further invaded by Danish immigration and the introduction of modern ways of life as the Danish government strives to bring Greenland into the twentieth century. In 1983 the first scheduled cruise service in Greenland was opened under the aegis of the Danish Tourist Board in conjunction with a new direct air service from Montreal to Godthaab.

One consequence of the new status has been the assignment of Greenlandic names to many places throughout the island. Greenland, for instance, is now named Kalaalit Nunaat. Godthaab is Nuuk. Angmagssalik is now Tasiilaq. Some Danish and other older names survive, but new maps are larded with Greenlandic designations not present in pre-1953 maps.

But material and cultural change has come almost solely to the more genial, habitable west coast and southern tip. By and large, the ice curtain has not lifted from the northeast coast. The radio and weather stations may have multiplied to eighteen, all operated by Danes, but they are nicknamed "devils' islands" because of their godforsaken isolation, and because it cannot be developed the whole northeast coast is dubbed "Greenland's back yard."

This would please Louise entirely. The glorious world she knew and loved remains in deep-freeze isolation, as forbidding to the casual traveler as ever, despite airplanes, helicopters, and snow-mobiles. The mighty fiords sleep on untouched, among the few remaining unsullied areas of the globe. As long as the inland ice cap holds a large portion of Greenland in its clutch and the South Greenland Current sweeps along the coast, this icy world will continue to serve as a "weather factory" of the North Atlantic. The northern end of the great island is further protected by Denmark's having turned it into a huge national park, protecting the wild creatures who dwell there.

A series of operations for intestinal cancer intruded upon Louise's action-crammed schedule at some point in her advanced years. At first she ignored her physician's urgings to adopt a more cautious pace and would pack her bags and be off at the first possible moment. But failing health and failing finances began to close in on her exuberant style and she passed her last days in a San Francisco convalescent center, so financially strapped she had to be supported by a few loyal friends. The evaporation of her wealth, particularly in view of her earlier sagacity and attention to careful investment, remains a mystery.

Not long before her death, Louise learned that the *Veslekari* had gone down in the ice in Newfoundland. A letter in imperfect English from Elling Aarseth & Company in Aalesund, Norway, from whom she had so often chartered the little vessel, answered her distressed inquiry. "I understand well that you were sorry when you saw *Veslekari*'s breakdown. She went down with the flag at the top. It was a good vessel and it is the only vessel that has got a whole book of 270 pages and 68 fotos. This book is of Norwegian and printed in 1957."

Louise died in the nursing home on September 14, 1972, two days before she would have been 85. During her last year she had expressed the hope to her long-time friend Dr. Walter Wood, a member of the 1933 expedition, that her ashes might be scattered over polar regions, preferably over Miss Boyd Land at the head of Ice Fiord in Greenland. Wood promised to do his best. Upon investigation after her death, he discovered that problems and costs connected with reaching Miss Boyd Land were insurmountable. For various reasons, some involving Danish permits, the only alternatives open were a seaborne approach from Denmark or Norway, or an aerial approach by helicopter, presumably from Iceland, to the head of Ice Fiord. Wood soon realized that with skyrocketing prices such a disposition of the ashes could possibly cost as much as Louise's $40,000 budget for her entire 1933 expedition.

He compromised. The last polar region Louise had visited had been Alaska, so he arranged through a friend at the Naval Arctic Research Laboratory at Point Barrow for her ashes to be dropped one hundred miles north of Point Barrow over the ice of the Arctic Ocean, a frozen world closely akin to the one Louise had loved.

SOURCES

INDEX

PHOTO CREDITS

SOURCES

Annie Smith Peck

Books by Annie Smith Peck:

A Search for the Apex of America: High Mountain Climbing in Peru and Bolivia, Including the Conquest of Huascarán, with Some Observations on the Country and People Below. New York: Dodd, Mead, 1911.

The South American Tour. New York: George H. Doran, 1913.

Industrial and Commercial South America. New York: E. P. Dutton, 1922.

Flying over South America: Twenty Thousand Miles by Air. Boston: Houghton Mifflin, 1932.

Annie Peck's mountain-climbing experiences in South America are best described in her book *A Search for the Apex of America*, and in her articles: "A Woman of the Andes," *Harper's Monthly Magazine* (December 1906); "The First Ascent of Huascarán," *Harper's Monthly Magazine* (January 1909); "How I Prepared to Climb Mt. Huascarán," *Collier's*, (March 13, 1909); "The Conquest of Huascarán," American Geographical Society *Bulletin* (June 1909); "Most Dramatic Event in My Life," *Delineator* (July 1909); and "My Home in Peru," *Harper's Bazaar* (May 11, 1911).

Contemporary comment on Annie's activities was found in *Outing* ("Practical Mountain Climbing" [September 1901], and "Mountaineering Feats" [August 1903]) and in *Review of Reviews* ("Woman's Conquest of the Andes" [October 1908]). The American Alpine Club supplied photographs, lecture brochures, and excerpts from the club's *Annals*, relating particularly to the controversy between Annie and Fanny Bullock Workman over Huascarán's altitude. *Scientific American* (February 12 and 26, and April 15, 1910) carried the exchange of letters between these rival climbers.

The National Archives are the source of a thirty-five-page correspondence between Annie and Commander Robert E. Peary, including a copy of her article entitled "Beware of Cook's Claims," from the *Brooklyn Daily Eagle* (December 11, 1910). *Scientific American* (July 1929) carried Annie's article "Aviation in and to South America." *The New Yorker* (October 3, 1936) recounted Annie's comical ascent of "El Popo."

Valuable insights came from Society of Woman Geographers members (now deceased) who knew Annie: Amelia Earhart's tribute on the book jacket of Annie's *Flying over South America* ("I felt myself an upstart beside her"); Berta N. Briggs's biography of Annie in *Notable American Women 1807–*

1950: A Biographical Dictionary, vol. 3 (Cambridge, Mass.: Harvard University Press, 1971); Blair Niles's recollections of Annie's last days in her *Peruvian Pageant: A Journey in Time* (New York: Bobbs-Merrill, 1937); and Reba Morse's oral history review (Archives, Society of Woman Geographers, Washington, D.C.). *A Dangerous Experiment: 100 Years of Women at the University of Michigan* (Center for Continuing Education of Women, University of Michigan, Ann Arbor, 1970), by Dorothy Gies McGuigan, provides a glimpse of Annie's student years. Brief reviews and appraisals of her career appear in *Lowell Thomas' Book of the High Mountains* (New York: Julian Messner, 1964); *On Top of the World: An Illustrated History of Mountaineering and Mountaineers*, by Showell Styles (London: Hamish Hamilton, 1967); and *The Roof of the World*, by Geoffrey Hindley, in the *Encyclopedia of Discovery and Exploration* (London: Aldus Books, 1971). On Matterhorn ascents before Annie's, *Matterhorn Centenary*, by A. H. M. Lunn (Chicago: Rand McNally, 1965), and *The Day the Rope Broke*, by R. W. Clark (New York: Harcourt Brace Jovanovich, 1965) were useful. Annie is included in *Annapurna: A Woman's Place*, by Arlene Blum (San Francisco: Sierra Club Books, 1980); *Women on the Rope: The Feminine Share in Mountain Adventure*, by Cicely Williams (London: George Allen & Unwin, 1973); *Women Who Changed Things*, by Linda Peavy and Ursula Smith (New York: Charles Scribner's Sons, 1984); *The National Cyclopedia of American Biography*, vols. 6 and 15 (New York: James T. White, 1916); *A Woman of the Century: Leading American Women in All Walks of Life*, by Frances E. Willard and Mary A. Livermore (Buffalo, N.Y.: Charles Wells Moulton, 1893); and *Who Was Who in America 1897–1942*, vol. 1 (Chicago: Marquis, 1966). The Peruvian embassy in Washington supplied data on the Huaylas Valley national park area and present-day Andean mountaineering, and about the earthquake that destroyed Yungay, Peru. Richard H. Howland, currently special assistant to the secretary of the Smithsonian Institution, was a former student of Annie's younger brother, William Thane Peck, the principal of Providence High School, and provided recollections of William's classroom stories of Annie's exploits.

Regarding Annie's sortie into the headwaters of the Amazon, *Exploring the Amazon*, by Helen and Frank Schreider (Washington, D.C.: National Geographic Society, 1970), and *Two Against the Amazon*, by John Brown (London: Hodder and Stoughton, 1952) were helpful as background on the debated question of the river's original source.

Delia J. Akeley

Books and articles by Delia J. Akeley:

"J.T., Jr.": The Biography of an African Monkey. New York: Macmillan, 1929. Illustrated with photographs by Carl E. and Delia Akeley.

Jungle Portraits. New York: Macmillan, 1930 (photographs).

"My First Elephant." In *All True: The Record of Actual Adventures That Have Happened to Ten Women of Today*. New York: Brewer, Warren & Putnam, 1931.

In *The Saturday Evening Post*: "Monkey Tricks," September 18, 1926; "Baboons," January 15, 1927; "The Little People," March 3, 1928; "Crocodiles," July 28, 1928.

"Jungle Rescue." *Collier's*, February 11, 1928.

"Table from Elephant's Ear." *Mentor*, May 1929.

"Elephants in the Fog." *Century*, October 1929.

"On Wings of Fire." *Saint Nicholas*, January 1930.

"Report on the Museum's Expedition to Africa." *Brooklyn Museum Quarterly* 12, no. 3 (July 1925); ''Among the Pigmies in the Congo Forest." *BMQ* 13, no. 1 (January 1926).

Carl E. Akeley's own reports on expeditions he shared with Delia were especially useful: *In Brightest Africa* (Garden City, N.Y.: Garden City Publishing, 1920); "Elephant Hunting in Equatorial Africa with Rifle and Camera," *National Geographic* (August 1912); and articles in *The American Museum Journal* (February and December 1912). Mary Jobe Akeley's two books, *The Wilderness Lives Again* (New York: Dodd, Mead, 1946) and *Carl Akeley's Africa* (New York: Dodd, Mead, 1951), provided background on Akeley himself. Interesting sidelights were found in Mary Hastings Bradley's *Alice in Jungleland* (New York: D. Appleton, 1922). Roy Chapman Andrews's *Beyond Adventure: The Lives of Three Explorers* (New York: Duell, Sloan & Pearce, 1924) includes a biography of Carl, with mention of Delia, and Mignon Rittenhouse's *Seven Women Explorers* (New York: Lippincott, 1964) includes a biography of Delia. The preeminent scholarly study of the Congo Pygmies is Paul Schebesta's *Les Pygmies* (Paris: Gallimard, 1940), translated from the German by François Berger. *Pygmy Kitabu*, by Jean-Pierre Hallet and Alex Pelle (New York: Random House, 1973), is a more recent report.

Voluminous newspaper coverage of Delia's exploits includes reports and interviews in old issues of the *Beaver Dam* (Wisconsin) *Daily Citizen*, the *Milwaukee Journal*, the *Brooklyn Daily Eagle*, the *New York Times*, the *New York Tribune*, the *New York World*, the *New York Evening Post*, the *New York Sun*, the *Washington Evening Star*, and the *Christian Science Monitor*. *Scientific American*, *Scientific Monthly*, *Literary Digest*, and *The Woman Citizen* were among the magazines carrying particularly useful articles. One of the most valuable sources for Delia's early years was *The News Review of Macmillan Company*, a small in-house news sheet, which ran a particularly revealing feature, "Woman of the Week: Delia Akeley," February 22, 1932.

Invaluable primary materials and personal recollections were made available by Delia's relative and friends (see Acknowledgments).

Marguerite Harrison

Books and articles by Marguerite Harrison (this is not an exhaustive list of Harrison's feature articles, nor does it include her regular news dispatches to the *Baltimore Sun* and Associated Press from her various European posts):

Marooned in Moscow: The Story of an American Woman Imprisoned in Russia. New York: George H. Doran, 1921.

Unfinished Tales from a Russian Prison. New York: George H. Doran, 1923.

Red Bear or Yellow Dragon. New York: George H. Doran, 1924.

Asia Reborn. New York: Harper & Brothers, 1928.

There's Always Tomorrow: The Story of a Checkered Life. New York: Farrar & Rinehart, 1935. (Published in England as *Born for Trouble* (London: Gallancy, 1936.)

"In Russian Prisons." In *All True: The Record of Actual Adventures That Have Happened to Ten Women of Today*. New York: Brewer, Warren & Putnam, 1931.

Translation from the German of *The Dissolute Years: A Pageant of Stuart England*, by Edward Stucken. New York: Farrar and Rinehart, 1935.

New York Times feature articles: "Turkey Mistrusts the Western World," January 25, 1925; "Women of the Orient," February 22, 1925; "Risky Motoring in Far Places," March 1, 1925; "Islam Limits Caliph to Spiritual Duties," July 5, 1925; "Reza Khan," December 6, 1925; "Gertrude Bell: A Desert Power," November 5, 1933.

Magazine articles: "Russia Under the Bolsheviks," *Annals of the American Academy of Political and Social Sciences*, March 1922; "Cross Currents in Japan," *The Atlantic Monthly*, July 1923; "Whirling Dervishes," *Asia*, July 1924; "I'm Not Afraid to Travel Alone," *Collier's*, February 21, 1925; "Turbulent Kurds Stage Another Uprising," *New York Times Magazine*, March 15, 1925; "Japan Guards Sakhalin, New Eldorado," *New York Times Magazine*, March 29, 1925; "The Bitter Bread of Exile," *Century*, November 1925.

As Marguerite was the first American woman imprisoned by the Bolsheviks, her initial incarceration in Moscow was actively covered by the American press, in particular the *Baltimore Sun,* from which two key articles are cited here: "Mrs. Harrison in Dire Straits in Moscow Cell" (April 18, 1921) and "Senator France Acts to Aid Mrs. Harrison" (April 21, 1921).

Regarding her second imprisonment by the Soviets, the *New York Times* printed: "Marguerite Harrison Will Be Released by Soviet" (February 18, 1923); "Marguerite Harrison Released from Prison" (February 20, 1923); "Official Word of Release Reaches Riga" (February 28, 1923); and "Mrs. Marguerite Harrison Blamed by Mrs. S. Harding, British Newspaper Woman, Who Says She Called Her a Spy and Was Responsible for Her Jail Sentence in Russia" (February 15, 1923).

For information about Marguerite's credentials as a spy, under the authority of the Freedom of Information Act, I consulted Marguerite's formerly restricted personnel file (File PF-39205), Military Intelligence Division, U.S. War Department, now catalogued in the National Archives and stored in the National Records Center, Suitland, Maryland. Marguerite herself probably never read any of this file, which does not include her own reports but consists of largely confidential correspondence between members of the various offices of the MID.

Useful viewpoints on this phase of her career came from "An American Newspaper Woman's Adventures in Soviet Russia," *Current Opinion* (May 1922), and "La Belle Marguerite, Journalist and Spy" by S. K. Ratcliffe, *The Observer* (April 26, 1936).

Background on the Bakhtiari came from *Caravan: Story of the Middle East,* by Carleton S. Coon (New York: Holt, Rinehart & Winston, 1962); *Road to Nineveh,* by Nora B. Kubie (New York: Doubleday, 1964); and *Early Adventures in Persia, Susiana, and Babylonia, Including a Residence among the Bakhtiyari* [sic] *and Other Wild Tribes, Before the Discovery of Nineveh,* by Sir Austen Henry Layard (new edition, Farnborough, England: Gregg International, 1971).

For details of the actual expedition, Merian C. Cooper's descriptions were invaluable: his book, *Grass* (New York: G. P. Putnam's Sons, 1925), with sixty-four illustrations from photographs by Ernest Schoedsack; three articles in *Asia,* "Grass: A Persian Epic of Migration" (December 1924, January 1925, February 1925); the *New York Times* article "Barefoot Nation Migrates Through Snow to Find Food: Three Americans, One a Woman, Take Part in Annual Trek of 30,000 Tribesmen" (August 31, 1924); and of course his documentary film *Grass,* a personal print of which was made available to me.

Among the many reviews of the film after its debut, reference is made here particularly to one from the *New York Times,* March 8, 1925 ("Persian Tribes Filmed on Brave Mountain Trudge"); a lengthy review in *The Literary Digest,* April 25, 1925 ("An Epic of Man's Fight with Nature"); and another from *The Outlook,* May 6, 1925 ("A Modern Migration").

Among works consulted on background history of the documentary film as an art form was Louis Jacobs's useful *Documentary Tradition, 1922–1970: From Nanook to Woodstock* (New York: Hopkinson & Blake, 1971).

Thomas Bullitt Harrison and his wife, Jeanne, were immensely informative, as was their loan of a scrapbook of newspaper and magazine clippings and letters, and first editions of Marguerite's books, in addition to other memorabilia.

The files of the Society of Woman Geographers supplied a few pictures of Marguerite, several letters, and her books.

A footnote to the 1925 film *Grass,* made, of course, in black and white, and silent: In 1972 the spectacle of the Bakhtiari migration was filmed in color and natural sound in a film entitled *People of the Wind,* produced by Anthony

Howarth and David Koff. Synopsis material describes the migration as "the largest movement of nomadic peoples in the world" and "the most hazardous test of human endurance still undertaken by an entire people." The techniques of modern cinematography at last could capture the full splendor of the epic, but the pioneering film *Grass* first made it known to the world.

Louise Arner Boyd

Books and articles by Louise Arner Boyd:

The Fiord Region of East Greenland. American Geographical Society, Special Publication, no. 18, 1935.

Polish Countrysides. American Geographical Society, Special Publication, no. 20, 1937.

The Coast of Northeast Greenland. American Geographical Society, Special Publication, no. 30, 1948.

"Fiords of East Greenland: A Photographic Reconnaissance Throughout the Franz Josef and King Oscar Fiords." *The Geographical Review* 4 (October 1932).

"The Louise A. Boyd Seven Arctic Expeditions." *Photogrammetric Engineering* (December 1950); published by the American Society of Photogrammetry.

Louise Boyd's own reports of her scientific expeditions to East Greenland, in her two books and in her articles about these voyages, provided the gist of the stories here. Since her two Arctic books are lavishly illustrated with her photographs and are supplemented by an accompanying case of route maps, hydrographic and terrestrial surveys, profile maps of fiord and ocean bottoms, and other scientific data, these are unusually complete sources of information. Most of the details about her 1928 hunt for the lost Norwegian explorer Roald Amundsen came from her succinct account submitted to the Society of Woman Geographers, while information about her 1941 expedition for the U.S. government was supplied by the National Bureau of Standards and its *Technical News Bulletin,* and the National Archives. Data on contemporary Greenland came from the Danish Tourist Board.

Friends and associates who knew Louise intimately provided descriptive insights about such personal aspects as her appearance, style of life, mannerisms, eccentricities, and organizational skills. Mrs. Gordon H. Fountain, a close friend who stood by Louise in her financially strained later years, contributed helpfully with an interview in her Oakland home, and later through correspondence and the trusting loan of Louise's diaries from her early European tours and a notebook from her 1964 Alaskan trip. Mrs. Edith Ronne of Washington, D.C., widow of the Antarctic explorer Captain Finn Ronne, offered recollections of visits to Maple Lawn and loaned letters and photographs. Mrs. Rose Saul Zalles of Washington, D.C., described Louise in her East Coast social context.

Dr. Walter A. Wood, assistant surveyor on Louise's 1933 East Greenland expedition, a member of the American Geographical Society at the time, and a former president of the Explorers Club, was informative and amusing in his accounts of Boyd as an expedition leader. Hon. James K. Penfield, U.S. consul in Greenland at the time Boyd made her 1941 expedition for our government, shared his memories of his encounter with her. Helpful information also came from the Marin County Historical Association, housed on the Maple Lawn grounds and an archive of many of Louise's papers. Others whose letters provided details are former AGS staff members (who also knew Louise through membership in the Society of Woman Geographers): Dr. Anastasia Van Burkalow, Alice Taylor, and the late Wilma Belden Fairchild. Files of the Society of Woman Geographers were particularly helpful with photographs and copies of Louise's cablegrams and reports.

Two popular articles in particular gave well-drawn impressions of Louise's place in San Francisco society: "Society Glitters in San Francisco," by Charlotte Curtis, *New York Times*, September 12, 1963; and an article by Stephen Birmingham in *Holiday*, April 19, 1961. Particularly complete obituaries appeared in the *New York Times*, *The Independent Woman*, and *The Geographical Review*. Numerous news stories about Boyd appeared in the *New York Times*, the *San Francisco Examiner and Chronicle,* the *Washington Post,* and the *Christian Science Monitor.* An excellent appraisal appears in *Encyclopaedia Arctica.*

(In 1978 the American Geographical Society donated its library, maps, and photographic collection to the University of Wisconsin-Milwaukee, among which was a large number of photographs of Poland and Greenland taken by Louise Boyd. New appreciation for Louise's work is evidenced by an exhibition of ninety photographs from this collection taken on her 1934 trip through Poland, which opened September 11, 1984, at the Golda Meir Library, University of Wisconsin-Milwaukee. Susan Gibson Mikoś, who organized the exhibition, entitled "Polish Countrysides," also produced a handsome booklet containing a biographical sketch of Louise and quotations from her descriptions of Poland, as well as a slide presentation, "Louise Boyd and Her View of the Vanishing Rural Life in Poland."

Meanwhile, the Marin County Historical Society is sponsoring a movement to obtain a United States postal stamp commemorating the centennial of Louise's birth in 1987.)

INDEX

Introduction

Annie Smith Peck

Delia J. Akeley

Marguerite Harrison

Louise Arner Boyd

PHOTO CREDITS

Frontispiece

Annie Smith Peck: courtesy Society of Woman Geographers. *Delia J. Akeley:* courtesy Dorothy Denning Stancheski. *Marguerite Harrison:* from *Marooned in Moscow* by Marguerite Harrison. *Louise Arner Boyd:* courtesy Edith M. Ronne.

Annie Smith Peck

5, 18, 23, 48, 52, 61: from *A Search for the Apex of America* by Annie S. Peck. *13, 33, 66:* courtesy Society of Woman Geographers. *14, 15:* from *The New Yorker*, October 3, 1936. *37:* National Archives, Washington, D.C.

Delia J. Akeley

71, 83, 85, 86, 87, 89 (top), 90, 96, 108, 139 (bottom): courtesy family of Martha Miller Bliven. *79, 89 (bottom), 115:* courtesy Patricia Howe Page. *111, 112:* courtesy Dorothy Denning Stancheski. *139 (top), 143:* from *Jungle Portraits* by Delia J. Akeley (New York: Macmillan, March 4, 1930). *151:* courtesy Society of Woman Geographers.

Marguerite Harrison

155, 169, 186, 189: from *Red Bear or Yellow Dragon* by Marguerite Harrison. *200, 201, 202:* courtesy Society of Woman Geographers. *219, 222:* from the film *Grass* by Merian C. Cooper.

Louise Arner Boyd

9087085
SBN 0-395-39584-4